Polish Contributions
to
South Asian Studies

Polish Contributions to South Asian Studies

EDITED BY DANUTA STASIK

Warsaw 2017

Reviewed by Dr Hab. Lidia Sudyka, Professor at the Jagiellonian University in Kraków

English text proofread by Steve Jones

Cover design by Agnieszka Miłaszewicz

Published with the financial support of the Chair of South Asian Studies of the Faculty of Oriental Studies of the University of Warsaw

ISBN 978-83-8017-145-9

DOM WYDAWNICZY ELIPSA

Typesetting and printed by:
Dom Wydawniczy ELIPSA
ul. Inflancka 15/198, 00-189 Warszawa
tel./fax 22 635 03 01, 22 635 17 85
e-mail: elipsa@elipsa.pl, www.elipsa.pl

Contents

Editor's Preface

This volume brings together the papers presented by Polish scholars at the ECSAS 2016 (European Conference on South Asian Studies 2016) – the 24th conference of the European Association for South Asian Studies (EASAS) that took place from 27 to 30 July 2016 at the University of Warsaw. It was co-organized by the Polish Oriental Society (PTO) and the University of Warsaw (Chair of South Asian Studies of the Faculty of Oriental Studies). This biennial event, the largest and most prestigious European conference concerned with research on South Asia, was held in Poland for the first time. The conference programme, including 49 panels[1] and the keynote lecture entitled *Asia, Europe and America in the Making of 'Caste'* by Professor Sumit Guha (Frances Higginbotham Nalle Centennial Professor in History) from the University of Texas at Austin attracted scholars from almost 40 countries. Thus, the event not only proved to be an exciting forum for academic interaction but also an excellent opportunity for Polish scholars, especially younger ones, to be more visible and audible than on other occasions when the ECSAS is organized abroad. In Warsaw, 35 out of 449 delegates were from Poland, which was the largest Polish participation ever in this series of conferences. The ECSAS 2016 also enjoyed higher participation than usual from other Central and Eastern European countries (15 delegates) and attracted a significant number of South Asian scholars – more than a hundred – representing Indian, Pakistani, Bangladeshi, Nepali as well as European academic institutions. This was – to a great extent –

[1] All the conference panels, the names of their participants and titles of their papers are available on the conference website: http://nomadit.co.uk/easas/ecsas2016/index.shtml, as is other information on the Warsaw ECSAS.

possible thanks to the generous grant of the Ministry of Foreign Affairs of the Republic of Poland for the PTO within the framework of 'Collaboration in the Sphere of Public Diplomacy 2016.' The conference also benefited from the support of BGK – Bank Gospodarstwa Krajowego, the partner of the University of Warsaw, who also actively participated in the event by giving a panel. I hereby extend my gratitude to the MFA and BGK for their support, and likewise to all those who helped in different ways to make the ECSAS 2016 a successful academic event introducing the University of Warsaw as a congenial venue for the scholars of South Asia.

Nine, out of twelve, papers read at the ECSAS 2016 by Polish delegates, are being published now in this volume entitled *Polish Contributions to South Asian Studies*. Taken together, they are meant to mark an improved Polish presence in European research on South Asia by presenting the substantial range of interests covered by South Asianists associated with Polish academia. Among the contributions, articles based on indigenous South Asian sources – both classical in Sanskrit, as well as modern in Hindi or Panjabi and early modern sources in Braj or Rajashtani – constitute the majority.

The volume opens with Danuta Stasik's article, 'A Polish Perspective on South Asian Studies,' in which a historical outline of Polish academic interest in South Asia is drawn. This is the only contribution in the whole volume that is not based on a paper read at the conference and has been added as an introduction to the volume. The remaining contributions have emerged from the papers presented at ECSAS 2016.

The first two articles concern Indian performative arts that in their original form were presented in Panel 02 'The Performing Arts in the Ritual Context,' convened by Bożena Śliwczyńska from the University of Warsaw. She is also the author of the paper 'Kūṭiyāṭṭam Theatre: The Aesthetic and Ritual Experience of the Performance,' in which she argues that the ancient Sanskrit theatre of Bharatamuni's *Nāṭyaśāstra* has survived in the form of Kūṭiyāṭṭam theatre and discusses it in terms of a refined and sublime combination of the aesthetic and ritual experience. The other Panel 02 paper is now published as Katarzyna Skiba's article 'Performing the Sacred in Kathak Dance,' in which its author, exploring the religious dimension of Kathak dance, demonstrates that an increasing tendency to spiritualize this dance tradition since the 1930s is a result of the appropriation of Kathak by Brahmin elites and urban middle classes, fostering its Hinduization and nationalization.

Olga Nowicka's article 'In the Footsteps of Śaṅkara: Mapping a Pan-India *Digvijaya* in the Local Space of Kerala' was originally presented in Panel 41

'Spatial and Visual Dimensions of Pilgrimage in South Asia' convened by Jörg Gengnagel (University of Heidelberg) and Vera Lazzaretti (Università degli Studi di Milano). It explores a specifically Keralan hagiographical tradition of Śaṅkara's conquest of the quarters of the land (*digvijaya*) and the process of constructing the physical space in which the pan-Indian legendary map of Śaṅkara's life can be relevant to a new geographic location and a peculiar local tradition.

Piotr Borek's 'Deification in a Secular Text. On Some Functions of Religious Content in Bhūṣaṇ's *Śivrājbhūṣaṇ*' (1673 AD) and Aleksandra Turek's 'Hostility or Solidarity? The Rājpūts and Jāṭs in the *Chāvaḷīs* from the region of Śekhāvaṭī' evolved from papers presented in Panel 24 'Secular Knowledge Systems in Early Modern Literary Cultures,' convened by Richard David Williams from the University of Oxford and Stefania Cavaliere from the University of Naples "L'Orientale". The first of these contributions is concerned with the *Śivrājbhūṣaṇ*, a late 17th-century poem, usually seen as a panegyric on Marathas' leader Śivājī. In his article, Piotr Borek argues that the poem was part of a planned enterprise meant to constitute the royal power of the newly consecrated king. The contribution by Aleksandra Turek, based on the *Chāvaḷīs*, rhymed works, transmitted orally, composed in Shekhavati, a Rajasthani dialect, at the turn of the 19th and 20th centuries, demonstrates that these regional works composed on the outskirts of the mainstream literature prove to be a good source for reconstructing the social reality of nineteenth-century Rajasthan.

A paper by Agnieszka Kuszewska (University of Social Sciences and Humanities, Warsaw) was originally presented in Panel 29 'Security Challenges in Contemporary India-Pakistan Relations' that was co-convened by her and Liladhar Pendse (University of California, Berkeley). Basing her article on the assumption that security challenges and conflicts remain central issues to the study of international relations, while examining the unresolved, protracted Indo-Pakistani conflict, she also demonstrates the crucial position of Afghanistan in the rivalry between New Delhi and Islamabad.

The three final contributions in the volume stem from Panel 17 'Self in Performance: Contemporary Life Narratives in South Asia,' convened by Monika Browarczyk from Adam Mickiewicz University in Poznań and Alaka Atreya Chudal from the University of Vienna. Justyna Wiśniewska-Singh in her article 'First-Person Narrative in the Early Hindi Novel,' having observed that the first-person narrative was absent during the initial period of novel writing in Hindi – i.e. in the last decades of the nineteenth century

– analyses this technique as implemented in a novel *Mādhavī-Mādhav vā Madan-Mohinī* by Kiśorīlāl Gosvāmī, published in 1909. Maria Skakuj-Puri in her paper 'Writing the Self: Literary Strategies in Dalip Kaur Tiwana's Autobiographical Writings,' while scrutinizing the writings of a Punjabi contemporary writer Dalip Kaur Tiwana, explores the narratives in her autobiographical works that start from women-centred, real life situations and are ultimately transformed into literary masterpieces, novels written in the first person. Monika Browarczyk in her paper '*Sobti Meets Haśmat. Ham Haśmat* by Krishna Sobti as an Experiment with Life Writing Form' based on *Ham Haśmat*, reminiscences of Sobti first published in 1977, addresses multiple readings of 'the self in performance' present in it and proves this work to be a unique creative experiment with a life writing form.

Lastly, it has to be noted that in view of the fact that the contributions to this volume have a number of words transliterated and transcribed from several languages, the Editor has not attempted to devise a unified system that might be used throughout this publication. Instead, care has been taken to maintain consistency within individual papers.

Danuta Stasik

Warsaw, January 2017

DANUTA STASIK

Chair of South Asian Studies, Faculty of Oriental Studies, University of Warsaw

A Polish Perspective on South Asian Studies*

1. LAYING THE GROUNDWORK

The earliest historically documented Indo-Polish contacts can be traced to as early as the fifteenth and sixteenth centuries. The name that appears first in this context is Gaspar da Gama alias Gaspar da India (?1450–1510), a Jew from Poznań, who is known to have become an adviser to the famous Vasco da Gama during his first voyage to India in 1498. This was possible thanks to Gaspar's knowledge of the country, its language(s) and culture.[1] Half a century later comes *Epitaphium Cretcovii*, a Latin epitaph found on the gravestone of Erazm Kretkowski (1508–1558) in The Pontifical Basilica of Saint Anthony of Padua in Italy.[2] Kretkowski was a Polish nobleman and an ambassador of Sigismund II Augustus, the King of Poland (1520–1572), to Suleiman the Magnificent (1494–1566), Sultan of the Ottoman Empire. The epitaph seems to testify to the fact that Kretkowski's voyages reached

* An earlier draft of this paper was read during the World Indology Conference held at Rashtrapati Bhavan in New Delhi from 21 to 23 November 2015.

1 For more see e.g.: Sanjay Subrahmanyam, *The Career and Legend of Vasco Da Gama*, Cambridge: Cambridge University Press, 1997; E.G. Ravenstein (ed.), *A Journal of the First Voyage of Vasco Da Gama, 1497–1499*, New York: Cambridge University Press, 2010, pp. 84–85; cf. also Ann Helen Wainer, *Jewish and Brazilian Connections to New York, India, and Ecology: A Collection of Essays*, Bloomington: iUniverse, 2012, p. 32.

2 It was composed by Jan Kochanowski (1530–1584), the most famous poet of the Polish Renaissance, one of the greatest Polish and Slavic poets prior to the nineteenth century, who used to write in Latin but later switched to the vernacular.

as far as India where he saw 'the rapid Ganges.'[3] The annals of history have also recorded Krzysztof Pawłowski (?–1603), a Polish noblemen, sailor and traveller who, on 20 November 1596, sent a letter from Goa to an unknown recipient in Kraków.[4] His letter, the first known account on India in Polish, not only betrays Pawłowski's pragmatic, appraising gaze[5] of a person overwhelmed by the riches India had been known for since the ancient times but also of someone curious about her culture.

However, the beginnings of a scholarly engagement in the subcontinent should be sought much later than in these earliest and later seventeenth and eighteenth-century contacts. It took almost three centuries before such an interest would develop in Poland. In this context, the works of Walenty Skorochód Majewski (1764–1835) and of Joachim Lelewel (1786–1861) in particular should be seen as the harbingers of this new-found curiosity.

Walenty Skorochód Majewski (1764–1835), a self-educated Sanskritist, was the author of the first Polish grammars of Sanskrit and Turkish. Małgorzata Wielińska-Soltwedel, introducing Majewski in her article devoted to him,[6] rightly notes: 'Probably the first man in Poland who, at least to a certain extent, learnt Sanskrit and who might be regarded as the precursor of Indological studies in Poland is Walenty Skorochód Majewski.'[7] He took really great pains to publish his works in which his conviction about the affinity of Sanskrit and Slavic languages in general, and Polish in particular, is vocalized. However, due to his insufficient command of Sanskrit, his works

---

3 ...*Te rapidus Ganges, gelidaeque Borysthensis undae,/ Te Tagus et Rhenus, te ripa binominis Istri,/ Et septem gemini noverunt ostia Nili*; quoted after Mirosław Lenart, 'Epitaphium Cretcovii świadectwem kontaktów padewskich Jana Kochanowskiego z otoczeniem Alvisa Cornara?' (http://neolatina.bj.uj.edu.pl/neolatina/main/reports.html, access 15.10.2015).

4 'Peregrynacja do Indii Krzysztofa Pawłowskiego w r. 1596,' in *Antologia pamiętników polskich XVI wieku*, ed. Roman Pollak, Wrocław–Warszawa–Kraków: Ossolineum, 1966; Stefan Stasiak, 'Les Indes Portugaises à la fin du XVIe s. d'après la Relation du voyage fait à Goa en 1596 gentilhomme polonais,' *Rocznik Orientalistyczny*, vol. 3, 1925 (1927), pp. 1–56.

5 On the concept of 'gaze' in the context of John Urry's 'tourist gaze' (*The Tourist Gaze*, London–Thousand Oaks–New Delhi: Sage, 2002, 2nd ed.) see: Krzysztof Podemski, *Socjologia podróży*, Poznań: Wydawnictwo Naukowe Uniwersytetu im. Adama Mickiewicza w Poznaniu, 2005 (2nd. ed.), pp. 74–91.

6 Małgorzata Wielińska-Soltwedel, 'Walenty Skorochód Majewski: The Precursor of Polish Indological Studies,' in *Theatrum Mirabiliorum Indiae Orientalis: A Volume to Celebrate the 70th Birthday of Professor Maria Krzysztof Byrski* (*Rocznik Orientalistyczny*, vol. 60, no. 2, 2007), ed. Monika Nowakowska and Jacek Woźniak, pp. 157–170.

7 Ibid., p. 157.

largely tended to be amateurish and full of mistakes.[8] His most important work in this context, *O Sławianach i ich probratymcach...* (*About the Slavs and Their Kindred...*,[9] 1816), the first Polish work on Sanskrit, was published in 1816, i.e. exactly two hundred years ago. Majewski planned it as a part of a bigger project that he could never complete because of a lack of funding, partly due to the fact that his views met with the distrust and criticism of the learned elite of Warsaw, where he lived and worked.[10]

Joachim Lelewel (1786–1861) as a renowned historian, professor of Vilnius University, who also lectured for a couple of years at the University of Warsaw, and an MP in the parliament of the 19th century Kingdom of Poland (Sejm of Congress Poland), is a different case. His work *Dzieje starożytne Indji ze szczególnem zastanowieniem się nad wpływem jaki mieć mogła na strony zachodnie* (*History of Ancient India with particular consideration of her influence on the Western parts*, 1820),[11] the first Polish work on the subcontinent, reveals Lelewel's fascination with India typical of, as John D. Stanley observes, 'the Romantics who saw in Indian culture and religion a route to the wisdom of the East,'[12] although he was not blinded by such an attitude. Although his history benefited a lot from Arnold Hermann Ludwig Heeren's (1760–1842) work,[13] Lelewel also offered a number of new and original insights, especially on the formation of Indian society and state.

---

8 Ibid., pp. 162–163.

9 Its very long title is given here in the format used in the records of the National Library in Warsaw: *O Słowianach i ich pobratymcach. Cz. 1, Obeymuiaca czytane na posiedzeniach działowych w latach 1813, 1814, 1815, tudzież na Posiedzeniu Publicznem Towarzystwa Królewskiego Przyiaciół Nauk dnia 30 kwietnia 1816 r. rozprawy o języku samskryptskim* [...], Warszawa: s.n., 1816 (https://polona.pl/item/633219/2/, access 30.10.2015). A digitalized copy of this and some other Majewski's works are also available there.

10 For more on W. Skorochód Majewski see e.g.: Wielińska-Soltwedel, 'Walenty Skorochód Majewski,' pp. 157–170; Barbara Podolak, 'Walenty Skorochód Majewski – zapomniany archiwista i pasjonat języków wschodnich,' *LingVaria*, vol. 7, no. 1(13), 2012, pp. 183–194 and Aleksander Batowski, 'Walenty Skorochód Majewski i jego naukowe prace,' in *Pismo zbiorowe*, vol. 2, ed. Józafat Ohryzko, Petersburg: Józafat Ohryzko, 1859, pp. 313–352 (http://polona.pl/item/12837703/4/, access 29.10.2015).

11 Joachim Lelewel, *Dzieje starożytne Indji ze szczególnem zastanowieniem się nad wpływem jaki mieć mogła na strony zachodnie*, Warszawa: N. Glücksberg, 1820 (http://jbc.bj.uj.edu.pl/dlibra/docmetadata?id=266177&from=publication, access 17.10.2015).

12 John D. Stanley, 'Joachim Lelewel (1786–1861),' in *Nation and History: Polish Historians from the Enlightenment to the Second World War*, ed. Peter Brock, John Stanley and Piotr Wróbel, Toronto: University of Toronto Press, 2006, p. 57.

13 Arnold Hermann Ludwig Heeren, *Ideen über die Politik, den Verkehr und den Handel der Völker der alten Welt*, Göttingen: Vandenhoek und Ruprecht, 1815.

2. An Overview of South Asian Studies in Poland

2.1. Introductory Notes

Yet another few decades had passed before Sanskrit found its way into the academic curricula in Poland as a founding subject of a branch of scholarship traditionally known as Indology. In nineteenth-century Poland, divided among three neighbouring countries (the Russian Empire, the Kingdom of Prussia and Habsburg Austria – NB. neither of them a colonizing state in South Asia[14]), with no direct exposure to India, this could not be and in fact was not an independent development. This was an offshoot of the emergence of Indology in nineteenth-century Europe, particularly in French and German-speaking countries. However, while academic interest in Sanskrit in Poland in the second half of the nineteenth century was a fact, due to historical and political reasons, what we may call the Polish tradition of scholarly research in this field could begin only at the turn of the nineteenth and twentieth centuries, especially thanks to such eminent Professors as Andrzej Gawroński (1885–1927) at the Jagiellonian University in Kraków (in the years 1916–1917) and since 1917 at Jan Kazimierz University in Lwów, Helena Willman-Grabowska (1870–1957) at the Jagiellonian University and Stanisław Schayer (1899–1941) at the University of Warsaw.

Before providing an overview of the history of South Asian studies in Poland, with special focus on the biggest centres in Kraków and Warsaw, where courses at all university levels (BA, MA and PhD) are offered, it seems reasonable to pay attention to the traditional name of this discipline – i.e. 'Indology' – by setting it in the broader context of the Polish and, more broadly speaking, Central European historical and political experience. This term, or the concept of 'Indology' as such, calls for special elucidation in view of how it is commonly understood in western English-speaking countries and in South Asia itself, where it has become virtually inseparable from postcolonial theory and discourse. Central in this context is Edward Said's formulation of Orientalism that, in general, designates 'a way of coming to terms with the Orient that is based on the Orient's special place in European Western experience,' and in particular the 'Western style for dominating, restructuring, and having authority over the Orient.'[15] The fact that should be

[14] Cf. Douglas T. McGetchin, *Indology, Indomania, and Orientalism: Ancient India's Rebirth in Modern Germany*, Madison-Teaneck, NJ: Fairleigh Dickinson Univ. Press, 2009, pp. 21–22.

[15] Edward W. Said, *Orientalism*, London: Penguin Books, 2003, pp. 2–3.

underlined here is that in Said's analysis the notion of 'Western' designates mainly the nineteenth and early twentieth-century French and British experience of the Orient as well as contemporary American Orientalism. Said left India out of his analysis, although his formulation of Orientalism not only provoked discussion about the study of India – i.e. Indology[16] – but also made the term itself disreputable.[17] Not going into detail about this – sometimes heated albeit inconclusive – discussion between advocates and critics of Said's Orientalism, it should be pointed out that in the Polish context representations of India were based, like in the Czech case discussed by Martin Hříbek,[18] on 'identity' rather instead of 'otherness' or 'difference,' and on 'equality' instead of 'superiority.' As a result the Polish understanding of the term 'Indology' has never strayed far from its etymology (gr. *Indós* + *logía* < *lógos*). Thus it has denoted the study of India – of the Indian subcontinent, and later of South Asia – her languages, literatures, cultures, history etc. from antiquity to the present, though, as should be emphasized, Indology was initially concerned exclusively with Sanskrit and ancient India. In fact, Western interest in Sanskrit, rooted mainly in the realization of its affinity with Indo-European languages, was the driving force behind the emergence of this discipline. Furthermore, there has certainly never been any notion of intent to dominate or restructure India. What is noteworthy in this context is that from the very beginning an important factor fuelling Polish interest in the study of India has not concerned pragmatics but rather a curiosity about the world, *jijñāsā* about other cultures and languages – a desire to know them. No matter how romantic it may sound, this has been clearly visible until the present day and evidenced by the numbers of undergraduate students admitted yearly by four Polish university centres of South Asian languages and culture – 12 up to 30 students by each of them![19]

---

16 See e.g.: Richard King, *Orientalism and Religion: Postcolonial Theory, India and 'the Mystic East,'* London and New York: Routledge, 1999, esp. pp. 82–95; Fred Dallmayr, *Beyond Orientalism: Essays on Cross-Cultural Encounter*, Albany: State University of New York Press, 1996 and McGetchin, Indology, *Indomania, and Orientalism*, esp. pp. 20–23.

17 More recent proofs of such a negative association can be found in a volume *Understanding India: Indology and Beyond*, ed. Jaroslav Vacek and Harbans Mukhia, *Acta Universitatis Carolinae. Philologica. Orientalia Pragensia*, vol. 18, no. 1, 2011.

18 Martin Hříbek, 'Czech Indology and the Concept of Orientalism,' in *Understanding India*, pp. 45–56.

19 Though in recent years, due to demographic decline, the number of candidates competing for one place has dropped and is much lower at the graduate level than it used to be.

2.2. The Jagiellonian University in Kraków

The beginnings of Polish Indology bring us to the Jagiellonian University in Kraków, established in 1364 – the oldest university in Poland and one of the oldest universities in Europe.[20] It was there, in Kraków, in 1860, that a German linguist – Professor Bernard Jülg (1825–1886) – inaugurated Indian studies in Poland at the university level with his lectures on Sanskrit grammar. Later, his work was continued at the Department of Comparative Linguistics by such eminent linguists as Jan Baudouin de Courtenay (1845–1929) from 1894 to 1898 and Jan Rozwadowski (1867–1935) from 1899 to 1926, as well as in the years 1912–1916 by Andrzej Gawroński, an excellent Indologist, linguist and one of the greatest Polish polyglots,[21] a co-founder and editor of *Rocznik Orientalistyczny* (*The Yearbook of Oriental Studies*), a journal published to this day.[22]

The Chair of Sanskrit at the Jagiellonian University was established in 1893 with Leon Mańkowski (1858–1909) as its head until 1906 but unfortunately he left no successor. In 1916, for a brief period of one year, Gawroński took the chair of Sanskrit but then he left for Lwów where he was appointed professor and Head of the Department of Contrastive Linguistics at Jan Kazimierz University. It is worth mentioning here that Gawroński is the author of the first Polish handbook of Sanskrit (*Podręcznik sanskrytu*, 1932), published posthumously in Kraków in 1932, an excellent work used until the present day at Polish universities. It took long eleven years, before in 1927 Helena Willman-Grabowska, an Indologist and Iranologist, began her lectures on Sanskrit. In 1928, after acquiring a French state *doctorat ès lettres*, she took the Chair of Sanskrit and Indian Philology. Interestingly,

---

20 For more on Indology in Kraków see e.g.: Iwona Milewska, 'Sanskrit Studies in Kraków,' *Cracow Indological Studies*, vol. 1, 1995, pp. 5–11; Lidia Sudyka, 'Indian Studies at the Jagiellonian University, Cracow,' in *Teaching on India in Central and Eastern Europe: Contributions to the 1st Central & Eastern European Indological Conference on Regional Cooperation (Warsaw, 15–17 September 2005)*, ed. Danuta Stasik and Anna Trynkowska, Warszawa: Dom Wydawniczy Elipsa, 2007, pp. 78–83; Marzenna Czerniak-Drożdżowicz, 'Indology in Cracow – Facing New Challenges, Viewing New Perspectives,' in *Understanding India*, pp. 131–136.

21 It is said that he knew 60 foreign languages, though Gawroński himself, questioned by someone, embarrassed acknowledged that he could 'speak and write in 40 languages but understand and read in about 100.' Eugeniusz Słuszkiewicz, 'Wspomnienie o Andrzeju Gawrońskim w dziesięciolecie zgonu,' *Rocznik Orientalistyczny*, vol. 12, 1936, pp. 217–219.

22 http://www.kno.pan.pl/index.php/rocznik-orientalistyczny.

Helena Willman-Grabowska was the first woman lecturer and professor (from 1929) in the history of the Jagiellonian University.[23]

After the outbreak of the Second World War, in Nazi-occupied Poland, all universities were closed. Paradoxically, after the end of war, due to political reasons, Professor Willman-Grabowska was expelled from the University in 1947, and from 1948 there were no regular degree courses in Indian studies, until 1973, when one of Professor Willman-Grabowska's disciples, Tadeusz Pobożniak (1910–1991), became the head of the newly opened Department of Indian Studies.[24] He did not limit his interest to Sanskrit but also introduced Hindi into the curriculum; himself he was especially interested in Polish Gypsies and their Romani language.

At present, after over forty years later of its unbroken academic activity, the department, functioning now under the name the Department of Languages and Cultures of India and South Asia within the structure of the Institute of Oriental Studies, enrolls students on undergraduate, graduate and PhD programs in classical and modern Indology (mainly Sanskrit and Hindi).[25] The department also publishes *Cracow Indological Studies*, a journal highly ranked by the Polish Ministry of Science and Higher Education.[26]

2.3. The University of Warsaw

The tradition of teaching and scholarship on South Asian topics, known as Indology, at the University of Warsaw goes back to 1918, the year that marks the restoration of Poland's independence. In that year, Jan Baudouin de Courtenay, an eminent linguist, known worldwide for his theory of the phoneme, moved from Kraków to Warsaw where he lectured on the comparative grammar of Indo-European languages, thanks to which Sanskrit was included as one of the subjects in the University of Warsaw curricula.[27]

---

[23] For more on Willman Grabowska see: Renata Czekalska, 'Helena Willman-Grabowska (1870–1957),' in *Złota Księga Wydziału Filologicznego UJ*, ed. Jan Michalik and Wacław Walecki, Księgarnia Akademicka, Kraków 2000, pp. 224–230 and Renata Czekalska and Agnieszka Kuczkiewicz-Fraś (eds), *Helena Willman-Grabowska. Orientalistka – uczona – popularyzatorka*, Księgarnia Akademicka, Kraków 2014.

[24] Selected articles of Tadeusz Pobożniak were edited by Agnieszka Kuczkiewicz-Fraś and Halina Marlewicz and published in *Cracow Indological Studies*, vol. 3, 2001.

[25] The department's website address: http://www.indologia.io.filg.uj.edu.pl/.

[26] http://www.indologia.io.filg.uj.edu.pl/badania/cracow-indological-studies .

[27] For more on Sanskrit studies in Warsaw see e.g.: Marek Mejor, 'Sanskrit Studies in Poland,' in *Teaching on India in Central and Eastern Europe*, pp. 36–43 and Anna

The formal beginnings of the Department of Indology, however, should be linked to Professor Stanisław Schayer (1899–1941), the founding father of the Oriental Institute of the University of Warsaw and its first director (1932). Initially only Sanskrit and subjects related to ancient India (especially philosophy) were taught at the department but soon modern languages also followed: in 1935, Bengali and in 1938, Hindi, taught by Schayer himself with the assistance of Hiranmoy Ghoshal (1908–1969), a Bengali from Calcutta, who came to Poland at the behest of Professor Schayer.[28] During this short seven-year period of its pre-war history, the department became a well-known centre for Indian studies, especially thanks to Schayer's profound works on Buddhism and Indian philosophy.

During the Second World War, as previously mentioned, in Nazi-occupied Poland, all universities were closed but in September 1939, the building of the Oriental Institute together with its newly assembled library collection was burnt as a result of an air raid. The department resumed its operation only in 1953 with Professor Eugeniusz Słuszkiewicz appointed as its Head and Grażyna Spychalska as his assistant. Considering the history of this institute, one should always bear in mind what Professor Byrski once noted: 'Let us never forget the titanic energy of our predecessors who were active immediately after the war. It was their limitless enthusiasm which made it possible for us now to think about becoming a full-fledged faculty[29] and about embracing in our research and teaching practically all Asian and African cultures, as well as those bordering Asia and Europe.'[30]

Initially the courses were entirely devoted to Sanskrit and classical Indian culture but that situation changed two years later when, in 1955, Tatiana Rutkowska (1926–2002), a graduate of the University of Leningrad and a pupil of Professor Aleksei P. Barannikov, joined the Department.

Trynkowska, 'Sanskrit Studies in Poland After the Second World War,' in Radhavallabh Tripathi (ed.), *Sixty Years of Sanskrit Studies (1950–2010)*, Rashtriya Sanskrit Sansthan, New Delhi 2012, pp. 213–236.

[28] For more on Hindi studies in Warsaw see: Danuta Stasik, 'Hindi Studies in Warsaw,' in *Teaching on India in Central and Eastern Europe*, pp. 92–101.

[29] Prof. Byrski's paper was read in 2005 – i.e. three years before the Institute of Oriental Studies was officially transformed into a faculty of the University of Warsaw (the Faculty of Oriental Studies) under the Act no. 332 by the Senate of the University of Warsaw (Monitor UW no. 1, 23.01.2008).

[30] Maria Krzysztof Byrski, 'Jubilee Retrospections,' in *India in Warsaw. Indie w Warszawie*, ed. Danuta Stasik and Anna Trynkowska, Dom Wydawniczy Elipsa, Warszawa 2006, p. 24.

It should be stressed here that the work begun in 1955 by Tatiana Rutkowska (the first person in Poland to receive a PhD degree in Hindi in 1968) forms the starting point of the unbroken and by now the sixty-year tradition of research on Hindi and Urdu language and literature in the post-war history of the department and in Poland. Until the beginning of the 1990s all the graduates of the Department for whom Hindi was the main subject, as well as those who learnt it in addition to other subjects, were Doctor Rutkowska's students.

Another expansion in the department's curriculum took place in 1957 after Hiranmoy Ghoshal returned to Poland and joined the university. He continued to teach Sanskrit and Bengali as well as other subjects at the department until his death in 1969.

A few years after the department resumed its activity, its first graduates began to supplement its teaching staff. Among them were: Alicja Karlikowska (Hindi and Urdu); Dr Agnieszka Kowalska-Soni (Hindi and Bengali); Professor Maria Krzysztof Byrski, a Sanskritist with doctoral degree from the Banaras Hindu University, an expert in classical Indian theatre, for many years (1971–1990) the head of the department, and in the 1990s the Polish ambassador to India; Andrzej Ługowski, an outstanding linguist and an erudite, demanding Sanskrit teacher; Artur Karp, a Sanskrit, Pali and Hindi teacher; Barbara Grabowska, professor of medieval Bengali literature and Elżbieta Walter, a specialist in modern Bengali literature.

Tamilology is the youngest branch of Indian studies in Poland. It was introduced as a new Indological discipline at the University of Warsaw in the 1970s thanks to the efforts of Professor Eugeniusz Słuszkiewicz and Professor M. Krzysztof Byrski. The beginnings of Tamil Studies are related to the figure of Dr. Ramanathan Sundaram (b. 1938), the first Tamil teacher in Poland, who came to Warsaw in 1972 and for seven years worked as a lecturer of Dravidian languages, teaching Tamil and Malayalam.[31]

In 1996, as a result of this expansion in the scope of academic interest into all the areas of classical and modern South Asia, the department was renamed as the Department of South Asian Studies and in 2008 it was upgraded to the status of the Chair of South Asian Studies. At present, this department,

[31] For more on Tamil studies see: Joanna Kusio, 'Tamil Studies in Poland,' in *Teaching on India in Central and Eastern Europe*, pp. 109–114 and Jacek Woźniak, 'Tamil Studies in Warsaw,' in *Tamil in Warsaw. Celebrating the 40th Anniversary of Tamil Studies at the University of Warsaw (2012/2013)*, ed. Danuta Stasik and Jacek Woźniak, Dom Wydawniczy Elipsa, Warszawa 2014, pp. 11–14.

well-known for its academic activities on national and international level, offers BA, MA and PhD courses in Indology with majors in Sanskrit, Hindi, Bengali and Tamil. It comprises a broad range of subjects and interests and counts as the leading centre for South Asian studies in Poland.[32]

2.4. The University of Wrocław and Adam Mickiewicz University in Poznań

Apart from Warsaw and Kraków, research on India on a regular basis is also conducted at the University of Wrocław[33] and Adam Mickiewicz University in Poznań[34] though teaching goes on a smaller scale and only courses at the undergraduate level are offered there.

The beginnings of Indological Studies in Wrocław go back to the first half of the nineteenth century, when Wrocław belonged to the German Empire, and are connected with Adolf Friedrich Stenzler (1807–1887), a German Indologist, a pioneer of Sanskrit studies in Germany, the author of a highly regarded textbook on Sanskrit. In 1833, he was appointed professor of the University of Breslau (then Schlesische Friedrich-Wilhelms-Universität zu Breslau) and was also eventually elected its Rector (1862–1863). A number of well-known German Indologists received their doctoral degrees under the guidance of Professor Stenzler, among whom were, for instance, Richard Pischel (1849-1908) and Lorenz Franz Kielhorn (1840–1908). In 1878, Stenzler was succeeded by Alfred Hillebrandt (1853–1927), another of his pupils, an academic and twice rector of the university (1901–1902 and 1910–1911), the author of *Vedische Mythologie* (1891–1902) translated into English in 1980 and published in India.[35]

With the geopolitical changes brought by the Second World War, Wrocław became part of Poland in 1945. Indological research at the University of Wrocław was resumed by Ludwik Skurzak (1900–1979), a student of such renowned scholars as Stefan Stasiak (1884–1962), Jean Przyluski, Sylvain Lèvi and Stanisław Schayer, whose work, based on Sanskrit, Greek and Latin

[32] The department's website address: http://www.indologia.orient.uw.edu.pl/.

[33] For more on Indian studies in Wrocław see: Joanna Sachse, 'Indological Studies at the University of Wrocław,' in *Teaching on India in Central and Eastern Europe*, pp. 69–77 and Trynkowska, 'Sanskrit Studies in Poland.'

[34] Trynkowska, 'Sanskrit Studies in Poland.'

[35] Alfred Hillebrandt, *Vedic Mythology*, 2 vols, Motilal Banarsidass, Delhi 1990.

sources devoted to Indian asceticism,[36] has been quoted by specialists until the present day. The difficult beginnings at Wrocław, where everything had to be built from scratch, and the very trying political circumstances, meant that in 1951, Indology was deleted from the university curricula. It was resumed only a year after the so-called 'Polish October' or 'Polish thaw,' in 1957, by Ludwik Skurzak and his pupil Hanna Wałkówska (1921–2013), a specialist in ancient Indian customs and law. In 1969, the department was renamed as the Department of Indian Philology. It was one of the units of the Institute of Classics. For many long years it was headed by Professor Wałkówska and until recently by her pupil – Professor Joanna Sachse, a scholar especially interested in ancient Indian civilisation and the study of the *Mahābhārata* and classical Sanskrit literature (*kāvya*).

At present (since 2009), the Department of Indian Philology in Wrocław[37] offers a regular BA program in the field of philology with a specialization in Indian philology and the culture of India, which is based not only on Sanskrit but also on Hindi.

A brief episode of Sanskrit teaching at Adam Mickiewicz University in Poznań can be dated to back to the 1920s, when Antoni Śmieszek (1881–1943) was appointed as Professor of 'the languages of the Ancient East, including Sanskrit.'[38] However this position was discontinued in 1933 and for a long time there was no teaching on Asian subjects in Poznań. The beginnings of the unbroken history of South Asian studies at Adam Mickiewicz University in Poznań can be dated to 1987 when Sanskrit and Hindi, then Tamil (1988) and much later also Tibetan (2001) as well as courses on South Asian culture were offered to the students of the Faculty of Modern Languages. Finally, in the 1999, thanks to the efforts of Professor Marek Mejor the Unit of South Asian Studies was established but for several years did not recruit their own students. In 2007, this unit's range of studies has

[36] Ludwik Skurzak, *Études sur l'origine de l'ascétisme indien*, Wrocławskie Towarzystwo Naukowe, Wrocław 1948.

[37] The department's website address: http://indologia.uni.wroc.pl/.

[38] Arkadiusz Jabłoński, Maciej Kanert, Marek Mejor and Halina Wasilewska, *Katedra Orientalistyki na Wydziale Neofilologii Uniwersytetu im. Adama Mickiewicza w Poznaniu*, ed. Jacek Swędrowski and Tomasz Wicherkiewicz (unpublished materials of the Chair of Oriental Studies, Faculty of Modern Languages, Adam Mickiewicz University in Poznań). I would like to acknowledge my gratitude to Natalia Świdzińska for sharing this material with me.

transformed into a regular BA course in classical Indology including Sanskrit and Tibetan, and modern Indology with Hindi and Tamil, and since 2013 it has offered a uniform BA program in Indian studies.[39]

3. CONCLUSIONS

Undoubtedly, we may say that in present-day Poland the lively interest in South Asia, South Asian languages and the wide range of related issues has also translated into more frequent direct contacts of Poles with this region. It is also true that the direct and indirect presence of South Asia in many spheres of our lives has been more and more pronounced (especially in the form of Indian popular culture, cuisine, a plethora of yoga and meditation classes etc.) which to a certain degree may pave the way for new needs and new possibilities in the field of South Asian studies.

To sum up, I would like to quote the words of Professor Stanisław Schayer, one of, if not the (!), most eminent among Polish Indologists of all times, that in fact may serve as the motto for this paper and my own research as well. In the 1930s, Professor Schayer wrote: 'Identifying Western culture with the notion of universal culture is a grave mistake. Whoever knows India and her culture will not make this mistake.'[40] Have we all done our homework properly?

BIBLIOGRAPHY

Batowski, Aleksander, 'Walenty Skorochód Majewski i jego naukowe prace', in *Pismo zbiorowe*, vol. 2, ed. Józafat Ohryzko, Petersburg: Józafat Ohryzko, 1859, pp. 313–352 (http://polona.pl/item/12837703/4/, access 29.10.2015).

Brock, Peter, John Stanley and Piotr Wróbel (eds), *Nation and History: Polish Historians from the Enlightenment to the Second World War*, Toronto: University of Toronto Press, 2006.

Byrski, Maria Krzysztof, 'Jubilee Retrospections,' in *India in Warsaw. Indie w Warszawie*, ed. Danuta Stasik and Anna Trynkowska, Warszawa: Dom Wydawniczy Elipsa, 2006, pp. 23–28.

39 The department's website address: http://orient.amu.edu.pl/index.php/katedra/struktura/indologia.

40 Polish original in Stanisław Schayer, 'Literatura indyjska,' in *Wielka Literatura Powszechna* (2nd ed.), Warszawa: Trzaska, Evert, Michalski, 1936, p. 225.

Czekalska, Renata, 'Helena Willman-Grabowska (1870–1957),' in *Złota Księga Wydziału Filologicznego UJ*, ed. Jan Michalik and Wacław Walecki, Kraków: Księgarnia Akademicka, 2000, pp. 223–230.

Czekalska, Renata and Agnieszka Kuczkiewicz-Fraś (eds), *Helena Willman-Grabowska. Orientalistka – uczona – popularyzatorka*, Kraków: Księgarnia Akademicka, 2014.

Czerniak-Drożdżowicz, Marzenna, 'Indology in Cracow – Facing New Challenges, Viewing New Perspectives,' in *Understanding India: Indology and Beyond*, ed. Jaroslav Vacek and Harbans Mukhia, *Acta Universitatis Carolinae. Philologica. Orientalia Pragensia*, vol. 18, no. 1, 2011, pp. 131–136.

Dallmayr, Fred, *Beyond Orientalism: Essays on Cross-Cultural Encounter*, Albany: State University of New York Press, 1996.

Heeren, Arnold Hermann Ludwig, *Ideen über die Politik, den Verkehr u. den Handel der vornehmsten Völker der alten Welt*, Göttingen: Vandenhoeck et Ruprecht, 1815.

Hříbek, Martin, 'Czech Indology and the Concept of Orientalism,' in *Understanding India: Indology and Beyond*, ed. Jaroslav Vacek and Harbans Mukhia, *Acta Universitatis Carolinae. Philologica. Orientalia Pragensia*, vol. 18, no. 1, 2011, pp. 45–56.

King, Richard, *Orientalism and Religion: Postcolonial Theory, India and 'the Mystic East,'* London and New York: Routledge, 1999.

Kusio, Joanna, 'Tamil Studies in Poland,' in *Teaching on India in Central and Eastern Europe: Contributions to the 1st Central & Eastern European Indological Conference on Regional Cooperation (Warsaw, 15–17 September 2005)*, ed. Danuta Stasik and Anna Trynkowska, Warszawa: Dom Wydawniczy Elipsa, 2007, pp. 109–114.

Lelewel, Joachim, *Dzieje starożytne Indji ze szczególnem zastanowieniem się nad wpływem jaki mieć mogła na strony zachodnie*, Warszawa: N. Glücksberg, 1820 (http://jbc.bj.uj.edu.pl/dlibra/docmetadata?id=266177&from=publication, access 17.10.2015).

Lenart, Mirosław, 'Epitaphium Cretcovii świadectwem kontaktów padewskich Jana Kochanowskiego z otoczeniem Alvisa Cornara?' (http://neolatina.bj.uj.edu.pl/neolatina/main/reports.html access 15.10.2015).

Majewski, W(alenty) S(korochód), *O Słowianach i ich pobratymcach. Cz. 1, Obeymuiaca czytane na posiedzeniach działowych w latach 1813, 1814, 1815, tudzież na Posiedzeniu Publicznem Towarzystwa Królewskiego Przyiaciół Nauk dnia 30 kwietnia 1816 r. rozprawy o języku samskryptskim* [...], Warszawa: Drukarnia Wiktora Dąbrowskiego, 1816 (https://polona.pl/item/633219/2/, access 30.11.2015).

McGetchin, Douglas T., *Indology, Indomania, and Orientalism: Ancient India's Rebirth in Modern Germany*, Madison–Teaneck: Fairleigh Dickinson Univ. Press, 2009.

Mejor, Marek, 'Sanskrit Studies in Poland,' in *Teaching on India in Central and Eastern Europe: Contributions to the 1st Central & Eastern European Indological Conference on Regional Cooperation (Warsaw, 15–17 September 2005)*, ed. Danuta Stasik and Anna Trynkowska, Warszawa: Dom Wydawniczy Elipsa, 2007, pp. 36–43.

Milewska, Iwona, 'Sanskrit Studies in Kraków,' *Cracow Indological Studies*, vol. 1, 1995, pp. 5–11.

Nowakowska, Monika and Jacek Woźniak (eds), *Theatrum Mirabiliorum Indiae Orientalis: A Volume to Celebrate the 70th Birthday of Professor Maria Krzysztof Byrski* (*Rocznik Orientalistyczny*, vol. 60, no. 2, 2007).

Pawłowski, Krzysztof, 'Peregrynacja do Indii Krzysztofa Pawłowskiego w r. 1596,' in *Antologia pamiętników polskich XVI wieku*, ed. Roman Pollak, Wrocław–Warszawa–Kraków: Ossolineum, 1966.

Podemski, Krzysztof, *Socjologia podróży*, Poznań: Wydawnictwo Naukowe Uniwersytetu im. Adama Mickiewicza w Poznaniu, 2005 (2nd. ed.).

Podolak Barbara, 'Walenty Skorochód Majewski – zapomniany archiwista i pasjonat języków wschodnich,' *LingVaria*, vol. 7, no. 1(13), 2012, pp. 183–194.

Ravenstein, E. G. (ed.), *A Journal of the First Voyage of Vasco Da Gama, 1497–1499*, Cambridge: Cambridge University Press, 2010.

Sachse, Joanna, 'Indological Studies at the University of Wrocław,' in *Teaching on India in Central and Eastern Europe: Contributions to the 1st Central & Eastern European Indological Conference on Regional Cooperation (Warsaw, 15–17 September 2005)*, ed. Danuta Stasik and Anna Trynkowska, Warszawa: Dom Wydawniczy Elipsa, 2007, pp. 69–77.

Said, Edward W., *Orientalism*, London: Penguin Books, 2003.

Schayer, Stanisław, 'Literatura indyjska,' in *Wielka Literatura Powszechna*, Warszawa: Trzaska, Evert, Michalski, 1936.

Skurzak, Ludwik, *Études sur l'origine de l'ascétisme indien*, Wrocław: Wrocławskie Towarzystwo Naukowe, 1948.

Słuszkiewicz, Eugeniusz, 'Wspomnienie o Andrzeju Gawrońskim w dziesięciolecie zgonu,' *Rocznik Orientalistyczny*, vol. 12, 1936, pp. 216–230.

Stanley, John D., 'Joachim Lelewel (1786–1861),' in *Nation and History: Polish Historians from the Enlightenment to the Second World War*, ed. Peter Brock, John Stanley and Piotr Wróbel, Toronto: University of Toronto Press, 2006, pp. 52–84.

Stasiak, Stefan, 'Les Indes Portugaises à la fin du XVIe s. d'après la Relation du voyage fait à Goa en 1596 gentilhomme polonais,' *Rocznik Orientalistyczny*, vol. 3, 1925 (1927), pp. 1–56.

Stasik, Danuta, 'Hindi Studies in Warsaw,' in *Teaching on India in Central and Eastern Europe: Contributions to the 1st Central & Eastern European Indological Conference on Regional Cooperation (Warsaw, 15-17 September 2005)*, ed. Danuta Stasik and Anna Trynkowska, Warszawa: Dom Wydawniczy Elipsa, 2007, pp. 92–101.

Stasik, Danuta and Anna Trynkowska (eds), *India in Warsaw. Indie w Warszawie*, Warszawa: Dom Wydawniczy Elipsa, 2006.

Stasik, Danuta and Anna Trynkowska (eds), *Teaching on India in Central and Eastern Europe: Contributions to the 1st Central & Eastern European Indological Conference on Regional Cooperation (Warsaw, 15–17 September 2005)*, Warszawa: Dom Wydawniczy Elipsa, 2007.

Stasik, Danuta and Jacek Woźniak (eds), *Tamil in Warsaw. Celebrating the 40th Anniversary of Tamil Studies at the University of Warsaw (2012/2013)*, Warszawa: Dom Wydawniczy Elipsa, 2014.

Subrahmanyam, Sanjay, *The Career and Legend of Vasco Da Gama*, Cambridge: Cambridge University Press, 1997.

Sudyka, Lidia, 'Indian Studies at the Jagiellonian University, Cracow,' in *Teaching on India in Central and Eastern Europe: Contributions to the 1st Central & Eastern European Indological Conference on Regional Cooperation (Warsaw, 15–17 September 2005)*, ed. Danuta Stasik and Anna Trynkowska, Warszawa: Dom Wydawniczy Elipsa, 2007, pp. 78–83.

Trynkowska, Anna, 'Sanskrit Studies in Poland After the Second World War,' in Radhavallabh Tripathi (ed.), *Sixty Years of Sanskrit Studies (1950–2010)*, New Delhi: Rashtriya Sanskrit Sansthan, 2012, pp. 213–236.

Understanding India: Indology and Beyond, ed. Jaroslav Vacek and Harbans Mukhia, *Acta Universitatis Carolinae. Philologica. Orientalia Pragensia*, vol. 18, no. 1, 2011.

Urry, John, *The Tourist Gaze*, London–Thousand Oaks–New Delhi: Sage, 2002 (2nd ed.).

Wainer, Ann Helen, *Jewish and Brazilian Connections to New York, India, and Ecology: A Collection of Essays*, Bloomington: iUniverse, 2012.

Wielińska-Soltwedel, Małgorzata, 'Walenty Skorochód Majewski: The Precursor of Polish Indological Studies,' *Theatrum Mirabiliorum Indiae Orientalis: A Volume to Celebrate the 70th Birthday of Professor Maria Krzysztof Byrski* (*Rocznik Orientalistyczny*, vol. 60, no. 2, 2007), ed. Monika Nowakowska and Jacek Woźniak, pp. 157–170.

Woźniak, Jacek, 'Tamil Studies in Warsaw,' in *Tamil in Warsaw. Celebrating the 40th Anniversary of Tamil Studies at the University of Warsaw (2012/2013)*, ed. Danuta Stasik and Jacek Woźniak, Warszawa: Dom Wydawniczy Elipsa, 2014, pp. 11–14.

Bożena Śliwczyńska

Chair of South Asian Studies, Faculty of Oriental Studies, University of Warsaw

Kūṭiyāṭṭam Theatre: The Aesthetic and Ritual Experience of the Performance

The ancient Sanskrit theatre of Bharatamuni's *Nāṭyaśāstra* has survived in Kūṭiyāṭṭam theatre[1] until our times. Kūṭiyāṭṭam (lit. 'acting together'), which originates from the South Indian state of Kerala, concentrates on staging Sanskrit dramas. Its long history covers twenty centuries or even more, if we take into consideration the evidence of the *Cilappatikāram* of Iḷaṅkō[2] where the name of a Kūṭiyāṭṭam actor is mentioned as well as the *Nāṭyaśāstra*'s rules adopted by the Kūṭiyāṭṭam theatre. In fact, we may call the tradition of this theatre 'Nāṭyaśāstra' in practice. Yet, Kūṭiyāṭṭam means more than enacting Sanskrit drama texts. Within its realm there are two more subforms based on the same performing tradition: Naṅṅyār Kūttu and Cākyār Kūttu, and both of them, unlike the Sanskrit drama Kūṭiyāṭṭam, are solo performances. Until the mid-20th century, the Kūṭiyāṭṭam theatre in all its complexity operated exclusively within temple premises and its performances were intended as a temple ritual in the annual cycle prescribed to certain temples of the Brahmanical order.[3] Nowadays the Kūṭiyāṭṭam stage performances, while performed in the temple, are still considered as a regular temple ritual.

---

[1] In this paper, I refer to my observances and experiences during my long term research work on the Kūṭiyāṭṭam theatre tradition in Kerala since 1998 onwards.

[2] Iḷaṅkō belongs to the period between the 2nd and 5th centuries or even earlier, thus his poem *Cilappatikāram* is a part of the Tamil Sangam literature.

[3] The orthodox temples were closed to the lower strata members of the Hindu society. Depending on the region of the modern state of Kerala, the temples of the Brahmanical

In most of these Brahmanical temples, there are special buildings called *kūttampalam* – lit. 'a temple of stage performance/theatre.' Their location within the overall temple layout is not accidental at all. The *kūttampalam* is situated in the first entry courtyard of the temple, on the right of the temple east-west axis (viewed from the *garbha gṛha*, or the temple's *sanctum sanctorum*). Inside the structure, a stage is arranged in such a way that the Kūṭiyāṭṭam artists always face the *garbha gṛha* and the statue (*mūrti*) of the temple's presiding deity. All *kūttampalam* architectural measurements have to relate to the same measurements of the *garbha gṛha*. Both buildings are in very close proximity, structurally as well as ritually. Let me point out that the ritual activities in the *garbha gṛha* and *kūttampalam* are never performed at the same time. According to the regular temple schedule, all prescribed rituals conducted in the *garbha gṛha* can only take place after the performance offerings have been concluded in the *kūttampalam*, and vice versa. Ritual actions held in both sacred temple structures are complementary to one another.

Since the Kūṭiyāṭṭam theatre ritual is performed within the temple grounds, the strict rules of ritual purity must be observed by all participants of the performance, especially by Kūṭiyāṭṭam exponents. They belong to two subcommunities of the *ampalavāsi* (lit. 'those living in the temple') milieu, namely Cākyārs (actors) and Nampyārs (musicians) and their womenfolk called Naṅṅyārs (musicians and actresses). Only the members of these communities are allowed to step onto the temple theatre (*kūttampalam*) stage and execute a ritual of the *nāṭya* performance. For centuries the Cākyārs, Nampyārs and Naṅṅyārs have been, and still are, the exclusive exponents of the ritual performed in the *kūttampalam* and, moreover, the ritual stage activity is their *kula-dharma*, or 'the duties and obligations of a family/clan.'[4] Their hereditary vocation holds a strong correlation with an idea expressed in the *Nāṭyaśāstra*: 'Gods are not so much pleased with worshipping [them] with garlands and scents, as they are always pleased with well-done[5] theatre

order started to be open to all members of the Hindu society in the late 1930s (1936 in Travancore) and the process was completed in the late 1940s (Kochi and Malabar).

4 Since the traditional Kūṭiyāṭṭam theatre exponents follow a matriarchal system of inheritance, they are custodians of their maternal family art tradition.

5 In the *Nāṭyaśāstra* text, the term *maṅgala* is used in the meaning 'happiness, welfare, bliss, anything auspicious.' Definitely a well-executed theatre performance is an auspicious issue, bringing happiness to all its participants.

performance.'[6] The stage activity of Kūṭiyāṭṭam exponents is definitely sanctified by the most authoritative text of Indian theatre.

As a religious ritual, the Kūṭiyāṭṭam theatre performance involves a series of strictly defined actions executed in the proper order. At the very beginning of all the stage activities, a stage lamp of three knots must be lit with the fire brought from the *garbha gr̥ha* (*śrīkovil*). The burning knots of the lamp represent the three fires of Vedic sacrifice (*yajña*) – i.e. *āhavanīya*, or eastern fire, *gārhyapatya* (western fire) and *anvāhāryaparana* (*dakṣiṇa* – southern fire).[7] Bringing the fire on stage establishes the presence of the Divine in the *kūttampalam*. It is a significant moment of ritual purity for the whole performance space (the stage, green-room and auditorium) as well as for the people involved in the *nāṭya* ritual act (performers and spectators). Referring to the Vedic sacred fires and invoking the gods to be seated on the stage (in the *puṟappāṭu* segment[8]) brings to mind the mutual correlations of theatre–*nāṭya* and sacrifice–*yajña*.[9] No wonder that the theatre performance is called *cākṣuṣa-yajña* – a sacrifice that is pleasing to the eyes, and in fact to all the senses. The Kūṭiyāṭṭam theatre performance definitely deserves to be regarded as a *cākṣuṣa-yajña* of the highest value.[10]

Let us first say a few words about the way in which the Kūṭiyāṭṭam enacts the Sanskrit dramas. First of all, a single act of the drama constitutes a full-fledged performance lasting for many days. However, the drama text is only one of three components, or segments, of the whole performance. It is preluded by the *puṟappāṭu* and *nirvahaṇa* segments.[11] The latter is

6 *na tathā gandhamālyena devāstuṣyanti pūjitāḥ / yathā nāṭyaprayogasthairnityaṁ tuṣyanti maṅgalaiḥ*// NŚ PSS, XXXVII, 29.

7 In the course of time, the three burning knots of the stage lamp started to represent the Hindu *trimūrti*, i.e. the gods: Brahmā, Viṣṇu and Śiva.

8 See the next paragraphs of the main text of this article.

9 For more about the concept of the *yajña* and *nāṭya* see: M. Christopher Byrski, *Concept of Ancient Indian Theatre*, New Delhi: Munshiram Manoharlal Publishers Pvt. Ltd., 1974, pp. 41–51.

10 The Kūṭiyāṭṭam performers do realize the value and sacred context of their hereditary art. See: Māṇi Mādhava Cākyār, *Nāṭyakalpadrumam*, Ceṟuturutti: Kēraḷa Kalāmaṇḍalam, 1973, pp. LXXIII–LXXV.

11 For more about the *puṟappāṭu* see: Bożena Śliwczyńska, 'The Ritual of Beginning. The Puṟappāṭu Segment of the Kūṭiyāṭṭam Theatre Tradition,' *Rocznik Orientalistyczny*, vol. 60, no. 2, 2007, pp. 357–361; Bożena Śliwczyńska, *Tradycja teatru świątynnego kudijattam*, Warszawa: Wydawnictwo Akademickie Dialog, 2009, pp. 127–138; about the *nirvahaṇa* see: Bożena Śliwczyńska, 'The Technique of Narration in the Kūṭiyāṭṭam Theatre Tradition,' in *India in Warsaw*, ed. Danuta Stasik and Anna Trynkowska, Warszawa: Dom

a flashback leading to the main story of the text enacted, while the former, the *puṟappāṭu*, which is definitely the ritual of the beginning,[12] always initiates the complex performance. The stage is consecrated with an offering to Gaṇapati (*Gaṇapati pūjā*) performed by a temple priest and made ready for stage activities carried out by the Kūṭiyāṭṭam performers. Then the gods of the stage (of the Universe) are invoked and their presence established.

The *puṟappāṭu* mainly consists of a series of songs praising the gods (*akkitta*) combined with certain choreographic patterns, called *nitya kriyās*, namely the 'acts that must always be done/performed.' The stage worship is meant to glorify and please the Divine (God) and is also for the benefit of all participants of the performance – i.e. the performers, the audience and the main spectator (the presiding deity of the temple). Let us mention here that there are performances made exclusively for the temple deity, without the presence of human spectators (*aṭiyanttira*). The *puṟappāṭu* segment is to be performed by the *sūtradhāra*, or stage-manager, and the master of theatre art (*nāṭyācarya*), if the first act of a drama text is enacted (this is mainly an outdated practice), or if other acts of the drama are enacted – by the main drama personage.

The *puṟappāṭu* can be multiplied in a complex performance. The first *puṟappāṭu* of a complex performance, or of a cycle of performances (Naṅṅyār Kūttu, Cākyār Kūttu and Sanskrit drama Kūṭiyāṭṭam), is marked with an important ritual action. The Cākyār or Naṅṅyār performing the *puṟappāṭu*, having completed the *nitya kriyās*, goes with the musicians (Nampyār and another Naṅṅyār) to the *garbha gṛha* to pay homage to the presiding deity of the temple and the main spectator of the performance. The human audience is welcome to accompany the performers in this ritual act. Having the deity's blessings and receiving a *prasādam* all come back to the stage of the *kūttampalam* to formally finish this segment of the performance. The rule is that only when the first *puṟappāṭu* is completed[13] can the next segments of the performance follow on consecutive days. We may say that the *puṟappāṭu* is a ritual within a ritual, the essence of the complex Kūṭiyāṭṭam as well as the Naṅṅyār Kūttu and Cākyār Kūttu. However, in the latter it has a different structure.

Wydawniczy Elipsa, 2006, pp. 285–292; Śliwczyńska, *Tradycja teatru świątynnego kudijattam*, pp. 138–148.

[12] I have defined the *puṟappāṭu* as the ritual of beginning and introduced the term to the literature of the subject. See the footnote above.

[13] It must be executed in the morning.

The Kūṭiyāṭṭam theatre tradition offers a whole spectrum of aesthetic experience. The poetical sentiments (*rasa*), being an essence of the *nāṭya* performance (according to Bharatamuni),[14] are generated in the performance to the extreme. All elements of the Kūṭiyāṭṭam theatre enacting art are highly intricate and subdued to create aesthetic values, or *rasa-sṛṣṭi*. The way a literary text is presented gives a lot of scope for elaboration and improvisation. The Kūṭiyāṭṭam theatre concept of leaving the text itself while adding new episodes or subepisodes to the main story offers unlimited possibilities to 'work' on emotions (*bhāva*) leading to poetical sentiments (*rasa*) and to display all undertones as well as overtones of existing emotions. The Kūṭiyāṭṭam theatre follows the concept of the *nava-rasa*, or nine poetical sentiments.[15] The stanza's recitation is multiplied as a whole or divided into small fragments, thus even the *bhāva*s and sentiments that are not present in the text lines or only slightly marked can be invoked. Between succeeding recitations of the stanzas or their fragments, the performers elaborate their contents much further with *āṅgika-abhinaya* – i.e. hand gestures, mime, facial expressions and appropriate body movements. The stanzas are not always divided and repeated; still their exposition can be very detailed and refers to the episodes as well as the *bhāva*s and *rasa*s not found in the recited stanza, while those present are highly elaborated and intensified. Such a way of presenting the text is found especially in the Naṅṅyār Kūttu whose sole subject is the story of Lord Kṛṣṇa – *ŚrīKṛṣṇacaritam*.[16] Here all the stanzas are recited in full in Sanskrit or Prakrit, by a Naṅṅyār musician, and enacted with *āṅgika-abhinaya* by the main Naṅṅyār actress.

Furthermore, in the Kūṭiyāṭṭam theatre the actor or actress, while elaborating the text, often change roles and thus enact different drama personages, which again provides an opportunity to invoke more aesthetic sentiments than in the text recited. All of this definitely intensifies the experience of the aesthetic sentiments, of the taste for the beautiful and the taste for the wonderful. No wonder that the *adbhuta-rasa*, or the sentiment of wonder, appears not only at the end of the performance to the audience's full contentment, but in fact is present during the whole

[14] For more on the rasa theory see: NŚ PSS VI.

[15] I.e. the eight poetical sentiments (*rasas*) of the *Nāṭyaśāstra* (*śṛṅgāra*, *hāsya*, *raudra*, *karuṇa*, *vīra*, *bībhatsa*, *bhayānaka*) plus *śanta-rasa* that was added later.

[16] For more on Naṅṅyār Kūttu and *ŚrīKṛṣṇacaritam* see: L.S. Rajagopalan, *Women's Role in Kūḍiyāṭṭam*, Chennai: The Kuppuswami Sastri Research Institute, 1997, pp. 88–95; Śliwczyńska, *Tradycja teatru świątynnego*, pp. 205–232.

performance accompanying other sentiments and as their aesthetic finale. The Kūṭiyāṭṭam theatre certainly earns its reputation as the kingdom of the rasa (*rasa-rājya*).[17]

Let me refer to one more offspring of the Kūṭiyāṭṭam already mentioned – the Cākyār (Prabandha) Kūttu. This genre of performance belongs to Vidūṣaka, or a jester, the only drama personage on the stage, although accompanied by two musicians – the Nampyār who plays the *miḻāvu* drum and the Naṅṅyār on the *talam*. Here Vidūṣaka is a great narrator telling stories of the divine and the mundane. The text is based on the epics (the *Rāmāyaṇa* and the *Mahābhārata*) and the *Purāṇa*s, although rearranged and composed by poets belonging to the wide circle of the Kūṭiyāṭṭam theatre.[18] The temple Cākyār Kūttu is seldom a one-day event, usually lasting several days (the longest Cākyār Kūttu cycle is 41 days). Yet, every day the performance begins with a sort of mini (*ceṟiya*) *puṟappāṭu* whose structure differs from the one mentioned earlier and is exclusively intended for the figure of Vidūṣaka. The moment Vidūṣaka enters the stage, he pays homage to the *miḻāvu* drum (as all Kūṭiyāṭṭam performers do), then he faces the stage proper to start a prescribed choreographic sequences (*tattu*). If one looks carefully, it can be noticed that with proper movements and steps he draws a mandala (*maṇḍala*) with the stage gods residing there. This is the way the gods are invoked to be seated and present.[19] Having completed the next portion describing his own nature, Vidūṣaka faces the lamp and the audience to recite a benediction stanza (*pīthīka*, or *nandī śloka*). Soon afterwards, he begins storytelling in his own very specific way. Thus, stanzas recited in Sanskrit and occasionally in Prakrit are followed by a long and elaborated explanation in Manipravalam.[20] The Cākyār Kūttu is undoubtedly the kingdom of *vāc* – the speech, and the *vācika-abhinaya*, or verbal acting, definitely governs the whole performance. Vidūṣaka 'translates' or rather

---

[17] The term frequently used by the Kūṭiyāṭṭam artists and their traditional recipients.

[18] For example, the most popular *prabandha* (story), thus a textual basis for the Cākyār Kūttu, exploring a subject of the *Rāmāyaṇa* is the *Rāmāyaṇaprabandham* composed by Koccāmpiḷḷī Maṭhattil Rāman Nampyār (also called Rāmapāṇivāda) of the 18th century. In the Cākyār Kūttu performances, original stanzas from both epics and Puranas are occasionally used as well.

[19] In the puṟappāṭu of other drama characters, such a divine mandala is also drawn, although with different choreographic patterns and some of them are accompanied by songs of praise (*akkitta*). For the *puṟappāṭu* of Vidūṣaka see: Śliwczyńska, *Tradycja teatru świątynnego kudijattam*, pp. 189–191.

[20] Manipravalam (*Maṇipravāḷam*) – the Sanskritized Malayalam language.

interprets all the stanzas word by word, phrase by phrase, beginning from the line or the word that he finds the most interesting for himself and the audience. He is allowed to criticize everything and everyone, and nobody should persecute him for any accusation. He is a polymath held in the highest esteem, a teacher explaining the sacred and profane to the initiates and the uninitiated, the one who praises, rewards and condemns; thus he is an unusual instructor of life. His lectures generate all poetical sentiments, definitely with the supremacy of the *hāsya rasa* (the comic sentiment). Had I been authorized to do so, I would have added one more poetical sentiment not yet in existence: *vidyā-rasa*, or the sentiment of knowledge, since Vidūṣaka is definitely a great *vidyā-guru*. One really learns a lot from him! Let me point out here that for those who listen to Vidūṣaka's stage-*adhayana* (a stage-lecture), he becomes the figure of *mahārṣi*. The audience pays full respect to him (an *aṣṭāṅga* bow is not rare)[21] at the beginning and the end of the performance. Vidūṣaka is a great redeemer in the world of the humans and the gods. For many members of the traditional audience, it is still a family religious obligation (*dharma*) to come for the Cākyār Kūttu; it is a unique ritual offering made for the sake of the entire living family and those who departed. It is believed that ancestors and all divine beings gather in the *kūttampalam* to listen to the Cākyār Vidūṣaka Kūttu together with ordinary humans, which is a perfect union of the divine and mundane, the sacred and profane.

The Kūṭiyāṭṭam theatre of unique complexity demands from its audience a profound knowledge of manifold rules governing all the stage presentations. The dedicated spectators of the Kūṭiyāṭṭam theatre are genuine *rasika*s, or connoisseurs. The same can be said about the performers, the executors of the *Nāṭyaśāstra*. No wonder that their dedication to the stage art as well as to the knowledge (*śāstra*) of theatre (*nāṭya*) theory and practice results in excellence to bring a fruit (*phala*) of the highest value (liberation, *mokṣa*). Bharatamuni says that those who always listen to the *Nāṭyaśāstra* (thus 'the knowledge of theatre') originating from Brahmā's mouth and put it into practice and those who witness performances will reach the same highest goal (*mahat phalam*) that is reached by the masters of the Veda (*gatirvedaviduṣām*) and performers of the Vedic sacrifice (*gatiryajñakāriṇām*).[22] Moreover, 'one

---

[21] Lit. '[prostrating] with all the eight limbs.'

[22] See: NŚ PSS, XXXVII, 26–28.

who attends both music and theatre performances, will gain the final good fortune[23] in union with the gods.'[24]

To sum up the discussion so far, it can be said that the Kūṭiyāṭṭam theatre of the temple tradition, meant to be a ritual offering, provides a refined and sublime combination of the aesthetic and ritual experience. It displays various emotions in all their tones, generating poetical and spiritual sentiments of the highest intensity. The performance provides an experience of the sacred art, leaving the participants with an immense feeling of spiritual/religious importance. In fact, we might call this all-embracing experience 'bhakti-rasa,' thus the sentiment of extreme devotional dedication. I refer here to Rūpa Gosvāmī's concept of poetical sentiments or rather one *bhakti* sentiment comprising all aesthetic sentiments.[25] The sacred ambience of the Kūṭiyāṭṭam theatre activities influences how the stage performance is presented and increases the aesthetic and religious ritual values experienced both by the Kūṭiyāṭṭam performers and the recipients of their unique art. The Kūṭiyāṭṭam *cākṣuṣa-yajña* definitely meets the individual expectations of each and every participant to the full.

Bibliography

Bharatamuni, *The Nāṭyaśāstra*, ed. Manmohan Ghosh, Calcutta: Asiatic Society, 1956, vol. 2. (NŚ Ghosh)

Byrski, M. Christopher, *Concept of Ancient Indian Theatre*, New Delhi: Munshiram Manoharlal Publishers Pvt. Ltd., 1974.

Māṇi Mādhava Cākyār, *Nāṭyakalpadrumam*, Ceṟuturutti: Kēraḷa Kalāmaṇḍalam, 1973.

23 ...the final good fortune [after his/her death, thus liberation (*mokṣa*)].

24 NŚ PSS, XXXVII, 30: *gāndharvaṁ ceha nāṭyaṁ ca yaḥ samyak pari (myaganu) pālayet / sa īśvaragaṇeśānāṁ labhate sadgatiṁ parām//*
Abhinavagūpta commenting on the second line says that since the word *īśvara* means god Śiva, so 'the highest good fortune is a union with Śiva (*śivasāyujyate*).' In another recension of the *Nāṭyaśāstra*, the second line of the verse mentions the company of Brahmin sages (*brahmarṣi*). NŚ Ghosh, XXXVI, 82.

25 Rūpa Gosvāmī (a theologian of Gauḍīya Vaiṣṇavism, the 16th AD) basically accepts eight *rasa*s of the *Nāṭyaśāstra*'s *rasa* concept (BRAS 2. 4. 114) to develop his own theory of one *bhakti-rasa*. What is important, the experience of the *bhakti-rasa* may differ, depending on the worshipper (*bhakta*), thus on the experiencing individual. For more see: Rūpa Gosvāmī, *Bhaktirasāmṛtasindhu*, with the commentaries of Jīva Gosvāmin, Mukundadāsa Gosvāmin and Viśvnātha Cakravartin, ed. Haridāsa Dāsa (with Bengali translation by Haridāsa Dāsa), Navadvīpa: Haribol Kuṭīr, 1945.

Nāṭyaśāstra of Bharatamuni with the commentary Abhinavabhāratī of Abhinavaguptācarya, ed. with introduction by R.S. Nagar, Parimal Sanskrit Series no. 4, vol. 1, Delhi: Parimal Publications, 1994, vol. 4 1989. (NŚ PSS)

Rajagopalan, L.S., *Women's Role in Kūḍiyāṭṭam*, Chennai: The Kuppuswami Sastri Research Institute, 1997.

Rūpa Gosvāmī (Gosvāmin), *Bhaktirasāmṛtasindhu*, with the commentaries of Jīva Gosvāmin, Mukundadāsa Gosvāmin and Viśvnātha Cakravartin, ed. Haridāsa Dāsa (with Bengali translation by Haridāsa Dāsa), Navadvīpa: Haribol Kuṭīr, 1945. (BRAS)

Śliwczyńska, Bożena, 'The Technique of Narration in the Kūṭiyāṭṭam Theatre Tradition,' in *India in Warsaw*, ed. Danuta Stasik and Anna Trynkowska, Warszawa: Dom Wydawniczy Elipsa, 2006, pp. 285–292.

Śliwczyńska, Bożena, 'The Ritual of Beginning. The Puṟappāṭu Segment of the Kūṭiyāṭṭam Theatre Tradition,' *Rocznik Orientalistyczny*, vol. 60, no. 2, 2007, Dom Wydawniczy Elipsa, Warszawa, pp. 357–361.

Śliwczyńska, Bożena, *Tradycja teatru świątynnego kudijattam*, Warszawa: Wydawnictwo Akademickie Dialog, 2009.

Katarzyna Skiba

Institute of Philosophy, Jagiellonian University, Kraków

Performing the Sacred in Kathak Dance*

This paper explores religious dimension of Kathak dance, demonstrating the various ways in which spirituality in modern Kathak performance and educational practices is expressed and emphasized. It investigates to what extent the sacral aspects of this dance are an inherent part of an older tradition, and which of them appear to be 20th-century innovations. In this regard, an attempt has been made to highlight the process of sacralization as a crucial tendency in the Indian dance revival (launched in the 1930s) that led to refashioning the preexisting *nautch* tradition into a form of classical Kathak. In order to underline the changes, reference will be made to 19th-century sources and research on this dance as well as the memories of senior Kathak artists, who shared their knowledge with the author of this paper during interviews conducted in India in 2014–2015. An attempt to contextualize the Kathak revival as part of broader political and socio-cultural transformations, linked with the process of national identity formation in late-colonial and postcolonial India, will be also made. Thus popular historiographies of the dance as part of the discourse on Kathak antiquity and its alleged religious roots will be taken into consideration. Interviews and observations carried out during dance festivals and Kathak classes in several national dance institutes

* The project was funded by the National Science Centre of Poland (NCN) on the basis of decision no. DEC-2013/09/N/HS3/02108 (*Transformation of the Classical Indian Dance Kathak in the Context of Socio-Cultural Changes*, 2014–2016). Some data come from the interviews and observations conducted in India in 2013–2014 as part of the research project *The Role of Sanskrit Literature in Shaping the Classical Dance Traditions in India*, funded by École française d'Extrême-Orient.

and private Kathak schools in 2013–2015 will be also analysed with the aim of determining how the dominant narratives on spirituality in Kathak, entangled in nationalist discourse, have been entwined with the dance praxis.

DELVING INTO THE HISTORY OF KATHAK

The history of Kathak is reconstructed in different ways. The majority of artists interviewed reproduce the dominant narrative, disseminated through Indian publications on Kathak, insisting that Kathak is a centuries-old tradition that sprung from Hindu temples. Next, it was brought to Rajput and Mughal courts, from where it was transmitted to modern dance academies and auditoria, thanks to the hereditary families of male Kathak performers, who are regarded as the founders of three leading schools of Kathak called *gharanas* (Hin. *gharānā*). However, there is not sufficient evidence that the dance forms associated with ancient storytellers or the dance presented in Akbar's court can be identified with Kathak. The majority of references that Kathak history writers have found in literature and miniature paintings are not detailed enough to recreate the dynamics of dance movement, such as its pace, rhythmical varieties of footwork, the speed, directions, or the number of pirouettes. The descriptions of dance techniques in Sanskrit treatises (such as, the *Nāṭyaśāstra*, the *Abhinayadarpaṇa* or the *Nartananirṇaya*), referred to by various dancers and writers, in detail do not correspond with Kathak.[1] We may presume that some traditions of storytelling along with Persian and Rajasthani dances may possible provide material for an understanding of the early Kathak structure. Nevertheless its ultimate, classical shape, combining a mostly Hindu narrative conveyed through mimes and gestures, with technical virtuosity and rhythmical improvisation, probably appeared much later.

As for the intricacies of Kathak history, it is worthwhile to take a look at the research of Pallabi Chakravorty[2] and Margaret Walker.[3] They argue that

[1] See, e.g., the comparison between these techniques and Kathak drawn by Mandrakanta Bose, *Movement and Mimesis, The Idea of Dance in the Sanskritic Tradition*, New Delhi: D.K. Printworld (P) Ltd., 2007.

[2] Pallabi Chakravorty, *Choreographing Modernity. Kathak Dance, Public Culture and Women's Identity in India*, doctoral dissertation, Philadelphia: Temple University, 2000; Pallabi Chakravorty, *Bells of Change*, Calcutta: Seagulls Books, 2008.

[3] Margaret Walker, *Kathak Dance: A Critical History*, unpublished PhD thesis, Toronto: University of Toronto, 2004 and Margaret Walker, *India's Kathak Dance in Historical Perspective*, Farnham–Burlington: Ashgate Ltd., 2014.

Kathak emerged from the process of the amalgamation and re-appropriation of various preexisting performing arts in the first half of the 20th century. Its components – taken from Muslim and Hindu religious and secular, village as well as court arts – were homogenized and standardized in the course of the so-called 'Kathak revival.'

Walker distinguishes two groups of performing communities that seem to have contributed most to the development of the tradition later termed as 'Kathak.' Firstly, in North India there were clans of male storytellers and musicians, who performed during religious festivals, rites and social gatherings – originally in the villages, in private houses and on temple grounds, and later, at royal courts – for the purpose of entertainment. According to Walker, these hereditary groups, that can be viewed as the 'forefathers' of Kathak, were heterogeneous, including *kathak*s, *bhand*s, *mirasi*s, *kalawant*s, *bhagat*s, *naqqal*s, *dhari*s and *dholi*s[4]. Secondly, there were communities of female singers and dancers, mostly identified with courtesan *tawaif*s (Hin. *tavāyaf*, Ur. *tawā'if*), who performed at the courts, private parties called *mehfil*s (Hin. *mahfil*) in the houses of rich landlords, in the courtesans' salons called *kotha*s (Hin. *koṭhā*), and in British cantonments. Female dancers in colonial North India, generally termed as *nautch* girls, were also divided into various groups and classes.

Since the aforementioned communities performed for different patrons and presented regionally diverse arts, the scope of this research is narrowed to the Lucknow *gharana* of Kathak, developed primarily in the region of Avadh and Bihar, later disseminated into many other corners in India, including Kolkata, Delhi, Bangalore, as well as abroad. It is commonly believed that this style of dance flourished in the court of Wajid Ali Shah (1847–1856), the last nawab of Awadh, where its specific qualities, like focus on erotic mood – *shringar* (Hin. *śṛṅgār*) and emotional expression – *bhaw* (Hin. *bhāv*),

[4] Hin. *kathak* – 'narrator, story-teller,' 'a Hindu caste of performers;' Hin. *bhāṁṛ* – 'a comic,' 'jester,' 'itinerant actor,' 'mime;' Hin. *mīrāsī* – 'a member of a Muslim community of professional singers and dancers;' Hin. *kalāvant* – 'an acrobat,' 'a vocalist,' lit. 'an artist;' Hin. *bhagat* – a Ramaite community of musicians and dancers in Rajasthan; Hin. *naqqāl* – 'a mimic,' 'an imitator,' 'an actor;' Hin. *ḍhāṛhī* – 'a community of itinerant singers and musicians (chiefly Muslim);' Hin. *ḍholī* – 'a community of (mostly Hindu) singers and drummers.' The aforementioned terms are explained differently in various sources, for more see: Walker, *India's Kathak Dance*, pp. 76–88. Walker also notes the fact that the artists employed by nawab Wajid Ali Shah's courts were referred as Bhagats, not the Kathaks, and there is neither mention of the Kathaks, nor the names of Birju Maharaj's ancestors in the nawab's books; ibid., pp. 132–133.

subtleties of acting – *abhinay* (Hin. *abhinay*), graceful postures, beauty – *khubsurati* (Hin./Ur. *k͟hūbsūratī*), and delicacy – *nazakat* (Hin./Ur. *nazākat*) evolved.

In an attempt to verify these assumptions, the two 19th-century Urdu treatises, ascribed to Wajid Ali Shah, can be examined. His *Banī*[5] *describes simple sequences of movements called gat*s (Hin. *gat*) that indeed resemble some Kathak movements in a simplified form. The *gat*s are illustrated with the drawings of male dancers. *Nājo*[6] includes a collection of *thumri* (Hin. *ṭhumrī*), *dadra* (Hin. *dādrā*), *hori* (Hin. *horī*), *stuti* (Hin. *stuti*) and *tarana* (Hin. *tarānā*) compositions – the musical genres to which Kathak is danced today. Walker also investigated other Urdu treatises and pointed out that in *Ma'dan al-Mūsīqī* (*The Mine of Music* by Muhammad Karam Imam, c. 1856) there is a description of twenty-one *gat*s and in *Sarmāya-i Iśrat* (*The Value of Pleasure* by Sadiq Ali Khan, c. 1874) twenty *gat*s are listed.[7] The latter treatise includes depictions of explicit and sexual movements, designed for women, aimed at the seduction of a sponsor and attracting clients, emphasizing the use of eye contact, amorous glances, smiles and constant fluid movement of the hips, breasts, waist, eyebrows, hands, feet, cheeks.[8] The *nautch* dances are also described in numerous letters and diaries of British colonists quoted and examined by Neville.[9]

The oldest living hereditary master of Lucknow *gharana*, Birju Maharaj, asked about the origin of Kathak, referred it to the art of his own ancestors, seven generations back, who lived in Kichikila village near Allahabad.[10] In the light of his account, the dancers and musicians, called *kathakar*s (Hin. *kathakār*), used to wander around, singing songs for Kr̥ṣṇa and Rāma. They performed in temples and in the houses of rich landowners – *zamindar*s (Hin. *zamīndār*), usually at ritual functions, like marriage, piercing of ears – *karn chhedan* (Hin. *karṇ chedan*), first shaving of head

[5] Vajid Ali Shah, *Banī*, Hindi transl. R. Taqi and K.M. Saxena, Lucknow: Uttar Pradesh Sangeet Natak Akademi, 1987.

[6] Vajid Ali Shah, *Nājo*, Hindi transl. Y. Praveen, Lucknow: Uttar Pradesh Sangeet Natak Akademi, 1989.

[7] Margaret Walker, 'Wounded with the Arrow of Her Eyelashes: Seduction and Sensuality in North Indian Dance,' in *Music, Dance and the Art of Seduction*, ed. F. Kouwenhoven and J. Kippen, Delft: Eburon Academic Press, 2013, pp. 305–306.

[8] Ibid.

[9] Pran Nevile, *Nautch Girls of India: Dancers, Singers, Playmates*, Paris–New York–New Delhi: Raj Kumar Publishers and Prakriti India, 1996.

[10] Birju Maharaj, personal communication, New Delhi, 18 February, 2015.

– *mundan* (Hin. *muṇḍan*), or religious festivals, such as Holi, Divali or Dashahra (Hin. *holī, divālī, daśahrā*). Their art of story-telling consisted of straightforward dance, accentuated by the sounds of anklet bells.

When the situation had become unstable, some of the families moved to other places, like Banaras, Ayodhya and Lucknow. Nawab Wajid Ali Shah called sixty members of Birju Maharaj's family to perform in the Lucknow court. In front of Muslim spectators, his ancestors started performing to Urdu poetry and developed more rhythmical sections of dance. Because of the long skirts they wore, they could not take more than three rounds at once. Instead, they elaborated subtle movements of wrists, fingers, shoulders, elbows and eyes, taking care of the movements' lines and synchrony.[11]

Birju Maharaj also remembered that because of *purdah* custom, only men could undergo proper training and perform. His daughter, Mamta Maharaj, is the first woman from his clan who appeared on stage. Previously, the only dancing girls were the courtesans – *tawaif*s. Some of them learned from their father and uncles. They presented good standards of Kathak and were skilled vocalists as well. During the gatherings, called *baithak*s (Hin. *baiṭhak*), organized at special occasions, *tawaif*s usually performed first. After their shows, comics called *bhand*s (Hin. *bhāṇḍ*) used to entertain guests. The soirees ended with a *kathakar*s' performance of the 'classical Kathak' and *thumri* songs in the early morning.[12]

From this account, it can be concluded that in 19th-century Lucknow, both male and female performing communities remained interconnected, sharing the same performance spaces and – to some extent – a similar repertoire. The memories of other senior Kathak *guru*s and biographies of courtesans also reveal that numerous *tawaif*s learned dance and music from male masters.[13] Their art had both religious and entertainment functions, and the space of artistic practice transcended the religious affiliations of the performers.[14] According to historian Saleem Kidwai, *tawaif*s were invited to perform at various functions, like marriages, or birthdays, because they were believed to bring auspiciousness, due to their liminal status: since they were not married,

---

11 Ibid.

12 Ibid.

13 Malka Pukhraj, *Song Sung True. A Memoir*, transl. and ed. S. Kidwai, New Delhi: Zubaan, 2003; Vikram Sampath, *My Name is Gauhar Jaan: The Life and Times of a Musician*, New Delhi: Rupa, 2010.

14 Ibid.

they could never become widows.[15] In the opinion of Veena Oldenburg, the culture of *kotha* represented both Islamic and Hindu culture, and there was mutual religious tolerance.[16] The performances were also ambivalent in regard of its secular/erotic and religious message. Depending on the context of the performance, the motif of *shringar(a)* could evoke various feelings, as well as specific gestures, glances and movements accompanying the presentation.

The courtesans established themselves as an influential group of women under the lavish patronage of the chief noblemen, merchants and the official elite.[17] They enjoyed a high social status and the great respect of the court. They frequently performed at the nawabi palaces and nobility houses, bringing respectability and prestige to cultural events. Young noblemen were sent to their salons to learn etiquette, the art of conversation, or appreciation of Urdu poetry. They were actively shaping trends in Hindustani music and Kathak dance.[18] Many *tawaifs* were also involved in politics and the anti-colonial movement. Therefore, after the revolt of 1857, British political propaganda aimed at reducing their influence. The colonizers initiated an anti-nautch movement that tarnished the reputation of *tawaifs*, equating them with mere prostitutes who profaned Indian music and dance.[19] The campaign made an impact on many Indians, who started to postulate 'purification' and a revival of the debased performing arts. The purification meant, in fact, the erasure of *tawaifs* from the cultural life of India and classical dance history alike (drawing a clear line of distinction between male and female performers).

In the course of the 'dance revival,' launched in the 1930s, the courtesans were replaced by middle class women, who became new disciples of the hereditary male dancers. Likewise, the whole system of transferring knowledge, art production and its social significance changed. Kathak – as one of the classical Indian dances – entered the public space and modern,

---

15 Saleem Kidwai, personal communication, Lucknow, 11 April, 2015.

16 Veena Talwar Oldenburg, 'Afternoons in the Kothas of Lucknow,' in *Lucknow: A City between Cultures*, ed. M. Singh, New Delhi: Academic Foundation, 2011, p. 72.

17 Ibid., p. 68.

18 Ibid., p. 69.

19 See, for example: *Nautches: An Appeal to Educated Hindus*, Pice Papers on Indian Reform, no. 29, Madras: The Christian Literature Society, 1893; *Opinion on the Nautch Question* (Responses to a letter dated 29th June 1893 sent to various gentlemen in the province (Punjab) on the subject on *nautch*), Lahore: Punjab Purity Association, 1894.

urban stages as a representation of national identity. Its Indo-islamic sources and aesthetics could well articulate the postulate of national unification above regional and religious differences, especially promoted in the Nehruvian period. The dance historiographies, books on the aesthetics of classical Indian dance, press reviews or lectures on classical Indian dance were instrumental in legitimizing its new, classical shape and respectable place in a postcolonial society.

Mythologizing Kathak Origin

The emphasis on the sacred origin of Kathak can be itself examined as part of the process of its sacralization. In the most popular opinions, circulated in print, as well as in the view of many Kathak dancers, Kathak history can be divided into three periods: Hindu/ancient (Hin. *prācīn kāl*), Muslim/ Mughal (Hin. *muġal kāl)* and modern (Hin. *ādhunik kāl*).[20] This narrative is reproduced on the dance stage, in numerous Kathak productions illustrating the dance history. Moreover, many Kathak dance shows are preceded by brief introductory lectures on Kathak history and aesthetics that underline the religious and ritual aspects and roots of the dance.

Most of the stories locate the beginning of Kathak in an old tradition of wandering bards called *kathaka*s, who spread Hindu stories through melorecitation, mime and body movement, first in the villages and temple courtyards, and later at the courts. In comparison to Birju Maharaj's view, this dominant vision of Kathak history dates back to Sanskrit sources, around two thousand years ago, explaining the etymology of the term 'Kathak.' There are numerous Indian publications referring to the fragments of the *Mahābhārata* (*Ādiparvan*) mentioning *kathaka*s who, along with ascetics, forest dwellers and Brahmins, recite sweet stories.[21] There are also similar stories, referring Kathak to *kushilava*s (Skt. *kuśilāva*), or the legendary sons of Rāma from the *Rāmāyaṇa*.[22]

---

[20] See, for instance: Māyā Ṭāk, *Aitihāsik paripreksya maiṃ kathak nr̥tya*, Naī Dillī: Kaniṣka Pabliśars, 2006.

[21] *kathakāścapare rājn śramaṇaśca vanaukasaḥ divyāhyāni ye cāpi paṭhanti madhuram dvijāḥ*; quoted after: Sunil Kothari, *Kathak. Indian Classical Dance Art*, New Delhi: Abhinav Publications, 1989, p. xvi. See also: Shovana Narayan, *Kathak – Rhythmic Echoes and Reflections*, New Delhi: Roli Books, 1998, pp. 8–9.

[22] Narayan, *Kathak – Rhytmic*, pp. 7–8.

The beginning of Kathak is often sourced in Hindu mythology, sometimes mixed with some historical facts. For instance, the artists who studied under Shambhu Maharaj, a hereditary master from Lucknow *gharana*, maintain that his guru used to say that his forefathers had seen Kr̥ṣṇa in a dream and he had ordered his clan to dance Kathak and that is how the dance lineage started.[23] In the light of such stories, carrying the legacy of Kathak seems to ascend to the role of divine mission, entrusted to the 'chosen' communities.[24]

According to Arjun Mishra, Kathak has its beginnings in Indra's heaven, where the divine musicians and dancers – *gandharva*s, *kinnara*s and *apsarase*s (Skt. *gandharva*, *kinnara*, *apsaras*) developed it.[25] Some dancers and historians from Lucknow (Arjun Mishra, Birju Maharaj, Saleem Kidwai) also mentioned the local custom of selecting the prettiest girl in the town for the title 'the bride of the city' (Hin. *nagarvadhū*), who was skilled in dance.

Some other artists (Uma Sharma, Rani Karna) and dance historians connect Kathak with the tradition of *ras-lila* (Hin. *rās-līlā*) and the community of *ras-dhari*s (Hin. *ras-dhārī*) from Vrindavan[26] – this assumption finds expression in various choreographic adaptations of *ras-lila* dance in Kathak.[27] The connection of Kathak with Krishnaite bhakti cults is also emphasized through stories, in which the deity spawns some elements of the Kathak technique – for example the 'dancing syllables' called *natwari bol*s (Hin. *naṭvārī bol*) are said to have been created when Kr̥ṣṇa subdued the aquatic monster Kāliya and danced on his head. On account of such stories, some

---

23 Maya Rao, personal communication, Bangalore, 27 January, 2014; Uma Sharma, personal communication, New Delhi, 27 March, 2014; Kumudini Lakhia, personal communication, Ahmadabad, 20 February, 2014.

24 Hereditary musicians and dancers are told to be secretive and keep the arcana of their art as a family secret, providing the best training to their own descendants (fieldwork notes 2015).

25 Arjun Mishra, personal communication, Lucknow, 7 February, 2014.

26 The comparison between Kathak and *ras-lila* tradition from Braj area is drawn by Hein, See: Norvin Hein *The Miracle Plays of Mathura*, New Haven: Yale University Press, 1972, p. 36.

27 For example, Uma Sharma, who learns the art of *ras* from *ras-dhari* performer Ladali Sharan from Vrindavan, composed a production combining Kathak with *ras* performance. Every year, on the occasion of *Sharad-purnima* (Hin. *śarad pūrṇimā*) she presents *ras-lila* dance in Birla Mandir in New Delhi, elaborated on the basis of the tenth chapter of the *Bhāgavatapurāṇa*. Group choreographies presenting the motif of *ras-lila* have been also choreographed by Birju Maharaj, Mohan Krishna and Chetna Jalan.

artists and dance historians postulate to call Kathak *natwari nritya* (Hin. *naṭvārī nṛtya*) – 'a dance by/about Kṛṣṇa' (Hin. *naṭvār* – 'the best dancer').[28]

Besides, many historians and dancers legitimize the sacred beginning of Kathak through reference to the *Nāṭyaśāstra* and the legendary story about the creation of theatre – *natya* (Skt. *nāṭya*) by Brahma. Kathak theorists also refer to the concept of *rasa* (Skt. *rasa*, Hin. *ras*) – an aesthetic 'taste,' formulated in the *Nāṭyaśāstra*, but more often in reference to its reinterpretation by Abhinavagupta, known as *navarasa* (Skt. lit. 'nine tastes'). In the light of this concept, the aesthetic experience can be equated with the metaphysical.

In their references to the *Abhinayadarpaṇa*, artists often use Ananda Coomaraswamy's translation. In comparison to other editions of this work[29], Coomaraswamy's translation includes passages on 'vulgar dancing' (Skt. *nīca nāṭya*) – i.e. 'in which the actress does not begin with prayer, etc.' 'Those who look upon the dancing of such a vulgar actress will have no children, and will be reborn in animal wombs.'[30] In his writing, Coomaraswamy repeatedly emphasized the sacred nature of dance, linking dance activity to the Hindu philosophy and the concept of *rasa*.[31] Praising its metaphysical dimensions, symbolized in an image of Śiva Naṭarāja – the Lord of Dance, he fostered the rehabilitation of Indian dance art and made the dancing Śiva the leading patron of classical Indian dance. He also inspired Western artists, like Ruth St. Denis and Ted Shawn, who created their romanticized adaptation of Indian dance, as well as Indian artists, to explore the spirituality in the degenerating *nautch* dance. The dissemination of his writing supposedly reinforced the enthusiasm for Sanskrit, instigated by British Orientalists, determining Indian historiographies, nationalist discourses of pan-Indian cultural heritage, including the classical dance history and aesthetics.

---

28 For instance, Vikram Siṃh, *Naṭvarī (Kathak) Nṛtya. Kramik Pustak Mala*, pt. 1, Laknaū: Rāy Bṛjeśvar Balī, 1984, p. 10.

29 Nandikeshvara, *Abhinayadarpanam*, transl. M. Ghosh, Calcutta: Firma K.L. Mukhopadhyay, 1957. Nandikeshvara, *Abhinayadarpana*: (text with English translation and notes), transl. C. Rajendran, Delhi: New Bharatiya Book Corporation, 2007.

30 Nandikeśvara, *The Mirror of Gesture, Being the Abhinaya Darpana of Nandikeśvara*, transl. Ananda Coomaraswamy and Gopala Kristnayya Duggirala, Cambridge: Harvard University Press, 1917, p. 17.

31 See: Ananda Coomaraswamy, 'The Dance of Shiva,' in *The Dance of Shiva, Fourteen Essays*, New Delhi: Rupa, 2013 (1st published 1918).

PURIFICATION OF INDIAN DANCE: MENAKA AND DAMAYANTI JOSHI

The Western visions of sacred Indian dance and the idea of the 'spiritual East' versus the 'material West' influenced the pioneers of dance revival and encouraged them to recreate its 'former glory.'[32] In the case of Kathak, the crucial contribution is assigned to Madame Menaka (Leila Sokhey), who refashioned the debased solo art of courtesans to the ballet form with group choreography, role division, costumes and ornaments, imitating old Indian temple sculptures and Ajanta frescos, and with libretto based on Sanskrit literature and stories about Hindu gods. Her performances articulating the religious dimension of Kathak were appreciated and patronized by prominent nationalists, like Jawaharlal Nehru, Rabindranath Tagore, Mahakavi Vallathol,[33] and nationalist groups, such as the Swastik League and Swadeshi League.[34]

Although she was the daughter of a Benagli lawyer and an English woman, Menaka was presented as a 'Brahmin lady.' This was instrumental in convincing a wider audience that ladies from respectable families can also learn the dance and perform it in public as an act of devotion and worship. In this process, Sanskrit literature became instrumental in enriching the repertoire with new stories (taken from the epics, puranas and Sanskrit dramas), facilitating the Hinduization of the dance and refining it with an aura of sanctity and sophistication. In the 1930s, Menaka choreographed *Malavikagnimitram* (an adaptation from Kālidāsa's *Malavikāgnimitra*), *Deva Vijaya Nritya* (based on puranic story about Śiva and Mohinī), *Krishna leela* (inspired by Vidyāpati's *Vaiṣṇāv padāvalī*), *Menaka Lasyam* (prelude to the story of *Śakuntalā*).[35] As she toured Europe in 1936–1937, these productions changed the Western imagination of Indian dance. Reviews from the European press describe Menaka's performances as: a 'wondrous world of Indian temple dances,' carrying a 'rich fragrance of ancient Indian art and culture,' creating 'a spiritual, magical atmosphere,' 'a recreation of the wonderland of ancient Indian mythology. This was dance that gave an insight into the beginning of time and creation. It captivated the senses and stirred the soul and left one under a magic spell.'[36]

---

32 See: Uttara Asha Coorlawala, 'Ruth St. Denis and India's Dance Renaissance,' *Dance Chronicle*, vol. 15, 1992, pp. 123–148.

33 Damayanti Joshi, *Madame Menaka*, New Delhi: Sangeet Natak Akademy, 1989, p. 31.

34 Ibid., p. 12.

35 Ibid., pp. 12–15.

36 Ibid., pp. 48–49.

This type of response seems to meet Menaka's expectations and goal, postulated in her paper 'Dance in India':

> We do not want our dance to become an exotic, erotic presentation for the delectation of the West. (…) It must have a solid basis. It must express the life and emotions of our nation and not be mere ethnographic posturing. (…) We have the richest of material to draw from and there is the extremely difficult traditional technique to be mastered. (…) In our efforts at reconstruction we can derive great knowledge from the study of paintings and sculpture. These sources and the study of the old Sanskrit texts bring out the fact that long before the Kathaka dances and the Kathakali dances flourished, plastic dancing had reached a very high state of development in our country. (…) Though the art of dance is decadent and the public appreciation is quite uncritical, all is not lost (…).[37]

Menaka was also a founder of the modern dance school Nrityalayam in Khandala, offering courses in Kathak, Kathakali and Manipuri, according to a designed curriculum. She probably took inspirations from her experience of studies of ballet and playing the violin in London. Her school attracted middle class women, whose high social background helped the dance to regain social respectability.

Following Menaka, one of her disciples, Damayanti Joshi, also drew inspiration from temple sculptures and miniature paintings. On the basis of sketches of dancing postures from Khajuraho temples, she composed solo ballets *Sur Sundari* and *Nayika Bedh*, referring to the concept of *nayika-bheda* (Skt. *nāyikā-bheda* – 'types of heroines') from the *Nāṭyaśāstra*. She did not want to be perceived as a dancer-entertainer, but as a creative artist. In her article about the artist, Rita Chatterjee explains:

> In Damayanti's dialogue, she often refers to the term dignity and respectability. Having brought Kathak out of the court ambience, dancers like Damayanti had to divest it of all the elements that could be associated with the court. Certain exaggerated gestures like biting the lips or raising the eyebrows unnecessarily were totally avoided by Damayanti. She emphasized that she never did *bhav* sitting down

[37] Madame Menaka, 'Dance in India,' *Sound and Shadow*, September 1933, quoted after: Joshi, *Madame Menaka*, source Appendix V, pp. 53–59.

> for it has an association with the court or the private dancing halls. She liked to do her *bhav* standing. Nor did she ever use *sarangi* as an accompaniment for it was traditionally associated with the court and private hall dancers (...). Damayanti wears costumes that were comfortable but not revealing. There are photographs of her in the *chooridar* but she mostly wore saris and *ghaghras*[38]

After 1947, as a cultural ambassador, representing the Indian nation on international stages, Joshi decided to dance only in saris. When she travelled abroad she used to begin her performances with an invocation to the nation of *Vande mataram*. To protect her own good reputation, after the performance she would never go out.[39]

Other Kathak artists also started to regard the promotion of classical dance as an act of their 'devotion' or an 'offering to the nation' termed as *rashtra bhakti* (Hin. *rāṣṭra bhakti*). The tendency to emphasize spiritualism, Sanskrit legacy, along with the role of hereditary masters in Kathak, has become particularly strong in national dance academies, like Kathak Kendra and dance departments of Indian universities, founded in postcolonial India. Many Kathak choreographers have turned to the *Mahābhārata*, the *Rāmāyaṇa*, the *Bhāgavatapurāṇa*, the *Gītagovinda* and works of Kālidāsa in search for inspiration.

FOUNDATION FOR MODERN DANCE PRACTICE AND RITUALIZATION OF TRAINING

In 1955, a hereditary dancer of Lucknow *gharana*, Shambhu Maharaj, was invited to Delhi to take a position of the first Kathak teacher in the Bharatiya Kala Kendra. His first disciples in the academy remembered that the dance he was teaching them in the 1950s was limited to Rādhā-Kr̥ṣṇa stories.[40] The few available archival recordings of his performances reveal that Shambhu's dance had a much slower pace than today's Kathak, little pirouettes – *chakkars* (Hin. *cakkar*) and less complicated footwork – *tatkar*

[38] C.S. Lakshmi and R.G. Shahani, *Damayanti Joshi: Manaka's Daughter (A Biographical Note based on the Visual History Workshop)*, Mumbai: Sparrow, 1998, p. 20.

[39] Ibid., p. 21.

[40] Uma Sharma, personal communication, New Delhi, 27 March, 2014; Kumudini Lakhia, personal communication, Ahmadabad, 20 February, 2014.

(Hin. *tatkār*). It largely consisted of *abhinaya*, also performed in the sitting position. Over the second half of the 20th century, Shambhu's nephew, Birju Maharaj, contributed a lot to enhance Kathak technique and broaden the scope of its repertoire.

Maya Rao, the first middle-class woman, who learned from Shambhu in the Bharatiya Kala Kendra and in the 1960s was sent to study choreography in Moscow – also evolved the classical performance format: starting from *vandanā*, progressing to *thāṭ*, *āmad*, *salāmī* to *tatkār*s, *toṛe* and *gat*s in the end.[41] Rao also took a lot of inspiration from the *Nāṭyaśāstra* in terms of stage design, lighting, space division and characterization. On the basis of this treatise, she reconstructed *purvaranga*[42], a plot structure consisting of five parts, and explored similarities between some units of movements described in this Sanskrit text (*karaṇa*s, *cari*s, *hasta*s) and Kathak technique.[43] In the Natya Institute of Kathak and Choroegraphy in Bangalore, founded by Rao, students learn Sanskrit and recite Sanskrit *śloka*s, sing Sanskrit *stuti*s (songs of praise, for instance, to Sarasvatī or Gaṇeśa) and compose one-act plays based on Sanskrit dramas.[44] Her disciples, like Nirupama and Rajendra, continue the research and use traditional shastric concepts, along with Sanskrit nomenclature in Kathak training and stage production. They also exhibit a very spiritual approach toward their art, calling their Abhinava Dance Studio in Bangalore 'the Temple of Kathak.'[45]

Nearly all the private and public Kathak schools, visited in India by the author of this paper, have the same marks of sacralization – a kind of altar with images of Hindu gods (usually Kṛṣṇa, Śiva Naṭarāja, Sarasvatī and Gaṇeśa), often standing next to the portrait of a dance guru, with a place for burning incense sticks. For example, in Abhinava Dance Studio, the

[41] Ashish Mohan Khokar, *Guru Maya Rao*, Bangalore: EKAH-Bios 2004, p. 43. It seems that only after acquiring the knowledge on Russian ballet techniques of stage production could she be acclaimed as a 'versatile choreographer' (ibid., p. 54) and teach choreography. The influence of ballet in Maya Rao's further artistic career can be diagnosed in enriching her methods of stage productions, although it is also an outcome of her study of the *Nāṭyaśāstra* and other Sanskrit texts (Maya Rao, personal communication, Bangalore, 27 January, 2014).

[42] Skt. *pūrvaraṅga* – preliminaries of a play, described in the *Nāṭyaśāstra*. It consists of a number of ceremonies, aimed at salutation and worship of gods, bringing benediction and removing obstacles.

[43] Maya Rao, 'Hastas in Kathak,' *Marg*, vol. 12, 1959, pp. 44–47.

[44] Fieldwork notes, Natya Institute of Kathak and Choroegraphy, Bangalore, January–March 2014.

[45] Nirupama and Rajendra, personal communication, Bangalore, 14 March, 2014.

big image of guru Maya Rao stands just behind the statue of Sarasvatī. In the classroom of guru Jaikishan Maharaj (Birju Maharaj's son) in Kathak Kendra, there is an altar with images of his legendary ancestors (Kalka, Bindadin, Achchhan), Sarasvatī and Kr̥ṣṇa. Similar altars are seen in gurus' houses, which are often open to disciples who come there for dance classes. Dancers tend to explain that the guru is worshipped by disciples almost as much as gods. Both the press and the artists' speech emphasize the relevance of *guru-shishya parampara* (Hin. *guru-śiṣya paramparā*) in contemporary Kathak training.

> In *guru-shishya parampara*, the guru will not tell you what to do in dance practice only, but also what you should do in your life. Guru is not only responsible for your body, but for your spirit and your soul. He is like your mother, father and a friend (…), Guru is a God (…).[46]

The high status of a dance teacher is expressed by numerous rules, commonly obeyed in Kathak classes. A Kathak class usually begins and ends with the students touching the guru's feet. In exchange, the teacher makes a symbolic movement over the disciple's head and his/her anklet bells, as a form of blessing. The disciples should sit lower than the guru and not question what he/she says.

The special relationship between student and teacher is also expressed and legitimized through the use of language. In older publications, we can find Urdu terms, such as *ustad* (Ur. *ustād*) for the teacher and *shagird* (Ur. *shāgird*) for a disciple. Birju Maharaj sometimes also used these terms while interviewed. But nowadays the terms *guru* and *shishya* for a teacher and a student respectively are in common use, highlighting the spiritual nature of the dance training and transfer of knowledge (in accordance with the previously mentioned concept of *guru-shishya parampara*).

Along with this, the concept of 'service for a guru,' termed as *guru-seva* (Hin. *guru-sevā*), is also claimed as part of Kathak training. Traditionally, this system required that a student lived in a guru's house and performed various domestic tasks in exchange for education. Nowadays, it is difficult to maintain the practice of sharing the same households, but some gurus still do not expect money for the dance classes, believing that the knowledge

[46] Chetna Jalan, personal communication, Kolkata, 10 March, 2015.

cannot be bought, but can only be gained through a student's dedication. The progress in dance education shall also proceed according to the guru's will. There is a kind of initiation rite called *ganda bandhan* (Hin. *gaṇḍā bandhan*) – 'tying a string' on a hand of disciple by his/her guru. The first public performance called *rang pravesh* (Hin. *raṅg praveś* – 'entrance into stage') is also celebrated as an entry into the dancing profession. Traditionally, the guru decides when this moment should come.

Although Kathak has been relocated from courts and salons to the democratized public spaces of schools and auditoria, the authority of hereditary dance gurus is still particularly strong in the modern dance academies. The supposed subordination to the guru's will and opinions prevents the students from exceeding the limitations of tradition, it also determines the extraordinary nature of the knowledge transfer. Thus, many Kathak students approach the dance practice as a means of spiritual development.

Dance as Devotion and Contemplation. The Transgressive Sacrality of Bhakti

The adoration, devotion and the great respect paid to a guru during dance training is also mirrored on stage. A classical performance often starts with a piece called *guru-vandana* (Hin. *guru vandanā*), including an invocation in Sanskrit to Brahmā, Viṣṇu, Maheśvara and the guru, likened to the Hindu deities. The invocation sequence, called *vandana*, was introduced into Kathak after the 1950s.[47] Sometimes, while presenting this part, the dancers spread flowers in front of the god's image and make gestures resembling those used in a Hindu prayer (see Fig. 1). There is also another short composition in Kathak, called *namaskar* (Hin. *namaskār*), in which the movements of a dancer imitate the act of an offering (*pūjā*). As noted by Pallabi Chakravorty, in the course of dance revival this piece replaced *salami* (Ur. *salāmī*) – a previous form of salutation, popular in the Muslim courts, expressing the respect for courtiers and a *nawab*, nowadays rarely seen on stage.[48] The act of praising a particular deity, like Śiva, Sarasvatī, or Gaṇeśa is also presented in various *stuti*s in a Kathak performance. Besides, Hindu gods

[47] Birju Maharaj, personal communication, New Delhi, 18 February, 2015.
[48] Chakravorty, *Bells of Change*, p. 145.

are depicted in many other parts of performance, like *kavitts* (Hin. *kavitt*), *parans* (Hin. *paran*) and *gats*.

Choreographers also use Hindi, Urdu and Bengali poetry to express their devotion in dance, especially by dancing to the compositions of bhakti poets (Sūrdās, Mirā Bāī) in Braj Bhasha. Numerous traditional songs, like *bhajans* and *thumris*, also evoke a *bhakti* mood and the predominant motif of separation – *virah* (Hin. *virah*), experienced by a cowherdess – *gopi* (Hin. *gopī*) longing for Kr̥ṣṇa, is contemporarily explained as a metaphor of the relationship between an individual soul – *jivatma* (Skt. *jīvātmā*) and the Universal Soul/God or Absolute – *paramatma* (Skt. *paramātmā*).[49] In *thumri*, the sensual content of older songs has been reinterpreted in terms of devotion to God,[50] which is additionally often clarified in an announcement preceding Kathak dance shows.

However, some dancers, when asked about their approach to the motif of *shringara*, often made a comparison to the human experience of love as an important basis for emotional expression in dance: 'Just like Rādhā is so immersed in thinking of Kr̥ṣṇa, you have to forget yourself in becoming one with God. There has to be a desire in your heart to unite with the God or a lover,' explained Chetna Jalan while talking about her choreography *Radhika* (2012).[51] According to Nirupama, '*shringara* is a universal feeling, that has many shades. Love requires a complete surrender to a lover.'[52] The motif of *viraha* and self-surrender to a beloved, lets the dancers express both their religious feelings, as well as their own experience of human love, regarded as parallel to each other. *Bhakti* is also regarded by Kathak artists in the category of *bhakti rasa*.

Moreover, the image of Rādhā and Kr̥ṣṇa seems to transcend religious divisions. Many former Muslim artists – *ustads*, or *tawaifs* – explored it in their compositions. The well-known example are *raha* performances, patronized by Wajid Ali Shah court (interpretations of *ras-lila* motif with some elements of Persian aesthetics). The biographies of Muslim *tawaifs*

49 See, for instance: C. Jyotishi, *Nayika Bheda in Kathak*, Delhi: Agam, 2009, pp. 123–125.

50 I have explored this shift from the sensual to the spiritual in my article 'A Heroine in Pangs of Separation or a Soul Longing for the Divine? Re-appropriated Voices in the Poetry of Kathak Dance Repertoire,' *Polish Journal of the Arts and Cultures. New Series*, 2016 (to be published).

51 Chetna Jalan, personal communication, Kolkata, 10 March, 2015.

52 Nirupama, personal communication, Bangalore, 14 March, 2014.

(Gauhar Jan, Malka Pukhraj) also reveal that they danced and sung to poems about Rādhā longing for Kr̥ṣṇa. Also today, some Muslim artists in India consider this theme as an integral part of Kathak art, 'the universal perception of God.'[53] Kathak dancers also draw parallels between the motif of *virah* and the divine spirituality and human love explored in Ghazals and Sufi compositions. For instance, Rani Karna explains:

> Kathak helped me find the path which leads to the union of *atma* and *paramatma* from a very young age. I would found the total surrender in the stories of Krishna and sakhis (…). The sufi's devotion of God involves no expectations of reward or fear of punishment and the sufi does not have any wishes and demands. The sufi way is taking the road towards fulfilment of love, to unite with the beloved and to become the instrument for the admiration of creation.[54]

For Rani Khanam, who also danced Kathak to Islamic poetry, dance is a path of communication and communion with god:

> There has always been a tradition of invoking the blessings of God before beginning any performance such as doing the *Ganesh Vandana*. Sufi compositions have the same underlying purpose of invoking the Almighty's grace. Hence I thought of using them for invocation in my performances.[55]

Rani Khanam also tried to dance to Koran verses including ninety-nine names of God through abstract forms of depiction. In her view, 'classical dance – in opposition to folk dances – is divine and spiritual, it is danced for the worship of God.'[56] It does not matter whether it is Hindu or Muslim god, therefore, though as a Muslim she does not restrain from exploring Hindu philosophy in her choreographies. For example, in *Yoga*, she presented the journey of salvation. In her opinion, 'when you control five senses (*indriya*s,

---

53 Rani Khanam, personal communication, New Delhi, 2 April, 2015.

54 Rani Karna on *Sajan Raheo Aa Ruha Mein* (Kathak dance presentation on the Sufi Poetry of Shah Abdul Latif), *The Director's Note*, Brochure of Sindhi Sufi Music Festival, 22–23 March 2014, New Delhi: IGNCA .

55 Praveen Shivashankar, 'Communion with God' (an interview with Rani Khanam), *The Hindu*, 15.06.2012.

56 Rani Khanam, personal communication, New Delhi, 2 April, 2015.

Hin. *indriy*) you can control the whole world – that is what both *Gita* and Koran say.'[57]

Many other Kathak artists also talk about the dance as a form of yoga, or a ritual of the body leading to the concentration of the mind. Since serious dance practice requires a lot of devotion and self-sacrifice, it is also regarded as *bhakti*, an act of devotion and dedication. Dance training is also referred to as a *sadhana* (Hin. *sādhanā* – lit. 'a means of accomplishing something,' 'a discipline undertaken to achieve a spiritual or ritual goal'). Chetna Jalan explains that every day practice (Ur. *riyāz*) is a form of *sadhana* and it can be also compared to the practice of *nam-smaran* (Hin. *nām-smaraṇ*) – repeatedly chanting the name of god, during which the heart opens and become peaceful.[58] She also draws comparison to yoga, understood as the state of union of an individual spirit with the supreme spirit. In her opinion, 'the divine energy may take the form of Krishna, Rama, or other deity – depending on which god you love and want to see.'[59]

In Kathak Kendra, on the doors of classroom it is written *sādhanālay* – lit. 'the place where *sadhana* is done.' During one of preparatory classes for diploma performances observed in this prominent dance institute, one of the students was practicing his/her own presentation, while others were constantly walking out of the classroom and coming back. Their guru, Jaikishan Maharaj got upset about this behaviour and explained to them that every dance class should be a *sadhana* for them – a time of immersion in contemplation. He also advised that before the class, students should prepare their mind. Similarly, the time of preparation before the dance show, putting on a costume and make-up, shall serve the purpose of spiritual transformation, enabling a dancer to become a character later enacted on stage.[60] However, in an interview, he admitted that nowadays, this aspect is becoming more and more neglected, as students are always in a hurry and absorbed with many other things.[61] Even if the attitude of a young generation of students changes, the dance productions still emphasize the religious importance of the dance and overflow with bhakti mood. There are also numerous strategies of ritualization of the performance space that maintain the religious atmosphere of a Kathak dance show.

57 Ibid.

58 Chetna Jalan, personal communication, Kolkata, 10 March, 2015.

59 Ibid.

60 Fieldwork notes, Kathak Kendra, New Delhi, April 2015.

61 Jaikishan Maharaj, personal communication, New Delhi, 18 April, 2015.

Fig. 1. Invocation to Krishna in Kathak performance, New Delhi, April 2015 (photo by the author).

Fig. 2. Kathak performance at the Natyanjali Dance Festival, Brihadeshvara Temple in Thanjavur, March 2014 (photo by the author).

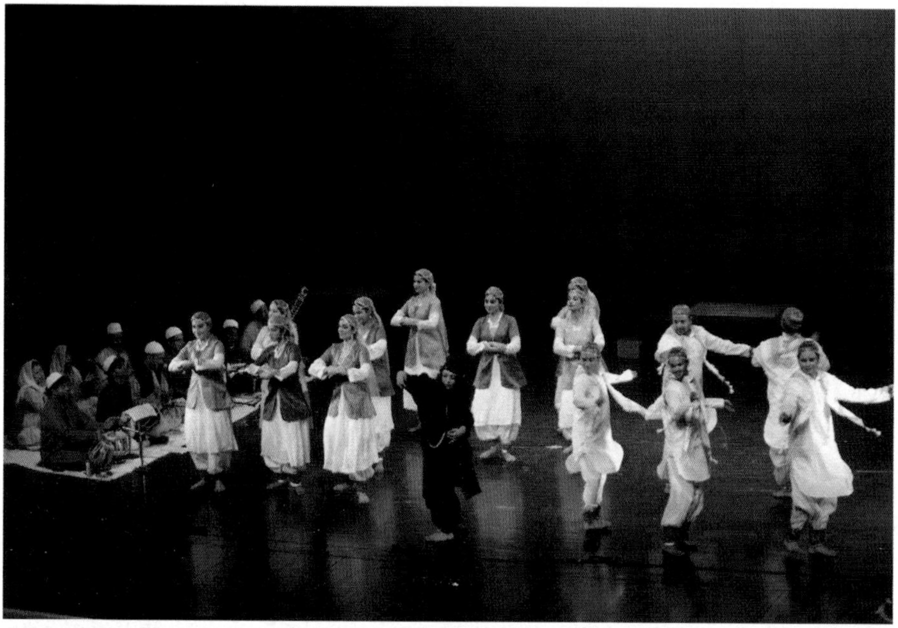

Fig. 3. Kathak and Sufi by Mamta Maharaj Group, Vasantotsava, New Delhi, February 2015 (photo by the author).

Fig. 4. Kathak performance, Khajuraho Dance Festival, February 2015 (photo by the author).

The Sacralization of Performance Space and Celebration of 'Unity in Diveristy' Through Dance

Kathak is often staged during religious festivities and national holiday celebrations. As part of the national dance festivals, held on the occasion of Hindu ceremonies, it is often presented against the background of old Hindu temples and other sacred spaces. Sometimes, it is a completely different religious environment than the alleged original spaces of Kathak demonstration – for example, the South Indian temples of Śiva (see Fig. 2). In such circumstances, the ritual elements of Kathak performance seem to be more intense and the dance concentrated on the particular motif or deity. Sometimes, the performance starts with burning a fire, offering flowers, worshipping an image of a deity, or the recitation of Sanskrit mantras. The stage is often adorned with statues of Hindu deities, candles and incense sticks.

Numerous 'national dance festivals' provide an opportunity to present Kathak together with other classical dance styles on the same stage – symbolizing the 'unity in diversity' of the 'Indian classical dance.' In recent years, one can observe the multiplication of innovative choreographies, in which Kathak is combined with other dance styles and musical traditions. For example, during Kathak Vasantotsav, organized by Kalashram (a private school of Birju Maharaj) in 2015, apart from a traditional presentation of all the three *gharana*s, Kathak was also juxtaposed with Sufi dance and music (Mamta Maharaj Group, see Fig. 3), *qawwali* (Dipanwita and Group), *kirtan*s (Maitreyee Pahadi Group), *Hari Katha* of Gujarat (Nirupama and Rajendra), traditional Rajasthani music (Pt. Rajendra Gangani) and Sikh music (Birju Maharaj Group and Saswati Sen). Besides, the Jaikishan Maharaj Group presented an adaptation of a *Krishna-lila* theme in the form of group choregraphy and the Ashimbandhu Bhattacharya Group staged a play on 'Swami Vivekananda's Thought' in Bengali. There was also a dance performance by the famous Bharatanatyam artist Alarmel Valli and the prominent Odissi dancer Madhavi Mudgal, in which the similarity between the two dance forms was exhibited. Generally, all the choreographies seemed to express devotion, transcending the borders between Hinduism, Islam, Sikhism and other religious as well as regional traditions, demonstrating also patriotic sentiments and celebrating India's 'unity in diversity.'[62]

62 Fieldwork notes, Vasantotsava, Kamani Auditorium, New Delhi, February 2015.

The events labelled as a 'national dance festival' are usually commercial, organized at historical sights and aimed at attracting tourists (see Fig. 4). Group choreographies, addressed to wide audiences, are the dominant forms of performance in this type of festivals. Recently, there have been more and more innovations and fusions between the classical dance styles, staged during these events. The atmosphere in the audience is often far from contemplative or ritual – people eat, chat, talk on their mobiles, take pictures, make movies and walk all the time.[63]

Nevertheless, some dancers say that they deeply experience the devotional dimension of their performance. For instance, Rani Karna remembered, when her group was permitted to dance inside Chidambaram temple on the occasion of Natyanjali in 2000, which was an unforgettable religious experience for them. They performed *arti* (Hin. *ārtī*) in front of Śiva's statue with lamps, bells and the accompaniment of musicians and then danced a few compositions on Shivaite themes (Ardhanareshvar, Siva Tandava, Siva Vandana, Dasa Mahavidya, or 'Ten incarnations of Durga').[64]

There are also smaller-scale festivals, sponsored by a religious community, which are not so publicized or advertised. One such less commercial event is the Sankat Mochan festival, held inside the temple of Hanuman in Benares, hosting both Hindu and Muslim artists. In 2015, Birju Maharaj and his son Deepak Maharaj, performed among crowds of devotees, inducing more vivid, spontaneous reactions and expressions of excitement than is usual in big auditoria.[65] Besides, Kathak is also celebrated as part of the syncretic Indo-islamic culture during festivals held near the Muslim monuments, like Taj Mahotsav in Agra. The various historical monuments in the background reinforce the aura of antiquity, mysticism and sophistication as inherent features of the great pan-Indian cultural heritage and the classical Indian dance alike.

CONCLUSIONS

An insight into the modern history of Kathak reveals an increasing tendency to spiritualize Kathak dance since the 1930s, both in the area of aesthetics, stage productions and training. This tendency was launched by the pioneers of

[63] Fieldwork notes, observations conducted at Natyanjali Dance Festival (Chidambaram, Thanjavur) 2014, Mamallapuram Dance Festival 2014, Khajuraho Dance Festival 2015.

[64] Rani Karna, personal communication, Kolkata, 13 March, 2015.

[65] Fieldwork notes, Sankatmochan Mandir, Varanasi, April 2015.

the 'Kathak revival' who sought to purify the art of Indian dance, considered to have been 'polluted' by courtesans, and rehabilitate it according to the modern tastes and notions of respectability, shared by new Indian practitioners and consumers of the dance art. The appropriation of Kathak by Brahmin elites and urban middle classes, fostered the Hinduization and nationalization of the dance, later supported by state patronage.

In reaction to Orientalist discourse, Indian nationalists tend to underline and revalue the supposed spirituality of India, in opposition to the 'materialist West.' The idea of the glorious Hindu/Vedic/Aryan past of India, with its Sanskrit legacy, became an essential element in the construction of national identity and historiography. These narratives imprinted the classicizing of the dance forms, refashioned as a representation of 'Indianness.' The revivalist initiatives, undertaken in the 1930s by Brahmin women, enriched Kathak with many elements from ancient Hindu culture (Sanskrit literature, Hindu temple sculptures, miniature paintings), making it basically Hindu, 'pure,' spiritual and devotional. However, in post-independence India, the patronage of governments under Nehru's and Indira Gandhi's leadership resulted in a positive re-evaluation of the Muslim component in Kathak tradition. Since then, Kathak has been promoted as an exemplification of the harmonious confluence of Hinduism and Islam, a part of the *Ganga–Jamuni tehzeeb* (Hin./Ur. *gāṅgā jamunī tahzīb*) – a syncretic culture of the Doab region of Ganges and Yamuna (idealized as an example of communal harmony).

The message of spirituality and mutual religious tolerance seems to be frequently evoked in contemporary Kathak productions. Nowadays, apart from Hindu and Muslim traditions, many other voices of religious, regional and ethnic groups are additionally articulated in the representation of India's 'unity in diversity,' demonstrated on the dance stage. In particular, the ideas of *bhakti* and Sufism, transcending religious affiliations, seem to gain popularity among contemporary Kathak artists. However, the spaces of dance praxis in state-sponsored dance schools and festivals seem to remain dominated by the marks and symbols of Hindu religiosity, which are adopted by non-Hindu practitioners (who do not exhibit their own religious identity in the class).

Furthermore, modern dance institutions and publications tend to support the dissemination of Sanskrit aesthetics in Kathak art, fostering its Hinduization. The implementation of the Sanskritized conventions and nomenclature may also facilitate explorations of the correspondence between Kathak and other classical dance forms, above the regional differences, reifying the concept of a pan-Indian 'classical dance.' The erasure of the old Muslim repertoire in modern dance practice seems to be more dictated by the wish to 'purify' Kathak from all the remnants of *tawaif* culture, more than from Islamic culture as a whole, which is today represented in the dance performance by such other devotional traditions as Sufi whirling and Qawwali music. The prevalent emphasis on the sacred rather than the secular/erotic in Kathak can also be considered a part of the efforts to distance the dance from the 'shameful' aspects of its past. Finally, the 'spirituality of the East' and cross-culturalism are additional qualities that are desirable in the global market of culture; therefore, economic factors too can be examined as factors in the emergence of the new, eclectic trends in Indian dance productions.

BIBLIOGRAPHY

Bose, Mandrakanta, *Movement and Mimesis, The Idea of Dance in the Sanskritic Tradition*, New Delhi: D.K. Printworld (P) Ltd., 2007.

Chakravorty Pallabi, *Choreographing Modernity. Kathak Dance, Public Culture and Women's Identity in India*, Doctoral Dissertation, Philadelphia: Temple University, 2000.

Chakravorty, Pallabi, *Bells of Change*, Calcutta: Seagulls Books, 2008.

Coomaraswamy, Ananda, *The Dance of Shiva. Fourteen Essays*, New Delhi: Rupa Publicatons, 2013 (1st published 1918).

Coorlawala, Uttara Asha, 'Ruth St. Denis and India's Dance Renaissance,' Dance Chronicle, vol. 15, no. 2, 1992, pp. 123–152.

Hein, Norvin, *The Miracle Plays of Mathura*, Yale University Press, 1972.

Joshi, Damayanti, *Madame Menaka*, New Delhi: Sangeet Natak Akademy, 1989.

Jyotishi, Chetna, *Nayika Bheda in Kathak*, Delhi: Agam Kala Prakashan, 2009.

Khokar, Ashish Mohan, *Guru Maya Rao*, Delhi: Ekah Bios, 2004.

Kothari, Sunil, *Kathak: Indian Classical Dance Art*, New Delhi: Abhinav Publications, 1998.

Lakshmi, C.S. and R.G. Shahani, *Damayanti Joshi: Manaka's Daughter (A Biographical Note based on the Visual History Workshop)*, Mumbai: Sparrow, 1998.

Nandikeśvara, *The Mirror of Gesture, Being the Abhinaya Darpana of Nandikeśvara*, transl. Ananda Coomaraswamy and Gopala Kristnayya Duggirala, Cambridge: Harvard University Press, 1917.

Nandikeshvara, *Abhinayadarpanam*, transl. M. Ghosh, Calcutta: Firma K. L. Mukhopadhyay, 1957.

Nandikeshvara, *Abhinayadarpana* (text with English translation and notes), transl. C. Rajendran, Delhi: New Bharatiya Book Corporation, 2007.

Narayan, Shovana, *Kathak – Rhythmic Echoes and Reflections*, New Delhi: Roli Books, 1998.

'Nautches: An Appeal to Educated Hindus,' in *Pice Papers on Indian Reform*, no. 29, 1893, Madras: The Christian Literature Society.

Nevile, Pran, *Nautch Girls of India: Dancers, Singers, Playmates*, Paris–New York–New Delhi: Raj Kumar Publishers and Prakriti India, 1996.

Oldenburg, Veena Talwar, 'Afternoons in the Kothas of Lucknow,' in *Lucknow: A City between Cultures*, ed. M. Singh, New Delhi: Academic Foundation, 2011, pp. 64–85.

Opinion on the Nautch Question (Responses to a letter dated 29th June 1893 sent to various gentlemen in the province (Punjab) on the subject on *nautch*), Lahore: Punjab Purity Association, 1894.

Pukhraj, Malka, *Song Sung True. A Memoir*, transl. and ed. S. Kidwai, New Delhi: Zubaan, 2003.

Sampath, Vikram, *My Name is Gauhar Jaan: The Life and Times of a Musician*, New Delhi: Rupa, 2010.

Shivashankar Praveen, 'Communion with God' (an interview with Rani Khanam), *The Hindu*, 15.06.2012.

Siṃh, Vikram, *Naṭvarī (Kathak) Nṛtya. Kramik Pustak Mala*, pt. 1, Laknaū: Rāy Bṛjeśvar Balī, 1984.

Rao, Maya, 'Hastas in Kathak,' *Marg*, vol. 12, 1959, pp. 44–47.

Ṭāk, Māyā, *Aitihāsik paripreksya maiṃ kathak nṛtya*, Naī Dillī, Kaniṣka Pabliśars, 2006.

Vajid Ali Shah, *Banī*, Hindi transl. R. Taqi and K.M. Saxena, Lucknow: Uttar Pradesh Sangeet Natak Akademi, 1987.

Vajid Ali Shah, *Nājo*, Hindi transl. Y. Praveen, Lucknow: Uttar Pradesh Sangeet Natak Akademi, 1989.

Walker, Margaret, *Kathak Dance: A Critical History*, unpublished PhD thesis, Toronto: University of Toronto, 2004.

Walker, Margaret, 'Wounded with the Arrow of Her Eyelashes: Seduction and Sensuality in North Indian Dance,' in Music, Dance and the Art of Seduction, ed. F. Kouwenhoven and J. Kippen, Delft: Eburon Academic Press, 2013

Walker, Margaret, *India's Kathak Dance in Historical Perspective* (SOAS Musicology Series), Farnham–Burlington: Ashgate Ltd., 2014.

Olga Nowicka

Department of Languages and Cultures of India and South Asia, Institute of Oriental Studies, Jagiellonian University, Kraków

In the Footsteps of Śaṅkara: Mapping a Pan-India *Digvijaya* in the Local Space of Kerala*

Most of Śaṅkara's hagiographies feature his conquest of the quarters of the land (*digvijaya*) as their dominant *topos*. According to popular accounts of philosopher's life, during a journey throughout India Śaṅkara was said to have travelled along with his disciples to the four corners of the Indian Peninsula and to have defeated doctrinal opponents representing other schools of thought in philosophical disputes.[1] During his triumphant tour, he was supposed to have established four seats of learning (*vidyāpīṭha*), meant for the propagation of the Advaita Vedānta doctrine, each affiliated with one of the four sacred places of pilgrimage (*dhāma*).[2] These institutions (*maṭha*) were situated at the farthest extremes of the subcontinent: Badrīnāth in the North, Śṛṅgerī in the South, Dvārakā in the West and Purī in the East. The headship of each of those *maṭha*s was said to have been entrusted subsequently to Śaṅkara's principal disciples: Toṭaka, Sureśvara, Hastmālaka and Padmapāda respectively.

A different version of this popular account remains in circulation in Kerala. According to the local hagiographic tradition, Śaṅkara founded four Advaita

---

* The text presented in this volume is a shortened version of the forthcoming article in *Cracow Indological Studies*, vol. 18, 2016.

1 W.R. Antarkar, *Śaṅkara-Vijayas. A Comparative and a Critical Study. Appendix*, Mumbai: Veda Sastra Pandita Raksha Sabha, 2003, p. 103.

2 William S. Sax, 'Conquering the Quarters: Religion and Politics in Hinduism,' *International Journal of Hindu Studies*, vol. 4, no. 1, 2000, p. 47.

Vedānta *maṭhas* in the city of Trichur only. These were Vadakke Maṭham (in Malayalam: 'Northern Maṭha'), Naduvil Maṭham ('Middle Maṭha'), Edayil Maṭham ('Maṭha In-between') and Thekke Maṭham ('Southern Maṭha'), each of them associated with one adjacent temple. Subsequently he attained *videha-mukti* ('liberation after death') in Vatakkunnathan Temple situated nearby.[3] Three of the mentioned monasteries have survived until today.

All the mentioned Keralan Advaita Vedānta institutions were built in one city, next to each other, just a few hundred meters away from Vatakkunnathan Temple. The physical space of Trichur was rearranged in order to actualize the ideological concept which gave it a symbolic meaning. Thus, the legendary map of Śaṅkara's life became recreated and inscribed in the specific geographic location of Trichur.

Thereby, in analysing this peculiar local tradition, the key concept seems to be the map itself – the map with its ability not only to represent the physical area but also to create and recreate the space along with the reality. Therefore, the literary cartography in this case may enable us to understand the cultural process of 'making the place,' giving it an importance and function along with symbolic values.[4] The map itself could be a practice or an instrument applied to spatial dimensions. Maps construct knowledge and produce identities. The process of creating reality by constructing the physical space seems to be relevant to Trichur.

The literary cartography assumes that maps do in fact make reality. John Pickles, while redefining the act of mapping, also noticed that maps indeed create spaces, geography, places, territories as well as people's identities.[5] But what seems to be crucial is that the notion of a map can be understood in a broader sense – the act of writing *per se* and creating geospatial descriptions in literary fiction can be already perceived as an act of mapping and cartographic activity. A writer, like a cartographer, designs a spatial arrangement of a territory by accepting an appropriate scale, making a specific selection of location, stressing the significance of a specific topographic points – thus a writer creates a narrative map. Narrative maps influence text recipients who during the reading process create (or rather

[3] Sreedhara A. Menon, *A Survey of Kerala History*, Kottayam: National Book Stall, 1970, p. 146.

[4] Barbara Piatti and Lorenz Hurni, 'Editorial. Cartographies of Fictional Worlds,' *The Cartographic Journal*, vol. 48, no. 4, 2011, p. 222.

[5] John Pickles, *A History of Spaces. Cartographic Reason, Mapping and the Geo-Coded World*, London: Routledge, 2004, p. 12.

recreate) their own maps of the fictitious territory. Thus the narrative maps primarily influence the mental maps of the readers. They cause the neutral places and spaces to become significant topographic points, recognizable from literature. Thereby narrative maps first of all produce mental maps of the text recipients by designing their territory imagination.[6]

Thus while analysing the phenomenon of the Trichur Advaita Vedānta *maṭhas* in question, what seems necessary is the deconstruction of the map which is inscribed in the Keralan legend of Śaṅkara. The shifts in the perspective of the narratives is also noteworthy: from macrocartography to microcartography – that is from a pan-Indian to a local level. As Piatti and Hurni put it: 'literary cartography indeed provides one possible approach by using symbolic language; the spatial elements of fictional texts are translated into cartographic symbols, which facilitates new ways to explore and analyse the particular geography of literature.'[7]

The strategy of *digvijaya* itself may be considered as a process of a symbolic acquisition of the outlined territory – the successful conquest of the world. The purpose of the ritual combat that is *digvijaya* intends to be a movement towards unity either at the political or metaphysical level under the guidance of a leader who is distinguished by his superior authority.[8] Most of Śaṅkara's hagiographies comprise the term *vijaya* in their titles. According to Antarkar's in-depth study, twelve of the twenty accounts on the philosopher's life examined by him feature this very title.[9] This fact clearly reveals the specific structure of the story intended to be focused, in the broader perspective, on the geographical movement, which was to be the spatial expansion. The aim of the conquest was supposed to be the establishment of Śaṅkara's presence throughout the subcontinent and the restoration of his authority based on the correct understanding of the orthodox sacred texts.[10] Thereby the hagiographers depict the image of a world conqueror who gains control over the chaos instigated by his doctrinal rivals by fully acquiring the space in its physical dimension. As a result, he consolidates the land in terms of Vedic dharma. As Bader states:

---

[6] Elżbieta Rybicka, *Geopoetyka. Przestrzeń i miejsce we współczesnych teoriach i praktykach literackich*, Kraków: Universitas, 2014, pp. 180–195.

[7] Piatti and Hurni, 'Editorial. Cartographies of Fictional Worlds,' p. 218.

[8] Jonathan Bader, *Conquest of the Four Quarters: Traditional Accounts of the Life of Śaṅkara*, New Delhi: Aditya Prakashan, 2000, p. 116.

[9] Antarkar, *Śaṅkara-Vijayas*.

[10] Bader, *Conquest of the Four Quarters*, p. 118.

'metaphysically, he becomes the sacred centre, the hub of the wheel, and restores the original unity which was lost in the demarcation of space. This is accomplished by establishing his presence in the four quarters of the land and yet at the same time remaining at the centre.'[11]

The validation of his world conquest and the following foundation of 'the kingdom' appears to be the coronation – i.e. ascending the throne of omniscience (*sarvajña-pīṭha*)[12] and establishing monastic centres referred to as the four seats of knowledge (*vidyāpīṭha*) in the four corners of India, where his principal disciples were subsequently installed as heads of those institutions. The referred episode of the Śaṅkara story evokes the motif of the royal consecration (*rājasūya*) used in the narrative. He is depicted as a ruler situated in the centre of the world, representing the axis mundi, who radiates in four cardinal directions.[13] This background concept of all Śaṅkara's hagiographies can be referred to as the doctrine of an 'exemplary centre,' defined by Clifford Geertz, which is primarily the general concept of nature and the foundation of the sovereignty. Originally, the principal aim of the *digvijaya* strategy was obviously the conquest of the world and the subsequent foundation of the capital city in the very heart of an empire. The 'exemplary centre' concept mentioned above refers to the theory that the court and the capital (with a king and his tutelary deity) are supposed to be the microcosmic version of the supernatural order – i.e. of the whole kingdom and the entire world at once. That was the exact projection executed on a smaller scale, which was designed to embody the religio-political order.[14] Geertz observes: 'It was not just the nucleus, the engine, or the pivot of the state, it was the state. The equation of the seat of rule with the dominion of rule, which the exemplary centre concept expresses, is more than an accidental metaphor; it is a statement of a controlling political idea – namely, that by the mere act of providing the model (...) the court shapes the world

[11] Ibid., p. 116.

[12] Among the major textual traditions we can found two variants of the identification of the place where Śaṅkara allegedly ascended the throne of omniscience. They were recognized as Kāśmīra (*Guruvaṃśa-kāvya*, Mādhava's *Śaṅkaradigvijaya*) and Kāñcīpuram (Cidvilāsa's *Śaṅkaravijaya-vilāsa*, Govindanātha's *Śaṅkarācāryacarita*, Rājacūḍāmaṇi-Dīkṣita's *Śaṅkarābhyudaya*, *Gururatnamālā* and *Suṣamā*). Vidyasankar Sundaresan, 'Conflicting Hagiographies and History: The Place of Śaṅkaravijaya Texts in Advaita Tradition,' *International Journal of Hindu Studies*, vol. 4, no. 2, 2000, p. 151.

[13] Bader, *Conquest of the Four Quarters*, pp. 119–120.

[14] Clifford Geertz, *Negara. The Theatre State in Nineteenth-Century Bali*, New Jersey: Princeton University Press, 1980, p. 13.

around.'[15] Therefore, all religious as well as political power was accumulated by a god-king figure only. Behind this concept hides the strategy, which consists of the idea that the arrangement of the physical space can influence popular imaginary. The aim of this procedure was to impose a specific paradigm for social order.

Hence, it can be argued that, while reading, it is especially important to pay particular attention to the landscape inscribed in Śaṅkara's hagiographies by the protagonist's wanderings. These were surely not ordinary journeys but rather the competition for expanding influences in order to strengthen authority in the pursuit of establishing their own tradition as paramount. It shows clearly the mutual association between specific places and a person. As William Sax notes: 'At stake was nothing less than the authority to define and thereby control space.'[16]

There is ample evidence to support the view that the emergence and dissemination of Śaṅkara's hagiographies tended to be strictly correlated with the growth of the Śaṅkara institutions. In the course of history, hagiographies were written, reworked and served as important sources of authority for future status claims on the part of individual *maṭhas*. Hagiographers, who were usually associated with a particular *maṭha*, mentioned specific places (like the place of Śaṅkara's final mortal abode etc.) in their works intentionally to strengthen the influences of the *maṭha*. The basic arguments in support for a *maṭha*'s claim for prestige mainly involved a new identification of the place of ascending the throne of omniscience, the location of Śaṅkara's final mortal abode and his personal involvement in the foundation of the *maṭha* in question. The figure of the deified philosopher must have served well the interest of the *maṭhas* and their appetite for religious splendour and political power.[17] In fact, beside Śaṅkara's life accounts widely known at the pan-Indian level and approved within the Daśanāmī monastic order,[18] there also exists a lesser known, regional hagiographic tradition originating in Kerala, which remains largely unrepresented in contemporary scholarship. The Śaṅkara

---

[15] Geertz, *Negara*, p. 13.

[16] Sax, *Conquering the Quarters*, p. 51.

[17] Sundaresan, *Conflicting Hagiographies and History*, pp. 112–113.

[18] The most widespread account happens to be the *Śaṅkaradigvijaya* of Mādhava featuring the pivotal episodes of Śaṅkara's life such as birth, ascending to the throne of omniscience (*sarvajña-pīṭha*) and the attaining of the *videha-mukti* in Kālaṭi, Kāśmīra or Himālayas respectively. Mādhava-Vidyāraṇya, *Śaṅkaradigvijaya: The Traditional Life of Sri Sankaracharya*, trans. Swami Tapasyananda, Madras: Sri Ramakrishna Math, 1996.

hagiographic tradition of Kerala seems to be independent to some degree. Its unique feature is a close association of Śaṅkara and his four disciples with the city of Trichur. To the best of my knowledge, at least four different hagiographic texts that represent this peculiar tradition remain extant. These are three Sanskrit texts: *Śaṅkarācāryacarita* by Govindanātha from c. the 17th century AD,[19] undated Puruṣottama Bhāratī's *Kūṣmāṇḍa-Śaṅkaravijaya*,[20] another undated and anonymous work entitled *Padmapādācāryacarita*[21] and *Śaṅkarabrahmānandavilāsam* a Malayalam text from the beginning of the 20th century AD[22] composed by Alathur Anujan Nambuthirippad.[23]

The peculiar, distinctive feature of this local hagiographic tradition is the strong association of the protagonist with the specific region, particularly in the case of Kerala. The events of the concluding part of Keralan stories of Śaṅkara's life inevitably take their readers/listeners to the city of Trichur. According to those accounts, the great saint achieves *samādhi* there, in the Śaiva Vatakkunnathan Temple, but prior to attaining the *videha-mukti*, he establishes in this very city all four *vidyāpīṭha*s, placed next to each other, just a few hundred metres away from the Vatakkunnathan Temple.[24]

---

19 The date of the composition of this text estimated as the 17th century is merely a proposition advanced by the previous generation of scholars. The poem itself gives no clue about when it was composed – except of Śaṅkara and his disciples, it does not refer to any historical personalities nor events from which a date could be deduced. The information obtained from Vidyasankar Sundaresan in a private conversation.

20 The text seems to be unique as it describes Śaṅkara and his four pupils as incarnations of the five Pāṇḍavas, who are in turn featured as partial incarnations of Śiva. It also relates the foundation of the Śāradā Temple in the site named Pammapura. Unfortunately, still not much is known about the author of this work. *The Śaṅkaravijaya Literature*, http://www.advaita-vedanta.org/avhp/sankara-vijayam.html (access 07.04.2016).
The common feature of these two Sanskrit hagiographies – *Śaṅkarācāryacarita* and *Kūṣmāṇḍa-Śaṅkaravijaya* – is the recognition of Śaṅkara's final disappearance of the abode as the Keralan Vr̥ṣācala Temple located in Trichur. However, they slightly differ in religious orientation while describing that episode. The first text appears to be more Vaiṣṇava in character as it depicts Śaṅkara praising Viṣṇu, and the second one looks to be more of Śaiva inclination as it features him composing a Haristuti and then uniting with Śiva in his abode. Antarkar, *Śaṅkara-Vijayas*, p. 129.

21 M.G.S. Narayanan, *Perumals of Kerala. Brahmin Oligarchy and Ritual Monarchy*, Thrissur: Cosmo Books, 2013, p. 385.

22 The information about existence of this text and the copy of the poem I owe to Dr hab. Cezary Galewicz.

23 As Prof. Chettiarthodi Rajendran informed me, although it is stated in the poem that it is written in Manipravalam, in fact the language in which the text is composed seems to be early 20th-century Malayalam.

24 Menon, *A Survey of Kerala History*, p. 146.

The first Swamiyar, or the pontiff, of the Vadakke Maṭham was said to be Toṭaka, the Swamiyar of the Naduvil Maṭham – Sureśvara, Swamiyar of the Thekke Maṭham – Padmapāda and of the Edayil Maṭham – Hastāmalaka. Subsequently, Śaṅkara's disciples appointed Nambudiri *saṃnyāsin*s ('ascetics') as their successors in charge of those institutions.[25] We can thus observe how the conception of pan-Indian Śaṅkara's *digvijaya* was precisely projected in the local microspace. The physical territory of Trichur was rearranged in order to actualize the ideological concept, which gave it a symbolic meaning. The legendary map of Śaṅkara's life became recreated and inscribed in the geographic location of one Keralan city only.

Nowadays, two of the *maṭha*s – Naduvil and Thekke, are still active religious institutions. The third one – Vadakke Maṭha, was transformed into a *vedapāṭhaśālā* called Brahmaswam Madham around 400 years ago. As claimed by the Nambudiris, who are in charge of that school, the then Swamiyar did not nominate his successor. However, the issue of the fourth *maṭha* is particularly interesting because this institution is actually missing. Although the local accounts say that originally four *maṭha*s were established, currently in Trichur there are only three of them. Some Nambudiris claim that the fourth *maṭha* was relocated outside the city but it seems quite probable that it has never existed and was used only in order to fulfil the ideological concept.

It is noteworthy that probably not all Nambudiris could accept *saṃnyāsa* ('renunciation of the world') from referred institutions. For instance, it seems that only Nambudiris from Śukapuram, Peruvanam and Iriññālakkuṭa Grāma possesing *bhaṭṭavṛtti* – i.e. lands given on service tenure by king to a Bhaṭṭa, usually a *mīmāṃsā* or *vyākaraṇa* teacher of high social status – and the right to performing *agnihotra* could accept *saṃnyāsa* from Naduvil Maṭha. It is possible that a similar restriction also concerned the remaining *maṭha*s. What is more, enumerated Nambudiri *grāma*s ('villages') belong to lineages that are said to keep the Vedic sacrificial tradition.[26] It seems that access to Śaṅkara institutions in Trichur was restricted only to the most privileged members of the Nambudiri community – the Nambudiri aristocracy.

Therefore, it seems probable that the Śaṅkara's hagiographic tradition in Kerala could primarily provide an elucidation for the origin of the Advaita

---

25 Ibid., p. 146.

26 Govindan V. Namboodiri, Śrauta Sacrifices in Kerala, Calicut: Calicut University Press, 2002, p. 57.

Vedānta *maṭha*s in Trichur and also determine the community in charge of them. Perhaps, it was through an appropriation of Śaṅkara's legend and an incorporation of the Advaita Vedānta doctrine into Nambudiri ideology that the Trichur *maṭha*s became influential institutions, wielding religious and political power in medieval Kerala.

The uniqueness of the local hagiographic tradition in question primarily presents itself in the peculiar act of mapping a widely known Śaṅkara's pan-India *digvijaya* in the local space of Kerala. It transposes the pan-Indian places associated with the life of Śaṅkara into the local sites of central Kerala, namely into the space of the Trichur city. Thus, the popular Keralan version of Śaṅkara's life features the place of the philosopher's final mortal abode as the Dakṣiṇa-Kailāsa – i.e. the important South Indian Śaiva Vadakkunathan Temple. Moreover, the great pan-Indian conquest of the four quarters (*digvijaya*) legitimated with the establishment of four *vidyāpīṭha*s is exactly projected in the smaller scale in the space of Trichur. It was in this city, according to the Keralan tradition, that the four Advaita Vedānta *maṭha*s (i.e. Northern, Middle, In-between and Southern) were founded by Śaṅkara and which were subsequently passed to the charge of Nambudiri Brahmins.[27] The names of those institutions clearly refer to the concept of acquiring space, subduing the earth. Indeed these names could be perceived as indexes and symbols at the same time. The act of naming a place appears to be a performative act that creates a new reality which is nothing more than a subjugation of a particular territory. The periphrastic, metaphoric and symbolic site names point to the geography-making processes.[28] Thus, by inscribing the *digvijaya* in the city of Trichur, it appears to simultaneously represent the capital and the microcosmic version of a whole kingdom – an entire world. Hereby, because of the particular arrangement of space (which in this case is the spatial transposition phenomenon) Trichur seems to constitute an exemplary centre. As Granoff emphasizes, places are primarily 'the ideas' more than tangible and sensible entities.[29] The authors and transmitters of the Keralan version of Śaṅkara's life account gave significant physicality and substantiality to the legend, which materialized

[27] Gouri Lakshmi L. Bayi, *Thulasi Garland*, Mumbai: Bharatiya Vidya Bhavan, 1998, pp. 127–132.

[28] Rybicka, *Geopoetyka*, pp. 197–198.

[29] Phyllis Granoff, 'Rāma's Bridge: Some Notes on Place in Medieval India, Real and Envisioned,' *East and West*, vol. 48, no. 1/2, 1998, p. 99.

into Śaṅkaric institutions located in Trichur.[30] As in Foucault's heterotopias,[31] Keralan *maṭha*s encapsulate a few spatio-temporal dimensions. At the same time, this phenomenon is about the place and detached from it, as this single place in fact juxtaposes several spaces.[32] It is a real site meant to be a local, microcosmic projection, connected with the great pan-Indian Śaṅkara tradition, which could be also perceived as 'the geographical equivalent of Sanskritization.'[33] The propaganda value of mythological paradigm, described by Granoff,[34] was also applied in this peculiar case, since in popular Keralan tradition, Śaṅkara was conceived by the god Śiva himself.[35] What is particularly interesting is the unique approach towards the personage of Śaṅkara in Kerala. In fact, most of his hagiographies do not associate him with any single, fixed geographical place. He represents an ideal of a *saṃnyāsin* who, as a true renouncer, should cut off all ties with his own community and with his native place, thereby transgressing his regional identity.[36] However, in Keralan tradition, Śaṅkara seems to be particularly connected with this region. As Veluthat notices, 'after he became a celebrity, he was shamelessly appropriated and the origin of anything that needed sanction in the Brāhmaṇa-dominated society of Kerala was attributed to him. Thus, the beginning of the Kollam Era,[37] the introduction of the graduated scale of untouchability for different castes,[38] the peculiar codes of conduct for the Brāhmaṇas of Kerala,[39] etc. were all presented as gifts of the great Advaita philosopher!'[40] Clearly, this also seems to be the case of the four Nambudiri *maṭha*s in question, established in the very heart of Kerala, namely, in the city of Trichur.

30 Granoff, 'Rāma's Bridge,' p. 100.

31 Michel Foucault, 'Des Espace Autres,' *Architecture, Mouvement, Continuité*, vol. 5, 1984, pp. 36-49.

32 Granoff, 'Rāma's Bridge,' p. 100.

33 Diana L. Eck, 'India's Tīrthas: "Crossings" in Sacred Geography,' *History of Religions*, vol. 20, no. 4, 1981, p. 336.

34 See more about the conception of mythological paradigm in Phyllis Granoff, 'Holy Warriors: A Preliminary Study of Some Biographies of Saints and Kings in the Classical Indian Tradition,' *Journal of Indian Philosophy*, vol. 12, no. 3, 1984, pp. 291–303.

35 As narrated in the Brahmanical Keralan chronicle *Keralolpatti*.

36 Bader, *Conquest of the Four Quarters*, p. 92.

37 Introduced in 825 AD.

38 *Tīṇṭal* 'unapproachability.'

39 These are the 64 *anācāras* intended for Nambudiri Brahmins.

40 Kesavan Veluthat, *The Early Medieval in South India*, New Delhi: Oxford University Press, 2013, p. 139.

Bibliography

Antarkar, W.R., *Śaṅkara-Vijayas. A Comparative and a Critical Study*, Mumbai: Veda Sastra Pandita Raksha Sabha, 2003a.

Antarkar, W.R., *Śaṅkara-Vijayas. A Comparative and a Critical Study. Appendix*, Mumbai: Veda Sastra Pandita Raksha Sabha, 2003b.

Bader, Jonathan, *Conquest of the Four Quarters: Traditional Accounts of the Life of Śaṅkara*, New Delhi: Aditya Prakashan, 2000.

Bayi, Gouri, Lakshmi, *Thulasi Garland*, Mumbai: Bharatiya Vidya Bhavan, 1998.

Eck, Diana L., 'India's Tīrthas: "Crossings" in Sacred Geography,' *History of Religions*, vol. 20, no. 4, 1981, pp. 323–344.

Foucault, Michel, 'Des Espace Autres,' *Architecture, Mouvement, Continuité*, vol. 5, 1984, pp. 36–49.

Geertz, Clifford, *Negara. The Theatre State in Nineteenth-Century Bali*, New Jersey: Princeton University Press, 1980.

Granoff, Phyllis, 'Holy Warriors: A Preliminary Study of Some Biographies of Saints and Kings in the Classical Indian Tradition,' *Journal of Indian Philosophy*, vol. 12, no. 3, 1984, pp. 291–303.

Granoff, Phyllis, 'Rāma's Bridge: Some Notes on Place in Medieval India, Real and Envisioned,' *East and West*, vol. 48, no. 1–2, 1998, pp. 93–115.

Gundert, Hermann (trans.), *Keralolpatti*, Thiruvananthapuram: International School of Dravidian Linguistics, 2003.

Mādhava-Vidyāraṇya, *Śaṅkaradigvijaya: The Traditional Life of Sri Sankaracharya*, trans. Swami Tapasyananda, Madras: Sri Ramakrishna Math, 1996.

Menon, Sreedhara A., *A Survey of Kerala History*, Kottayam: National Book Stall, 1970.

Namboodiri, Govindan V., *Śrauta Sacrifices in Kerala*, Calicut: Calicut University Press, 2002.

Narayanan, M. G. S., *Perumals of Kerala. Brahmin Oligarchy and Ritual Monarchy*, Thrissur: Cosmo Books, 2013.

Piatti, Barbara and Lorenz Hurni, 'Editorial. Cartographies of Fictional Worlds,' *The Cartographic Journal*, vol. 48, no. 4, 2011, pp. 218–223.

Pickles, John, *A History of Spaces. Cartographic Reason, Mapping and the Geo-Coded World*, London: Routledge, 2004.

Rybicka, Elżbieta, *Geopoetyka. Przestrzeń i miejsce we współczesnych teoriach i praktykach literackich*, Kraków: Universitas, 2014.

Sax, William S., 'Conquering the Quarters: Religion and Politics in Hinduism,' *International Journal of Hindu Studies*, vol. 4, no. 1, 2000, pp. 39–60.

Sundaresan, Vidyasankar, 'Conflicting Hagiographies and History: The Place of Śaṅkaravijaya Texts in Advaita Tradition,' *International Journal of Hindu Studies*, vol. 4, no. 2, 2000, pp. 109–184.

Veluthat, Kesavan, *The Early Medieval in South India*, New Delhi: Oxford University Press, 2013.

Piotr Borek

Department of Languages and Cultures of India and South Asia, Institute of Oriental Studies, Jagiellonian University, Kraków

Deification in a Secular Text. On Some Functions of Religious Content in Bhūṣaṇ's *Śivrājbhūṣaṇ* (1673 AD)*

The textual analysis that forms the crucial part of this article is based on *Śivrājbhūṣaṇ*,[1] a late 17th-century *rītigranth*, or book of poetics (lit. 'the book on the method'), the content of which used to be reduced by historians of Hindi literature to a simple panegyric of Marathas' leader Śivājī. As one may read in the poem, its author, Bhūṣaṇ – who was a Kānyakubja Brahmin, son of Ratināth, born in Trivikramapura at the bank of Yamuna river[2] – completed the composition of this poetic treatise in May 1673.[3] To identify the possible functions of his *rītigranth* it is necessary to observe that the composition had been completed shortly before Śivājī's first coronation. We read that Bhūṣaṇ was one among many talented men (*gunī*) who came to

* The research on *Śivrājbhūṣaṇ* is conducted in the frame of the research grant of the National Science Centre of Poland (NCN), decision number UMO-2012/07/N/HS2/00734.

1 The transliteration of Modern Hindi and Braj terms, names and titles follows the rules applied in: R.S. McGregor, *The Oxford Hindi-English Dictionary*, Delhi: Oxford University Press, 1993. In quotations from Braj poetry, intra-syllabic and final 'a' is never dropped in view of its metrical value. Anglicized versions of proper names are used in my own translations of Braj passages. In several Sanskrit terms and names, the intra-syllabic and final 'a' is always retained.

2 *dvija kanoja kula kasyapī ratinātha kau kumara / basata tribikramapura sadā jamunā-kaṇṭha suṭhāra* / (VM 1994, v. 26).

3 *samata satraha sentīsa para suci badi terasi bhānu / bhūṣana sivabhūṣana kiyau paṛhau sakala sugyāna* / (VM 1994, v. 356).

Śivājī's court in order to praise royal qualities,[4] although there is some other textual evidence mentioning that Bhūṣaṇ was one of the official court poets of Śivājī. Such information is conferred to us originally from two *bakhar*s, Marathi chronicles.[5] One of them is *Sabhāsad bakhar* from c. 1694 AD, the other – much later – *Ciṭnīs bakhar* from c. 1811 AD.[6] Śivājī's accession to the throne was not a result of succession. Thus it should be understood as equal to the proclamation of a new kingdom that denotes an event critical for legitimizing a new political entity. Śivājī became Bhūṣaṇ's patron in the sense common for the courts where *rīti* poets were hosted and therefore he was the one who commissioned the composition of *Śivrājbhūṣan*. The characterization of the leader runs across a number of stanzas in praise of his strength, bravery and martial prowess, fame, wealth and generosity. In the poem counting 347 stanzas,[7] over thirty may indeed be read as a deification

---

[4] *desani desani teṃ gunī āvata jacana tāhi / tinameṃ āyau eka kabi bhūṣana kahiyai jāh[i] /* (VM 1994, v. 25).

For the English translation of the above quoted stanzas and a more detailed study on textual evidence on the poet's life and circumstances of his poem's composition, see: Piotr Borek, 'The Reliable Poem. A 17th-century Hindi Poet in his Words,' *Cracow Indological Studies*, vol. 17, 2015, pp. 39–46.

[5] Indian scholars who published on Bhūṣaṇ present the biographical data of the poet either as well-known, with no need to look for further sources (eg. Bhagīrath Prasād Dīkṣit, *Mahākavi Bhūṣaṇ*, Ilāhābād: Sāhitya Bhavan Limited, 1953), or they link them with an 1811 chronicle, *Ciṭnīs bakhar* (eg. Rājmal Borā, *Bhūṣaṇ*, Naī Dillī: Sāhitya Akādemī, 2004, pp. 15–16). The introduction to the first edition of Bhūṣaṇ's texts (Gaṅgaviṣṇu Śrīkr̥ṣṇadās, *Bhūṣaṇ granthāvalī*, Hatarpur, c. 1895) provides reference to a text titled *Śivachatrapatīcaritra* which is probably Surendranāth Sen's Hindi translation of *Sabhāsad bakhar*, i.e. the Marathi chronicle by Kr̥ṣṇāji Anant Sabhāsad, an elder official in the court's administration. I hereby express my sincere gratitude to Uday Shankar Dube for providing me with a photocopy of otherwise unavailable Śrīkr̥ṣṇadās' edition of Bhūṣaṇ's texts.

[6] On the importance of *bakhar* sources for Marathas' historiography see: Prachi Deshpande, *Creative Pasts. Historical Memory and Identity in Western India 1700–1960*, New York: Columbia University Press, 2007, for the information on two chronicles referring to Śivājī's court see: pp. 20–21 of Deshpande's study.

[7] Out of 347 stanzas almost one third are definitions of literary figures. The illustrations form the rest of the *rītigranth*, less the introductory portions containing invocations to deities (Skt. *maṅgalacaraṇa*), the hero's and poet's genealogies (Skt. *vaṃśavarṇana*) and a description of Raigaṛh, Śivājī's new capital (Skt. *nagaravarṇana*).

The number 347 refers to the edition by Viśvanāth Prasād Miśra (Viśvanāth Prasād Miśra (ed.), *Bhūṣaṇ granthāvalī*, Naī Dillī: Vāṇī Prakāśan, 1994 (VM 1994) which I call the short recension in contrast to several other editions (eg. Miśra, Śyāmbihārī (ed.), *Bhūṣaṇ granthāvalī*, Vārāṇasī: Nāgarīpracāriṇī Sabhā, 1989 (MB 1989)). The text of the V.P. Miśra's edition is also the closest to an early manuscript of *Śivrājbhūṣan* I refer to occasionally for textual clarifications (MS).

of the ruler. However, the set of images they contain suggests that the choice was not accidental and must have aimed at fulfilling a political agenda possibly lying behind the production of this text.[8]

Another well-known text which was commissioned by Śivājī at more or less the same time, and which probably belonged to the same political enterprise, was Gāgā Bhaṭṭ's *Śrīśivarājābhiṣekaprayogaḥ*. Composed in Sanskrit, it provokes less doubts about its possible functions. The text on the procedure of the religious ceremony of consecration was meant 'to impress on to the King and the people that the kingdom belonged to God Indra and that Shivaji as his and their representative had been ordained to rule and protect it.'[9]

In this article, an attempt has been made to show that the stanzas which contain *alaukik* elements, especially the references to divine beings, have been designed to display the royal worthiness of the emerging ruler in tune with the traditional concepts of kingship. These elements form a reasonably coherent and uniform picture and thus enable us to add an argument for the political foundations of *Śivrājbhūṣaṇ*. The most important characteristic of this picture is its proximity to the widespread traditional ideas of kingship, and especially to the concept of *rājadharma*.

Early in the text of *Śivrājbhūṣaṇ* we find two stanzas where Śivājī seems to be deified, but – as I propose – they should be read rather as a proclamation of Śivājī's worthiness as a ruler. By being loaded with divine figures or obvious references to them these illustrations immediately identify the qualities of the hero with traditional concepts of kingship. The first example is one of the most famous *kavitt*s, recited till now by Indians who are eager to demonstrate their familiarity with Bhūṣaṇ's oeuvre:

> Just as Indra for demon Jambha, lava for water, the king of Raghu clan for impudent Ravana,

---

[8] Given the fact that the inhabitants of the dominium could not understand the highly elaborate poetry, nor probably even the language in which it had been composed, one cannot perceive them as possible addressees of Bhūṣaṇ's work. The argument about possible recipients, i.e. kings and other nobles, also fortifies the assumption about the political foundations of this composition.

[9] Vasudeo Sitaram Bendrey (ed.), *Coronation of Shivaji the Great – Gāgābhaṭṭakṛtaḥ Śrīśivarājābhiṣekaprayogaḥ – or the Procedure of the Religious Ceremony performed by Gagabhatta for the Consecration of Shivaji as a Hindu King*, Bombay: P.P.H. Bookstall, 1960, p. 55.

Wind for the clouds, Shambhu for the lord of love, twice-born king Rama for Sahasrabahu,
Jungle fire for tree-branches, cheetah for a herd of deer – Bhushan [says] – as the king of game for an elephant,
Light (*teja*) for overwhelming darkness, Kanha for Kansa, so is Shivaji the Lion for the clan of *mlecchas*.[10]

Poets would call [him] Karna, archers – Karna's conqueror, so many wounds has he made in the enemies' torsos.
Kings call [him] Shesha holding the earth [as] he has erased the pride of the other kings.
Bhushan says: maharaja Shivaji, no one who sees your royal deed reaches the secret.
Adil [Shah] would say [he is] atrocious, Kutub [Shah] – [he is] a storm wave, the conquerors of Nizam [Shah] – [he] is god.[11]

The crucial figures relevant for the subject under discussion are Indra, Rāma, Śiva, Sūrya, Arjuna and the serpent Śeṣa.[12] In Bhūṣaṇ's text, all of them would come back several times, shaping the targeted image and strengthening it. I refer to all of them but Rāma, whose frequent appearance in the poem calls for a separate discussion.

John Duncan Martin Derrett in his polemics on Gonda's work entitled *Ancient Indian Kingship from the Religious Point of View*[13] discusses the

---

10 *indra jima jambha para bāṛava jyauṃ ambha para rāvana sadambha para raghukularāja hai / pauna bāribāha para sambhu ratināha paa jyauṃ sahasrabāhu para rāma dvijarāja hai / dāvā drumadaṇḍa para cītā mṛgajhuṇḍa para bhūṣana bituṇḍa para jaise mṛgarāja hai / teja tama-aṃsa para kānha jima kaṃsa para yauṃ malecchha-baṃsa para sera sivarāja hai /* (VM 1994, w. 50).

11 *kabi kahaiṃ karana karanajita kamanaita arina ke urana meṃ kīnau imi cheu hai / kahata dharesa dharā dharibe kauṃ sesa aiso aura dharādharani kau meṭyau ahameu hai / bhūṣana bhanata mahārāja sivarāja terau rājakāja dekhi kou pāvata na bheu hai / kaharī audila maujalaharī kutuba kahai nijāma ke jitaiyā kahaiṃ deu hai /* (VM 1994, v. 67).

12 There are more stanzas containing similar lists of divine beings to whom Śivājī is being compared, eg.: *sāhitanai sivarāja to jasa āja bhūṣana bigara kalanka canda ura āniyatu hai / eka hī ānana pañcānana gani tohi gajānana gaja-badana binā bakhāniyatu hai / eka sīsa hī sahasasīsa mānyau dharādhara duhūṃ dṛga sauṃ sahasadṛga māniyatu hai / duhūṃ kara sauṃ sak(/h?)asakara jāniyatu tohi duhūṃ bāhu sauṃ sahasabāhu jāniyatu hai /* (VM 1994, v. 61).

13 Jan Gonda, 'Ancient Indian Kingship from the Religious Point of View,' *Numen*, vol. 3, fasc. 1, 1956, pp. 36–71.

mutual incompatibility of familiar attributes of Indian kings.[14] The attribute that can be associated with several passages of *Śivrājbhūṣaṇ* is the concept of *bhūbharaṇa*. In the above-cited stanzas read as a proclamation, this royal feature is represented by reference to the serpent Śeṣa. *Bharaṇa*, primarily meaning 'carrying' (here precisely carrying *bhū* – the Earth), further on has various realizations, if not under the form of Śeṣa, than as references to other *alaukik* beings which are associated with the role of Earth's supporter. In another stanza, next to this role – characteristic for both Śeṣa and the World-Elephants – another quality crucial in building the image of the legitimate kingship has been assigned to Śivājī:

> The heaviness of Earth [rests] only on your arms, it is just a talk that [it rests] on the serpent Shesha, World-Elephants and Himalayas. Your descending gives nourishment [and] supports the world. There is no god's role in it at all.
> Oh, son of Shahji the Lion, great king Shivaji, the poet Bhushan says that your life[15] is successful.
> Your sword brings death to *mleccha*s,[16] [thus] the Death is useless [and] disgraced on the surface of the Earth.[17]

Nourishment, or *poṣana* which may refer to *bharaṇa* understood simultaneously as maintaining, nourishing and as sponsoring sacrifices to secure the rain, was equally important and underlined in the ancient scriptures. Gonda states, 'Above all, the sovereign is indeed responsible for rainfall and this not only through his fitness as a ruler, but also by his presence itself.'[18] Instead of mentioning such sacrifices directly, Bhūṣaṇ compares his patron to Indra in various ways, including a stanza in which the coming of Śivājī, though unwanted by some, is identified with the coming of rain.[19]

---

14 John Duncan Martin Derrett, 'Rājadharma,' *The Journal of Asian Studies*, vol. 35, no. 4, 1976, pp. 597–609.

15 Lit. 'living.'

16 The term *mleccha* means 'barbarian,' 'non-Aryan' or just 'non-Indian,' but it may also denote a sinful or non-believing person.

17 *tere hī bhujāni para bhūtala kau bhāra kahibe kauṃ seṣanāga himācala hai / terau avatāra jaga-poṣana bharanahāra kachu karatāra kau na tā madhu amala hai / sāhitanai sarajā samaththa sivarāja kabi bhūṣana kahata jībau tero hī saphala hai / terau karavāla karai mlecchanakau kāla bina kāja hota kāla badanāma bhūmitala hai /* (VM 1994, v. 81).

18 Gonda, 'Ancient Indian Kingship from the Religious Point of View,' p. 42.

19 *camakati capalā na pherata phiraṅgaiṃ bhaṭa indra kī na cāpa rūpa bairakha samāja kau / dhāe dhūri ke paṭala megha gajibau na sājibau hai dundubhī-avāja kau /*

Next to carrying and maintaining the Earth, *bhūbhojana*, or shortly enjoying the Earth, is another concept that should be identified with Indra who fertilizes her (the Earth) with rain. Indra appears in the text in different functions as well. The idea of Śivājī as the enjoyer or husband of the Earth might be referred to tacitly by comparisons to Indra in different functional contexts. However, another argument can be proposed here in order to sustain the hypothesis that Bhūṣaṇ intended to suggest that his patron complies with the royal function of enjoying the Earth. Namely, in the whole text one does not find a single piece of information about Shivaji's family.[20] Such a lack of references to the private realm of the king's life should be understood as a result of the poet's deliberate decision, perfectly in tune with the character of this *vīr-ras* poem and its political functions. Śivājī without his family – wife and children – appears both as a leader entirely committed to his dominium and the worthy husband of the Earth.

Portraying a king as Indra was more often aimed at defining him as 'courageous and energetic' and – as we further read in Gonda's study – 'the length and strength of his arms are renowned. The whole world is subject to the power of his arms.'[21] In *Śivrājbhūṣaṇ*, such illustrations, which we may consider points of departure for displaying the function of a protector, i.e. *bhūpālana* (sometimes also *prajāpālana*, i.e. 'protecting the people'), appear several times.

Let us consider the following stanza:

> Hey, as many mountains are on the earth and the ocean,
> They gained happiness, having heard about his unparalleled grace.
> Hey, in the hearts rise waves of desire
> To come close to Shahji's son, says Bhushan.
> Hey, how many seek for his protection,
> Fearing to make enmity against his sword like a thunderbolt.

---

bhvaisilā ke ḍarana ḍarānī ripurānau kahaiṃ piya bhajau dekhi udau pāvasa kī sāja kau / ghana kī ghaṭā na gajaghaṭani sanāha sāja bhūṣana bhanata āyau saina sivarāja kau / (VM 1994, v. 76).

20 For Indian literary historians the absence of any mention of the royal family in Bhūṣaṇ's oeuvre was so striking and unbelievable that it served to them as a proof of existence of other poems that deal with this subject. This is how eg. Śyāmbihārī Miśra interpreted the presumed lacuna. Cf. MB 1989, p. 5.

21 Gonda, 'Ancient Indian Kingship from the Religious Point of View,' p. 40.

Hey, Shivaji the hero, full of lustre[22] – Indra on the Earth,
Overtook all the summits and fortified them.[23]

This excerpt is so explicit that it is almost devoid of poetic taste. Bhūṣaṇ not only builds a complete picture of his patron who is Indra on the Earth, full of lustre (*teja*) and holding a thunderbolt (*vajra*), but he also provides the context and reason for this comparison: this king proved capable of protecting.[24] According to Gonda's reading of a portion of the *Mahābharata*, 'A priest without knowledge and a king without protecting power are but wooden elephants.'[25] Also in the *Mahābharata* he finds other important opinions on kingship: 'Behave like the sun which protects (*pati*) and destroys all creatures by its rays' and 'protecting one's subjects is form of old tapas (asceticism, the word meaning primarily "heat, warmth").'[26]

Though in the quoted stanza *tejavāna*, or 'full of lustre,' is an element of comparison with Indra,[27] in many other passages of the poem, Śivājī's *teja* refers to Surya, another deity of primarily protective power. As we have seen, such a reference is present in the famous stanza referred to above as a proclamation.[28] In a *kavitt* containing a list of attributes of a good ruler,

22 Or: imposing.

23 *jete haiṃ pahāra bhuva pārāvāra māhiṃ tina suni kai apāra kṛpā gahe sukha phaila hai / bhūṣana bhanata sāhi tanai ke pāsa, āibe ko caṛhī ura hauṃsani kī aila hai // kiravāna bajra soṃ bipaccha karibe ke ḍara, āni ke kiteka āe sarana kī gaila hai / maghava mahī maiṃ tejavāna sivarāja bīra, koṭa kari sakala sapaccha kiye saila hai //* (MB 1989, v. 66 – corresponds to VM 1994, v. 62. The MB version of this stanza is more coherent with the preceding definition.)

24 Also in the description of the royal capital, Bhūṣaṇ in order to illustrate the excellence of Śivājī's fort in Raigarh uses comparison with Indra's court: *jā para sāhitanai sivarāja suresa kī aisī sabhā [subha] sājai / yauṃ kabi bhūṣana jampata hai lakhi sampati kauṃ alakāpati lājai / jā madhi tīnahu loka kī dīpati aisau baḍau gaṛhu rāya birājai / bāri patāla sī mācī mahi amarāvati chabi ūpara chājai /* (VM 1994, v. 15).

25 Gonda, 'Ancient Indian Kingship from the Religious Point of View,' p. 38. He continues providing a quotation from the *Mahabhārata*: 'Among the godlike characteristics of a good king the protection which he affords to his subjects is often mentioned in the first place: "Hear an account of that king of the world, of the life of your illustrious father: he was noble and virtuous, and a protector of his subjects. Like Dharma incarnate he protected the four orders, keeping them in their respective duties. Blessed with fortune or welfare (*śrīmān*) and with matchless prowess he protected the earth, and so on."'

26 Ibid., p. 38.

27 'Famous kings are described as exceeding all beings in strength, outshining all in lustre (*tejas*), transcending all in majesty;' ibid. p. 40.

28 'Light for overwhelming darkness (...)' in VM 1994, v. 50.

the reference to Śivājī's protective power precedes praise of his good fame and generosity:

> [Oh!] Powerful Lion, your energy (*teja*) is like that of the maker['s] of the day [and] the maker of the day shines with flood of your energy.[29]

In another stanza, which can be read in the context of the function of protecting (but again also of carrying), Bhūṣaṇ:

1) displays Śivājī's ability to hold the Earth (by comparison to Śeṣa);
2) makes reference to Sūrya in the context of protection;
3) depicts Śivājī as the one who extinguishes the fire of poverty,
or calms the Earth with water, and additionally
4) talks about fame, another royal attribute:
Bhushan [says]: he deprived the shahs of [their] splendour with [his] strong courage/energy similar to Sun['s].[30]

A *dohā* providing a similar context of comparison with Surya is also worth considering here:

> Shivaji, your energy (or: manliness) is similar to the Sun['s], the source of conquering the enemies' splendour.
> How obvious [it is that Shivaji] is proud – the ocean's fire is equal to it.[31]

According to the *Vāyupurāṇa*, 'Kings are indeed said to protect the earth with the force of their two arms.'[32] Again in the context of the *Mahābharata*, Gonda notes: 'Remarkably enough the epithet *mahābāhu-* is also given to Viṣṇu, the protector god par excellence, who is said to owe this title to the

[29] *terau teja sarajā samaththa dinakara sau hai dinakara sohai tere teja ke* [*nike* – MS] *nikara sau* / (VM 1994, v. 48).

[30] *bhūṣana tīkhana teja taranni sauṃ sāhana kauṃ kiyau pānipagīnau* [*/pāṃnipa hīnau* – MS] / (VM 1994, v. 65).

[31] *siva pratāpa to tarani sama ari-pānipa-hara mūla / garaba karata kita bidita hai baṛavānala tā tūla* (VM 1994, v. 41).

[32] Gonda, 'Ancient Indian Kingship from the Religious Point of View,' p. 40.

fact that he bears heaven and earth on his mighty arms.'[33] The association of Śivājī with Viṣṇu, usually as the powerful *mahābāhu*, is performed in *Śivrājbhūṣaṇ* as a manifestation of *bhūpālana* – the protecting aspect. The king becomes one who – thanks to his offensive skills – protects other kings or nobles. Bhūṣaṇ mentions the names of Udaybhānu, Amarsiṃh and Mānsiṃh[34] whose death became a huge loss for Aurangzeb and his predecessors, and thus summarizes:

> Without the advice of Shahji's son, Shivaji [with] strong arms, which padshah's kingdom does not collapse?[35]

Later on, the use of *mahābāhu* serves entirely to display the leader's offensive skills:

> Holder of the south,[36] holder of forbearance, the Long-lived[37] takes the forts and fortresses [and] gives to their holders the gates of dharma.
> [The one with] strong arms, son of Shahji snatches away great countries and kills shahs.
> Shivaji the Lion defeats the armies of enemies in fight, cuts off the opponents' heads with [his] sword.
> Bhushan says: Bhonsle reaches the summits of fame, the victory of the Destroyer feeds Shiva's attendants.[38]

---

33 Ibid.

34 The three are historical figures. They were Rajput allies of the Mughal emperors. Amarsiṃh (1559–1620), known from modern historiographical accounts as Amar Singh I, was the ruler of Mewar, Mānsiṃh – known as Man Singh I (1550–1614) – the ruler of Amber, while Udaybhānu was the fort-keeper under Jaisiṃh known as Jai Singh I (1611–1667), Mānsiṃh's great-grandson.

35 *sāhisua mahābāhu sibājī salāha bina kaune pātasāha kī na pātasāhī murakī* (VM, v. 140).

36 Śivājī's dominium was situated in the Deccan. His emerging power became a threat to Aurangzeb's domination in the south of the Indian Subcontinent.

37 Corresponds to the adjective *khumāna*, a frequent epithet of Śivājī, often replacing his name and used as a substantive.

38 *dacchina-dharana dhīra dharana khumāna gaṛha leta gaṛhadharana koṃ dharama-duāru dai / sāhi naranāha ko sapūta mahābāhu leta muluka matāha* (*/mahāna* – MB 1989) *chīno sāhana koṃ māru dai / saṅgara meṃ sarajā sivājī ari-sainana koṃ sāra hari leta hai duana sira sāru dai / bhūṣana bhvaisilā jaya-jasa ke pahāra leta harajū ko hāra haragana koṃ ahāru dai /* (VM 1994, v. 226).

The notion of the gates of dharma that appears in the above-cited stanza is another crucial element linking Śivājī's figure with the traditional forms of rulership. As Heesterman states with reference to ancient India, there was no unified view of kingship. However '(t)aken together the different statements agree on one point, namely, that kings are somehow necessary for the protection of the people through the maintenance of the moral order or dharma.'[39] Bhūṣaṇ hardly ever deals with only one royal attribute in a single stanza. Usually, as we have already seen, he joins several associations with the divine figures, thus combining in one stanza at least two elements that display royal worthiness. The same happens in the passage quoted above. Though it contains a reference to the god Śiva in the context of his destructive power, it opens with a reference to *dharma*. However, this is not a single case where the presence of Śiva serves to draw an image of Śivājī as a protector of *dharma*. Unlike in the case of other deities, the king is never compared to Śiva, but rather projected as his servant,[40] like, for instance, in the following passage where he is identified with the goddess Kālī. Here she or he (Kālī or Śivājī) will feed Śiva's ghosts with enemies, or *mleccha*s:

> Everyone says that Shivaji's hands are sword, but Bhushan having thought it over says:
> Kali descended at Creator's request to conquer *mleccha*s and free the Earth from burden.
> [She/He] mashes proud enemies, grinds [demons] Chanda and Munda and carefully drinks [their] blood not leaving a single drop.
> [She/He] erases the hunger of the ghosts [servants] of her/his own lord and thus adorns the lord, Master of Ghosts.[41]

[39] Jan Cornelis Heesterman, *The Inner Conflict of Tradition. Essays in Indian Ritual, Kingship, and Society*, Chicago and London: The University of Chicago Press, 1985, p. 108.

[40] This reflects the Śivaite religious traditions of the royal family. Śiva belonged to the main family deities of Śivājī's family and the king himself is known as the devotee of Bhavānī, the ferocious aspect of lord Śiva's consort. The cult of Bhavānī is popular in Maharashtra from at least the 12th century CE when the first temple devoted to her cult has been established in Tuljapur.

[41] *sivājī ke kara kiravāna hai kahata saba bhūṣana kahata yaha karikai vicāra kauṃ / līnau avatāra karatāra ke kahe teṃ kālī mlecchani harana udharana bhuvibhāra kau / maṇḍikai ghamaṇḍa ari caṇḍamuṇḍa cābi kari piyata rakata pībeṃ* (/*bībece va* (?) – MS) *lāvati na bāra kauṃ / nija bharatāra-bhṛtya bhūtana kī bhūkha meṭi bhūṣita karata bhūtanātha bharatāra kauṃ* / (VM 1994, v. 78).

The power to protect *dharma* by erasing the *mleccha*s, and simultaneously an important point of Śivājī's political agenda, has been also expressed in the proclamation quoted above.[42] It is also not astonishing that this royal attribute can be illustrated by the king's identification with Arjuna, already shown as the 'conqueror of Karna, [as] so many wounds he has made in the enemies' torsos.'

Summing up, it can be said that while looking for the divine elements in Bhūṣaṇ's poem it is difficult to find those which do not respond to the widespread traditional concepts of kingship. From this point of view, *Śivrājbhūṣaṇ* is not a mere deification, or a panegyric where comparisons to deities, no matter how frequent, have been interweaved in order to please the patron or display his divine nature in the eyes of his subjects. If various comparisons of Śivājī to several gods were meant to deify him, they were not primarily aimed at augmenting royal power, but rather at constituting it. Not only the attentive reading of the respective stanzas, but also the circumstances of its composition suggest that the poem was part of a planned enterprise. Vast preparations for *rājābhiṣeka*, coronation, or more literarily – royal consecration, also included composing texts that constituted a new political entity in various fields. If Bendrey may be believed, the Sanskrit text of Gāgā Bhaṭṭ's *Śrīśivarājābhiṣekaprayogaḥ* was the one meant to impress on to the king and the people. In the case of *Śivrājbhūṣaṇ*, multiple references to various deities traditionally linked with *rājadharma*, suggest that the circle of its potential addressees was not limited to Śivājī and the inhabitants of his dominium, but to other rulers and nobles more conversant with the traditional ideas of kingship as well. Also the vernacular language of the composition – widely in use in the courts of the other co-players in the geopolitical network of the Mughal Empire, primarily Rajputs – seems to support the argument about the supralocal function of this text.

[42] 'Just as (...) Kanha for Kansa, so is Shivaji the Lion for the clan of *mleccha*s' in VM 1994, v. 50.

Bibliography

Primary sources

MB 1989 = Miśra, Śyāmbihārī (ed.), *Bhūṣaṇ granthāvalī*, Vārāṇasī: Nāgarīpracāriṇī Sabhā, 1989 (1st ed. 1907).
VM 1994 = Miśra, Viśvanāth Prasād (ed.), *Bhūṣaṇ granthāvalī*, Naī Dillī: Vāṇī Prakāśan, 1994 (1st ed. 1953).
MS = Ms. no. 54 of 1898–99, new no. 27, *Śivrājbhūṣaṇ*, Location: Bhandarkar Oriental Research Institute in Pune.
Śrīkr̥ṣṇadās, Gaṅgaviṣṇu, *Bhūṣaṇ granthāvalī*, Hatarpur, c. 1895.

Secondary sources

Bendrey, Vasudeo Sitaram (ed.), *Coronation of Shivaji the Great – Gāgābhaṭṭakr̥taḥ Śrīśivarājābhiṣekaprayogaḥ – or the Procedure of the Religious Ceremony performed by Gagabhatta for the Consecration of Shivaji as a Hindu King*, Bombay: P.P.H. Bookstall, 1960.
Borā, Rājmal, *Bhūṣaṇ*, Naī Dillī: Sāhitya Akādemī, 2004.
Borek, Piotr, 'The Reliable Poem. A 17th-century Hindi Poet in his Words,' *Cracow Indological Studies*, vol. 17, 2015, pp. 29–48.
Derrett, John Duncan Martin, 'Rājadharma,' *The Journal of Asian Studies*, vol. 35, no. 4, 1976, pp. 597–609.
Derrett, John Duncan Martin, '*Bhū-bharaṇa, bhū-pālana, bhū-bhojana*: An Indian Conundrum,' *Bulletin of the School of Oriental and African Studies*, vol. 22, no. 1/3, 1959, pp. 108–123.
Deshpande, Prachi, *Creative Pasts. Historical Memory and Identity in Western India 1700–1960*, New York: Columbia University Press, 2007.
Dīkṣit, Bhagīrath Prasād, *Mahākavi Bhūṣaṇ*, Ilāhābād: Sāhitya Bhavan Limited, 1953.
Gonda, Jan, 'Ancient Indian Kingship from the Religious Point of View,' *Numen*, vol. 3, fasc. 1, 1956, pp. 36–71.
Heesterman, Jan Cornelis, *The Inner Conflict of Tradition. Essays in Indian Ritual, Kingship, and Society*, Chicago and London: The University of Chicago Press, 1985, pp. 108–127.

ALEKSANDRA TUREK

Chair of South Asian Studies, Faculty of Oriental Studies, University of Warsaw

Hostility or Solidarity? the Rājpūts and Jāṭs in the *Chāvaḷīs* from the region of Śekhāvaṭī

This paper, based on *Chāvaḷī* poems, aims to demonstrate that regional, peripheral works transmitted orally on the outskirts of the mainstream literature prove to be a good source for reconstructing social reality. This seems to be especially true with regard to inter-caste co-operation in a particular region of India, such as the Śekhāvaṭī[1] region of Rājasthān in the 19th century. It will be argued that *Chāvaḷīs* propagate inter-caste solidarity, putting particular stress on successful co-operation between Rājpūts and Jāṭs.

Chāvaḷīs[2] are rhymed, oral works, composed in the Śekhāvaṭī dialect (i.e. northern Mārvāṛī) around the turn of the 19th and 20th centuries. Therefore, their extant text, written down and published, is not complete. It is available in three slightly different versions published in 1947, 1973 and

[1] The area is named after Rāo Śekhā (the offshoot of the Kachvāha Rājpūts from Jaypur) who in the 15th century captured the region between Sīkar and Jhuñjhunū̃.

[2] Rhymed poems about Ḍūṅgjī and Javārjī are generally entitled *chāvaḷī* as all of them begin with the invocation in which the word *chāvaḷī* is used in the sense of singing the glory (*chāvaḷī*) of the story's heroes, e.g.: 'I'm singing the glory of the heroes in all directions' (*Mardā̃ rī chāvaḷī maĩ cyāra kūṇṭa mẽ gāū̃*). *Rājasthān Gaṅgā. Sāhitya rī Timāhī Patrikā* (ed. Kiraṇ Nāhaṭā), no. 2–4, Aprail-Disambar 2013, pp. 21, 43, 61. Cf. Aleksandra Turek, 'A Good Villain: the Bravery of the Dacoits from the Śekhāvaṭī Region of Rājasthān,' *Indologica Taurinensia* (Proceedings of the Conference 'Patterns of Bravery. The Figure of the Hero in Indian Literature, Art and Thought,' ed. Tiziana Pontillo), vol. 40, 2014 (2015), p. 380.

1986.[3] Judging by a passage from the 1986 version, it seems likely that the poem was composed and transmitted by local singers of the Bhopā caste in the region of Śekhāvaṭī:[4]

> Why not to believe Bhopā [who tells] all [these] stories.
> [Thanks to them] Śekhāvats became immortal [and] the rest went [back] home.
> Blessed [and] fortunate [is] Bhopā who [can be] proud of the heroes.
> Being proud of them, [he] composed verses about the heroes [and] sang [them].[5]

The heroes praised in *Chāvaḷīs* are highwaymen. These poems were composed to commemorate the deeds of a local gang of dacoits who were marauding in Rājasthān in the first half of the 19th century. Taking into account the significant fact that the gang of highwaymen consists of representatives of various social classes from the region of Śekhāvaṭī such as the Rājpūts, Jāṭs, Gūjars,[6] Mīṇās[7] and Nāīs,[8] it is justified to analyse these works in a broader context as works that spread a message of inter-caste co-operation in the region, rather than as works merely limited to relating the adventures of the Śekhāvaṭī outlaws.

The four main characters commemorated in the poem are historical figures. The chief of the group is Rājpūt Ḍūṅgar Siṅgh, known in the poem as Ḍūṅgjī, the *ṭhākur* of Baṭhoṭh village (the modern district of Sīkar). There

---

[3] *Rājasthān Gaṅgā*; cf. Turek, 'A Good Villain,' p. 380.

[4] Apart from a mention about an anonymous narrative folk-poem known as *Chāvaḷī*, Hiralal Maheshwari gives a list of seven poets as composers of poems on Ḍūṅgjī-Javārjī story: Likhamīdān Ūjaḷ, Śaṅkardān Sāmaur, Budhājī Āsiyā, Girvardān Kaviyā, Gaṅgādān Sāndū, Rāmdayāl Kaviyā and Tejdān Āsiyā. Maheshwari does not give, however, more details. Hiralal Maheshwari, *History of Rajasthani Literature*, New Delhi: Sahitya Akademi, 1980, p. 194.

[5] *Bhopā ne to sagaḷī vātā̃, ko kāinī vīsāsa / Śekhavaṭyā to ammara vai gyā, bākī rai gī vāsa / Bhopā kā to dhanna bhāga, jo sūrā̃ para itarāya / Sūrā̃ para itarāya, sūra kā kavitta baṇā kai gāya.* Verses 1131–1134 of the 1986 version: *Rājasthān Gaṅgā*, p. 103.

[6] *Gūjar* – a community of cowherds, milkmen.

[7] *Mīṇā* – 'the most populous tribe in the state. (...) They claim kshatriya descend and call themselves Mina Thakur. They claim to be original rulers of the area till the Rajputs defeated them and made them their subjects. (...) They have been under category of Scheduled Tribes;' K.S. Singh (ed.), *People of India. Rajasthan*, vol. 38, part 2, Mumbai: Anthropological Survey of India–Popular Prakashan PVT. LTD., 1998, p. 651.

[8] *Nāī* – the caste of barbers.

is also his devoted cousin, the *ṭhākur* of the Paṭodā village – Rājpūt Javāhar Siṅgh, known as Javārjī, and Ḍūṅgjī's two companions Karṇiyā Mīṇā and Loṭiyā Jāṭ, both from Baṭhoṭh village. The story narrated in *Chāvaḷīs* is also known as *Ḍūṅgjī–Javārjī*.[9]

Rājpūts

Before proceeding to the analysis of *Chāvaḷīs*, let us briefly introduce the two Rājasthānī communities – the Rājpūts and Jāṭs – with particular reference to the region of Śekhāvaṭī, as this introduction seems crucial for the better understanding of the content of these texts.

The Rājpūts were the ruling class of Rājasthān until the abolition of feudalism – i.e. the *jāgīrdārī* and *zamīndārī* systems – in the 1950s.[10] It should be mentioned here that the emergence of the Rājpūts, who are of mixed origin, serves as a good example of social mobility and of a new pattern of social order in medieval India that posed a challenge to the Brahmanical order.[11] This is the reason why it is more appropriate to describe Rājpūts rather as a community than as a caste, although they soon began to claim their *kṣatriya* genealogy through bardic literature composed by Cāraṇ bards.[12] In Rājasthān, only Rājpūts had the right to land (even Brahmins could only be granted land with the permission of a local Rājpūt feudal lord). Social structure and inter-caste relations in Rājasthān were thus quite unique and substantially different from other parts of India. K.L. Sharma aptly notes, 'For example, the "caste model" of Indian society implies determination of all other aspects

[9] Cf. K. Sahal, *Rājasthānī lok gāthā koś*, Jodhpur: Rājasthānī Sāhitya Saṁsthān, 1995, pp. 45–51.

[10] K.L. Sharma, *Caste, Feudalism and Peasantry. The Social Formation of Shekhawati*, New Delhi: Manohar, 1998, p. 54.

[11] For more information see: Jai Narayan Asopa, *Origin of the Rajputs*, in *History and Culture of Rajasthan (From Earliest Times upto 1956 A.D.)*, ed. Shyam Singh Ratnawat and Krishna Gopal Sharma, Jaipur: Centre for Rajasthan Studies, University of Rajasthan, 1999, p. 40; B.D. Chattopadhyaya, 'The Emergence of the Rajputs as Historical Process in Early Medieval Rajasthan,' in *The Idea of Rajasthan. Explorations in Regional Identity*, ed. Karine Schomer, Joan L. Erdman, Deryck O. Lodric and Llyod I. Rudolph, vol. 2, Delhi: Manohar–American Institute of Indian Studies, 2001, p. 161.

[12] Cf. Shyam Singh Ratnawat and Krishna Gopal Sharma (eds), *Cāraṇ sāhitya paramparā. Essays on Bardic Literature. Professor V.S. Bhatnagar Felicitation Volume*, Jaipur: Centre for Rajasthan Studies, University of Jaipur, 2001.

of social life by the ideology of pure and impure, but in Rajasthan caste was never an encompassing system. In fact, feudalism encompassed caste to a large extent.'[13] This scholar also notes that in the Rājasthān caste and class commingled, the terms *zamīndār* and Rājpūt became synonymous.[14] In princely states, the ruling class formed of all kinds of *rājās*, *rāvals* and feudal chiefs while landowners consisted of only less than 5 per cent of the total population, thus about 95 per cent were subject to them.[15] These numbers can serve as an argument that the rich and vast bardic Rājasthānī literature (*cāraṇ sāhitya*) deeply rooted in the Rājpūt milieu cannot be treated as representative of all aspects of Rājasthānī culture and its social reality. Such poems as *Chāvaḷīs*, which one may classify *a priori* as insignificant, regional works from the outskirts of the mainstream literature and lacking in literary values, come, however, from the majority voice of this 95 per cent of the population of Rājasthān. Therefore, this is the reason why such works should not be ignored by scholars.

Jāṭs

In terms of numbers, the Jāṭs are the second significant community in Rājasthān. They are the most dominant agricultural group in the region and, in fact, in the whole North-West of India. Their origin is uncertain. Some scholars trace it to the Vedic Aryans or Yādava tribe, whereas others are of the opinion that the Jāṭs come from Indo-Scythian stock.[16] Nevertheless, the Jāṭs can be described as a group with a well-defined identity which has been aptly summarized by a historian named Qanungo: 'The Jat is a Jat after all, whether he be a Hindu, Sikh or Muslim,'[17] and is the most ambitious community strongly determined to change their social status. In Rājasthān, they were considered *śūdras* by Rājpūts and hence severely punished by them for the Jāṭs' claim to be accepted as *kṣatriyas*. Hostility between the Rājpūts and Jāṭs in Rājasthān is very well known and has become almost legendary.

[13] Sharma, *Caste, Feudalism and Peasantry*, p. 15.

[14] Ibid., p. 39.

[15] Ibid., p. 44.

[16] Cf. K.R. Qanungo, *History of the Jats*, New Delhi: Originals, 2013 (1st published 1925).

[17] Ibid., p. 1.

In the opinion of Sharma, 'caste based rivalry between Rajputs and Jats may be treated in essence as class-based animosity rooted in feudalism.'[18]

Especially in the region of Śekhāvaṭī, the Jāṭs were never the landlords' favourites and land-grants were never given to them.[19] Various negative stereotypes and prejudices about the Jāṭs function in present-day Rājasthān (and in fact in all of North India). For example, they are accused of burning the emperor Akbar's bones[20] and of the devastation of the relicts of the Mughal imperial grandeur (by a Jāṭ king who usurped the black marble throne of the emperor Jahā̃gīr and, as a result of this act, the throne cracked, as can still be observed today).[21]

There are also many sayings and proverbs describing the Jāṭs as stubborn, cunning, unreliable, ill-tempered, quarrelsome or unable to be kept under control, which can be exemplified by a few of the following instances: 'Don't believe a Jāṭ to be dead till his 13th day [i.e. after-death *śraddhā* ceremony in his honour] is over;'[22] 'Who is boss for a Jāṭ and what [kind of rich,] fried food has Rābaṛī?;'[23] 'One should never trust credit given by a Jāṭ who wears white cloths and eats meat;'[24] 'Where is Jāṭ there is ostentation.'[25] There is also a Jāṭ counting rhyme: 'one Jāṭ [means] Jāṭ, two Jāṭs [mean] delight, three Jāṭs [is] a company, four Jāṭs [is] an army.'[26] The fact that there exist so many proverbs and plenty of stories about the Jāṭs' wits and

---

18 Sharma, *Caste, Feudalism and Peasantry*, p. 14.

19 Ibid., p. 78.

20 Cf. Qanungo, *History of the Jats*, p. 201.

21 Ibid., p. 127.

22 Raj. *Jāṭ nai maryā jad jāṇie jab uskī terahā̃vī ho le*; ibid., p. 90. The following proverb has an identical sense: 'don't believe a Jat to be dead till his fortieth day is over' (*Jāṭ marā jab jānie jab cālīsā hoya*); http://www.jatland.com/home/Rajasthani_Language_Idioms_and_Phrases (access 30.09.2016). The term *cālīsā* means here a Muslim rite performed forty days after a death; R.S. McGregor, *Oxford Hindi-English Dictionary*, New Delhi: Oxford University Press, 2012, p. 313.

23 Raj. *Jāṭ ko kāī jajmān ar Rābaṛī ko kāī pakvān?* Manohar Siṁh Rāṭhauṛ, *Rājasthānī kahāvatā̃*, Bīkāner: Ujās Granth Māḷā, 2001, p. 107. *Rābaṛī* or *Raikā* – a community of nomad camel herders in Rājasthān and Gujarāt. For more information on Rābaṛī see: Singh, *People of India*, 1998, pp. 765–768.

24 H. *safed kapṛe pahanne vāle aur māṁs khāne vāle Jāṭ kī ṛṇaden par kabhī viśvās nahī̃ karnā cāhie;* http://www.nidanaheights.net/culture-proverbs.html (access 02.10.2016).

25 Raj. *Jāṭ jaṭhai ī ṭhāṭh*; Rāṭhauṛ, *Rājasthānī kahāvatā̃*, p. 108.

26 H. *Jāṭ pahāṛā: ek Jāṭ – Jāṭ, do Jāṭ – mauj, tīn Jāṭ – kampanī, cār Jāṭ – fauj*; http://www.jatland.com/home/Rajasthani_Language_Idioms_and_Phrases (access 30.09.2016).

cunning[27], maybe be a result of their non-subordination to ruling groups of a higher status and this also helped to spread the Jāṭs' bad image.

Thus in Śekhāvaṭī, the Rājpūts and Jāṭs are the two main communities. No caste except the Jāṭs made demands for social equality with the Rājpūts in this region.[28] Sharma, explaining the social situation in Śekhāvaṭī, argues, 'It is invariably reported that the peasantry, particularly the Jat peasants, were maltreated by the Rajput *jagirdars*. Let us clarify here that the non-Rajput grantees/sub-grantees (including the Brahmins) never maltreated the Jat *kisans*.'[29] In 19th-century Śekhāvaṭī, Jāṭ and Rājpūt relations were particularly tense. The Jāṭs were most affected by the feudal rule which resulted in peasant movements whose agitations began to intensify especially in the first half of the 20th century (particularly in 1934–1937). The term peasant movement in the region of Śekhāvaṭī should really be called the Jāṭ movement as it was formed mainly by this caste. Demands for 'social honour' to be granted the Jāṭs along with access to the privileges of higher castes played an important role as well.[30] The Śekhāvaṭī Jāṭs neighboured the Jāṭ kingdom with its established royal dynasty in Bharatpur.[31] It is worth noting here that this kingdom was founded by the Jāṭ Cūṛamaṇ who 'began his career as the leader of a gang of highwaymen, plundering caravans and wayfarers.'[32]

Rājpūt–Jāṭ Relations in *Chāvaḷīs*

As has already been mentioned, in *Chāvaḷīs* the gang of the Śekhāvaṭī dacoits is led by the Rājpūt Ḍūṅgjī. The Rājpūt supremacy in the gang is unquestionable. All have a lot of respect for him and his cousin Javārjī. However, an interesting aspect of the story is that all his actions are successful essentially due to the help of the Jāṭ Loṭiyā who is in fact always accompanied by the Mīṇā man (known as Karṇiyā or Sāṁvatiyā Mīṇā), whereas in all

[27] Cf. collection of Jāṭ folk-stories in Vikramsiṁh Rāṭhauṛ, *Jāṭõ kī lok kathāẽ*, Jodhpur: Rājasthānī Granthāgār, 2014.

[28] Sharma, *Caste, Feudalism and Peasantry*, p. 82.

[29] Ibid., pp. 82–83.

[30] Ibid., p. 84.

[31] Until 1947, the region of Rājasthān consisted of 22 princely states (19 ruled by Rājpūts, 2 by Jāṭs and one by a Muslim). Ibid., p. 112.

[32] Qanungo, *History of the Jats*, p. 27.

three versions of the *Chāvaḷī* more stress is put on the figure of Loṭiyā Jāṭ, who is given voice in the story while Mīṇā is not. Loṭiyā Jāṭ is not a stereotypical but personified character, one who speaks in the first person singular. Rājpūt Ḍūṅgjī contributes ideas for action, but it is Loṭiyā Jāṭ who indicates what should be done and how. In the same way, other Rājpūts rely on the smart advice of Loṭiyā Jāṭ – e.g. how to set free Ḍūṅgjī from the jail in Āgrā Fort. He addresses Javārjī with the following words:

> 'Dear son of the Śekhāvats!' interrupted Jāṭ Loṭiyā 'Listen,
> Hold on with your idea, [let's] use the stratagem of my mind.'[33]

Ḍūṅgjī, entrusting the task to Loṭiyā Jāṭ, says that he is the best of men, the king of spies.[34] The Rājpūt dacoit praises him with the following words: 'Oh Loṭiyā ! Bravo for your caste. An excellent Jāṭṇī gave [you] birth.'[35] On another occasion, the figure of Jāṭ is also presented in a positive way as a brave warrior ready for confrontation in fight in the following passage:

> Loṭiyā Jāṭ gave a challenging shout: 'Oh Śekhāvats, listen to [my] words,
> Hand over a hatchet to me [and] see [what are] the hands of a Jāṭ.'[36]

In all the three versions, formulas describing Loṭiyā Jāṭ and his Mīṇā companion as very wise, having the minds of a skilled master or vizier regularly appear: 'Loṭiyā Jāṭ [and] Karṇiyā Mīṇā [have] vizier's mind;'[37] 'Loṭiyā Jāṭ [and] Sāṁvatiyā Mīṇā [have] skilled master's mind;'[38] 'A lot of passion aroused in Karṇiyā Mīṇā and Loṭiyā Jāṭ, [they have] an intelligent mind.'[39]

---

33 *Jāṭa Loṭhyo kevā lāgo, suṇa Śekhāvata lāla jī / thā̃ kī akkala revā do, ne mhā̃ kī akkala cāla jī*; 1986 version: *Rājasthān Gaṅgā*, p. 84. This formula reoccurs in this version in a slightly different form but in the same meaning: *thā̃kī buddhi revā do ne, mhārī buddhi cāla jī*; ibid., p. 90.

34 *Maradā̃ mẽ tū̃ marada āgalo, heryā̃ro tū̃ lāṭa*. 1947 version: ibid., p. 21.

35 *Raṅga re thārī jāta Loṭiyā! Bhalo Jāṭaṇī jāyo*! Cf. almost identical verse 680, 709 in the 1986 version: ibid., pp. 26, 86–87.

36 *Baṛakai bole Jāṭa Loṭiyo suṇa Śekhāvata bāta jī / Kuhāṛī sū̃po mere hātha mẽ dekho Jāṭa rā hātha jī*. 1973 version; ibid., p. 54.

37 *Loṭyo Jāṭa Karṇiyo Mīṇo, akalā̃ mā̃y ujīra*. 1947 version: ibid, p. 21.

38 *Loṭyo Jāṭa Sāṁvato Mīṇo, akala vaḍo ustāda*. 1973 version: ibid., p. 45.

39 *Mīṇo-Loṭhyo ghaṇā ūbake, akkala kā husiyāra*. 1986 version: ibid., p. 70.

Despite the fact that the story is also known under the name *Ḍūṅgjī–Javārjī*, one gets the impression that the most crucial character is Loṭiyā Jāṭ as the focus of the story concentrates on the episodes narrating his deeds and the realization of plans suggested and carried out by him. Ḍūṅgjī sends him to carry out reconnaissance to determine which place should be plundered. When Ḍūṅgjī is arrested by *firaṅgīs*, or the soldiers of the East India Company, only Loṭiyā Jāṭ accepts the challenge to set him free – 'all his relatives refused, all chieftains refused. Only Loṭiyā Jāṭ accepted the challenge.'[40] His courage, strength and wisdom as well as his solidarity with Rājpūt Ḍūṅgjī are emphasized in all the three versions of the poem. However, the following words that Loṭiyā addressed to Ḍūṅgjī seem to contradict what we learn from historical sources about the social tension in Śekhāvaṭī. Thus it seems they should be understood as a desirable option and not the actual reality:

> Neither do I want a land for myself, nor villages.
> Consider [me as] your blood relative, for me you are brother in religion.
> In the entire world, no relative exceeds the brother in religion.
> Sāṁvatiyā [Mīṇā] and Loṭiyā Jāṭ will take revenge like real brothers.
> No fortress nor cantonment will hold back Nīṭharvāl[41] Jāṭ.[42]

Even more striking is the fragment in which Loṭiyā Jāṭ lists things that are inaccessible to the Jāṭs in the region of Śekhāvaṭī. He declares that he does not want these things, although he mentions them. If we keep in mind that land was never given to the Jāṭs in Śekhāvaṭī, maybe his words should be understood in exactly the opposite way – i.e. he reveals the Jāṭs' aspiration to gain land.

---

40 *Sārā naṭagyā bhāī-bhatījā, saba naṭagyā umrāva. Bāvaṛtā vīṛā nai jhelyo eka Loṭiyai Jāṭa*. 1947 version: ibid., p. 25. In the 1986 version, a similar verse appears in the same sense: '*Ṭhākurs* did not accept the challenge, [only] Loṭhiyā Jāṭ accepted' (*Bīṛo to nī liyo ṭhākarā̃, leve Loṭhyo Jāṭa jī*); ibid., p. 89.

41 *Nīṭharvāl* – the caste name of Loṭiyā Jāṭ.

42 *Nī cāve mhā̃ ke bāga bagīcā, nī cāve mhā̃ ke gāma / Thā̃ ko lāge saggo kāko, mhā̃ ko dharama ko bhāī / Dharma bhāī tī baṛo jagata māī̃, koī saggo nāī̃ / Bhāī sarīkho badalo degā, Sāṁvatyo ara Jāṭa / Nī̃ rokegā kilā chāvaṇī, Nīṭharvāla Jāṭa*. 1986 version: *Rājasthān Gaṅgā*, p. 84.

> Neither do I want villages and *jāgīrs*[43], nor land[44] for myself.
> Neither do I want a hereditary tenure, nor fame for myself.[45]

After Ḍūṅgjī's spectacular escape from the Āgrā Fort, which was possible due to the tricks of Loṭiyā Jāṭ, the dacoit comes back home and says to his wife:

> Oh Rānī, do not congratulate me! Congratulate Loṭiyā Jāṭ.
> I did not come myself. Loṭiyā Jāṭ has brought me [here].[46]

> Perform the *ārtī* [ceremony] for Loṭiyā Jāṭ and pay respect to Mīṇā. (...)
> Loṭiyā Jāṭ and Sāṁvatiyā Mīṇā have brought [me] after setting free from the jail.
> [They] have fulfilled dharma [like] real brothers, even for a moment [I] did not suffer misfortune [from them].[47]

MESSAGE OF SOLIDARITY IN *CHĀVAḶĪS*

In this context, an important question could be raised: Can we reconstruct social reality on the basis of the story about dacoits who contest the social order and always exist on the margins of a society?

If we take into consideration the harsh rules of feudalism, the hostility between the Rājpūts and Jāṭs in the region of Śekhāvaṭī and the fact that both Ḍūṅgjī and Loṭiyā Jāṭ are local heroes (even deified) for the Śekhāvaṭī folk, we can treat *Chāvaḷīs* as the voice of the common people for building a bridge between the Rājpūts and Jāṭs who act together for the good of the poor. It seems that the positive image of Jāṭ characters in the poem is not incidental and has its roots in the emphasis on solidarity that is prominent

---

43 *Jāgīr* – 'an estate, a freehold (as formerly given by government, in return for services).' McGregor, *Oxford Hindi-English Dictionary*, p. 366.

44 The Rājasthānī word *pāṭ* can be translated in various ways, e.g. as 'cloth,' 'garment,' 'silk garment,' 'throne' or 'land.' Cf. Lāḷas, *Rājasthānī sabad kos*, vol. 3, part 1, p. 2453.

45 *Nī cāve mhāre gāma jāgīrā̃, nī cāve mhāre pāṭa jī / Nī cāve mhāre ammara paṭṭo nī cāve mhāre nāma jī*. 1986 version; *Rājasthān Gaṅgā*, p. 89.

46 *Mhā̃ne matā̃ badhāvo, Rāṇī ! Badhāvo Loṭiyo Jāṭ / Mhẽ āpai nahī̃ āyā, mhā̃ne lyāyo Loṭiyo Jāṭ*. 1947 version: ibid., p. 33.

47 *Loṭyā Jāṭa kī karo āratī, Mīṇā ne leo vadāya / (...) Loṭhiyo Jāṭa Sāṁvatyo Mīṇo, kāḍha jela to lyāyā / Bhāī sarīkho dharama nibhāyo, chanika nī ṭallā khāyā*. Ibid., p. 101.

in the story. There are lists of groups such as the Rājpūt clans of Śekhāvat, Vīdāvat, Tomvar, Pamvār, Meṛtiyā, Narūkā, but also the *yogī* communities of Gosāīs and Dādūpanthīs who unite in the campaign to release Ḍūṅgjī from the British jail in Āgrā. Particular emphasis is also placed on the role of Loṭiyā Jāṭ as the person who calls for inter-caste solidarity. He says to the Rājpūts:

> 'Write orders [and send them] to every village, call for union of relatives.
> Get warriors of each [lord] together.
> By [sending] *lākh*s of messages, raise a wish for union.'
> No relatives came [but] chieftains showed up.
> Mīṇā [people] mounted [camels and horses and] Muslim Jāṭs [arrived] in great numbers.
> Gūjars and Rabarīs got ready, a huge army appeared.[48]
> Maharaja of Mīṅgaṛā [joined them] with prince Tamman Siṅgh.
> Shepherds mounted [horses and camels, the same as did people from] Mevātī [region and] Sardār Hari Siṅgh.
> Bīdāvat [Rājpūts] and [brave] lions of Loṛhasar and Pīmsāgan [showed up].
> Megh Siṅgh of Ḍiggī [arrived with an army] mounted on camels.
> Dātār Siṅgh of Dāntā [joined] with Metāb Siṅgh,
> [And] Bhop Siṅgh, Bhopāl Siṅgh, Ude Siṅgh Sardār.
> Bhopās have arrived [and] Bhāṭs, Cāraṇs, Nāīs and Tamolīs[49].[50]

Not only is inter-caste solidarity declared but also reconciliation between Hindus and Muslims:

---

[48] Or 'there was a huge splendour.' Some of a number of meanings of the noun *ṭhāṭh*/*ṭhāṭ* are as follows: 'splendour,' 'pomp,' 'adornment,' 'crowd,' 'army.' S. Lāḷas (ed.), *Rājasthānī–Hindī saṁkṣipt śabdkoś*, vol. 1, Jodhpur: Rajasthan Oriental Research Institute, 1986, p. 524; Badrī Prasād Sākariyā and Bhūpatirāy Sākariyā (ed.), *Rājasthānī Hindī śabdkoś*, vol. 1, Jaypur: Pañcśīl Prakāśan, 1993, p. 498.

[49] *Tamolī* – the caste of betel (*pān*) producers.

[50] *Gā̃va-gā̃va paravāṇo likha do, bhāī banda leo bulāya jī / Harīka-harīkā jujhārā̃ ko, ekaṭa leo baṇāya jī / Lakha-lakha kāgada bhāī bandā̃ ne, karyo malaṇ ko cāva jī / Bhāī banda to āyā koīnī, caṛha āyā umarāva jī / Mīṇā caṛhgyā, Bābarī, ūbaratī kā Jāṭa jī / Gūjara ne Rebārī caṛhgyā, macagī ṭhaṭṭama ṭhāṭha jī / Mīṅgaṛā kā mahārāvajī, kaṁvara Tammana Sī̃ lāra jī / Gāyara caṛhyā, maṛha Mevātī, Harisīṅgha saradāra jī / Bīdāvata ara Loṛhasarī kā, Pīṁsāgana kā nhāra jī / Ḍiggī kā to Meghasīṅgha jī, ūṇṭā para asavāra jī / Dāntā kā Dātāra Sīṅgha jī, Metāba Sīṅgha ke lāra jī / Bhopasīṅgha Bhopālasīṅgha, Udesīṅgha saradāra jī / Bhopā āyā, Bhāṭa, Cāraṇā, Nāī aura Tamolī.* 1986 version: ibid., pp. 88–89.

Relatives joined [and] united, may God keep [them] happy [and] prosperous.
Hindus and Muslims stood with Ḍūṅg Siṅgh.[51]

If we keep in mind the nineteenth-century expanding domination of the British in India, the story bespeaks a common enemy for the Śekhāvaṭī folks. The Rājpūts, Jāṭs and other castes unite in order to preserve the *status quo*, which seems to be challenged by the new, unknown reality of an upcoming new epoch. We should also remember that the heroes of *Chāvaḷī*s are historical figures and records on them can be traced in archives. Thus first one feels a compulsion to repeat after Gayatri Spivak: 'Can the subaltern speak?'[52] And in the context of the *Chāvaḷī* works, the obvious answer seems to be: 'Why not believe Bhopā [who tells] all [these] stories?'

BIBLIOGRAPHY

Asopa, Jai Narayan, *Origin of the Rajputs, in History and Culture of Rajasthan (From Earliest Times upto 1956 A.D.)*, ed. Shyam Singh Ratnawat and Krishna Gopal Sharma, Jaipur: Centre for Rajasthan Studies, University of Rajasthan, 1999.

Chattopadhyaya, 'The Emergence of the Rajputs as Historical Process in Early Medieval Rajasthan,' in *The Idea of Rajasthan. Explorations in Regional Identity*, ed. Karine Schomer, Joan L. Erdman, Deryck O. Lodric and Llyod I. Rudolph, vol. 2, Delhi: Manohar–American Institute of Indian Studies, 2001, pp. 161–191.

Lāḷas, Sītārām (ed.), *Rājasthānī sabad kos, Rājasthānī-hindī bṛhat koś*, 7 vols, Jodhpur: Caupāsnī Śikṣā Samiti, 1962–1978.

Rājasthānī–Hindī saṁkṣipt śabdkoś, vol. 1, Jodhpur: Rajasthan Oriental Research Institute, 1986.

Maheshwari, Hiralal, *History of Rajasthani Literature*, New Delhi: Sahitya Akademi, 1980.

McGregor, R.S., *Oxford Hindi-English Dictionary*, New Delhi: Oxford University Press, 2012 (1st published 1993).

Qanungo, K.R., *History of the Jats*, New Delhi: Originals, 2013 (1st published 1925).

Rājasthān Gaṅgā. Sāhitya rī Timāhī Patrikā (ed. Kiraṇ Nāhaṭā), no. 2–4, Aprail-Disambar 2013.

Rāṭhauṛ, Manohar Siṁh, *Rājasthānī kahāvatā̃*, Bīkāner: Ujās Granth Māḷā, 2001.

Rāṭhauṛ, Vikramsiṁh, *Jāṭõ kī lok kathāẽ*, Jodhpur: Rājasthānī Granthāgār, 2014.

---

[51] *Kāke bhatīje joṛī juṛagī, bhalī kare bhagvān jī / Ḍūṅgasīṅgha ke lāre vhai gyā, hindū musalmāna jī*; ibid., p. 98.

[52] For more information see: Gayatri Chakravorty Spivak, 'Can the Subaltern Speak?,' in *Marxism and the Interpretation of Culture*, ed. Cary Nelson and Lawrence Grossberg, Urbana and Chicago: University of Illinois Press, 1988, pp. 271–315.

Ratnawat, Shyam Singh and Krishna Gopal Sharma (eds), *Cāraṇ sāhitya paramparā. Essays on Bardic Literature. Professor V.S. Bhatnagar Felicitation Volume*, Jaipur: Centre for Rajasthan Studies, University of Jaipur, 2001.

Sahal, Kr̥ṣṇabihārī, *Rājasthānī lok gāthā koś*, Jodhpur: Rājasthānī Sāhitya Saṁsthān, 1995.

Sākariyā, Badrī Prasād and Bhūpatirāy Sākariyā (eds), *Rājasthānī Hindī śabdkoś*, vol. 1, Jaypur: Pañcśīl Prakāśan, 1993.

Sharma, K.L., Caste, *Feudalism and Peasantry. The Social Formation of Shekhawati*, New Delhi: Manohar, 1998.

Singh, K.S. (ed.), *People of India. Rajasthan*, vol. 38, part 2, Mumbai: Anthropological Survey of India, Popular Prakashan PVT. LTD., 1998.

Spivak, Gayatri Chakravorty, 'Can the Subaltern Speak?,' in *Marxism and the Interpretation of Culture*, ed. Cary Nelson and Lawrence Grossberg, Urbana and Chicago: University of Illinois Press, 1988, pp. 271–315.

Turek, Aleksandra, 'A Good Villain: the Bravery of the Dacoits from the Śekhāvaṭī Region of Rājasthān,' *Indologica Taurinensia* (Proceedings of the Conference 'Patterns of Bravery. The Figure of the Hero in Indian Literature, Art and Thought,' ed. Tiziana Pontillo), vol. 40, 2014 (2015), pp. 377–389.

Internet sources

http://www.jatland.com/home/Rajasthani_Language_Idioms_and_Phrases (access 30.09.2016).
http://www.nidanaheights.net/culture-proverbs.html (access 02.10.2016).

AGNIESZKA KUSZEWSKA

Institute of Social Sciences, University of Social Sciences and Humanities, Warsaw

India-Pakistan Conflict Escalation and De-Escalation: the Dynamics of Contemporary Security Challenges*

1. INTRODUCTION

In the second decade of the 21st century, security challenges and conflicts remain central issues to the study of international relations. This assumption retains its unique importance with reference to the multi-faceted security problems and challenges in Indo-Pakistani relations. The unresolved, protracted conflict between these two states has its roots in colonial times and in 1947, when the British divided their empire into two dominions: India and Pakistan, on the basis of the 'two nation theory.' This theory argued that Muslims and Hindus, the largest religious communities in the subcontinent, are two distinct nations unable to live together. This was the indirect result of the *divide et impera* principle based on the manipulative exploitation of religious differences between these communities, which was strengthened and widely used during British rule in India. This was followed by an unprecedented rise in inter-communal violence and brutal massacres, affecting Hindu, Muslim and Sikh people. The extreme violence peaked during the time of the Partition and has traumatized many families in India and Pakistan. This, along with the first escalation of the conflict in the 1948 Kashmir war, had a tremendous impact on shaping the national

* Work on this paper has been supported by the National Science Centre of Poland (NCN). Research Project: 'Human rights and India's and Pakistan's policy towards Kashmir' (2012/05/B/HS5/00726).

consciousness, a virulent exclusive ideology based on mutual acrimony and distrust, fostered by military and political leaders of both India and Pakistan. It laid the groundwork for decades of hostilities between the two states and strengthened the military component, especially in Pakistan. However, nowadays the military role and argument of strength is also bolstered by the Hindu nationalist policy of BJP-ruled India.

Over decades, the persistent conflict, the arms race along with its nuclear aspect, have shaped the security structure in South Asia. The escalation-prone relations between India and Pakistan have left their pernicious mark on the prospect of mutual harmony and the likelihood of political and economic cooperation in the whole region remains significantly hindered. Until now all the attempts aimed at seeking a satisfactory resolution of the contentious issues have turned out to be ineffective. Whereas the conflict remains a crucial element of contemporary regional security challenges, its dynamics serve as a useful case study in post World War II conflict research and analysis. The realities of the India-Pakistan rivalry may undoubtedly serve as a thought-provoking point of reference in the theoretical debate on international security on local, regional and supra-regional levels.

The ongoing conflict has been escalating and de-escalating over the last few decades and remains the crucial point of reference in the regional strategies of both countries. Consequently, the media, scholars and other commentators have adopted different appellations to elucidate the South Asian realities and complexity of the crisis-prone dynamics of the Indo-Pakistani rivalry: a conundrum, a tinderbox, a juggernaut, a rollercoaster, 'sibling rivalry,' etc.[1] The peace process has been derailed by the lack of a framework for the final resolution of the Kashmir dispute and other bones of contention. The continuous instability, terrorist activities and sudden bursts of violence along the Line of Control, the *de facto* border dividing Indian and Pakistani Kashmir, remain an irresolvable challenge in this most protracted post World War II conflict. The sharp escalation of the situation in the Indian-administered Kashmir Valley in the summer of 2016 has directly contributed to the additional worsening of the already rocky bilateral relations.

---

1 Mobashar Jawad Akbar, *Tinderbox. The Past and Future of Pakistan*, New Delhi: HarperCollins, 2011, Stephen P. Cohen, *Shooting for a Century. Finding Answers to the India-Pakistan Conundrum*, Noida: HarperCollins, 2013, Navnita Chadha Behera, *Demystifying Kashmir*, Washington: The Brookings Institution Press, 2006, p. 277, John Keay, *Midnight's Descendants. A History of South Asia Since Partition*, New York: Basic Books, 2014, p. 350.

The major questions which should be raised with reference to the dynamics of contemporary security challenges between India and Pakistan are as follows: how to discuss the contemporary structure of conflict dynamics in general and in India-Pakistan relations in particular? What are the essential direct and indirect factors shaping the security related challenges and contributing to the conflict escalation?

The conceptual and theoretical framework of the problem analysis will be based on crucial elements which determine the conflict life cycle. The deliberations will be focused on current challenges in India-Pakistan relations in the context of geopolitical dynamics and major internal as well as external challenges. The direct and indirect issues which shape and/or hinder progress in improving bilateral India-Pakistan relations will be highlighted.

2. Conflict Escalation – Theoretical Analysis

Power politics among the states and its impact on the regional political environment, growing significance of non-state actors resorting to violence, and domestic insecurity which may spill the conflicts across the borders, should be perceived as crucial factors responsible for fostering instabilities. Interstate conflicts are often connected with territorial disputes which involve the alleged necessity to protect religious and/or ethnic minorities living in adjacent states. This may turn into a driving force behind aggressive ideology, nationalism and antagonistic rhetoric, supplemented by building the negative image of the enemy (foe-friend dichotomy), dehumanization of rival state citizens, religious/ethnic minorities, etc.

It is generally assumed that each conflict escalates through certain distinguished stages which constitute the so-called conflict life cycle. For example, Johan Galtung's conflict model was based on a triangle: contradiction (as the root of actual or perceived incompatibility of goals[2]), attitude and behaviour.[3] Escalation is a mark of conflict in its dynamic form, a specific increase in conflict, a tactical step that marks a qualitative difference in conflict

[2] Johan Galtung, Carl G. Jacobsen and Kai Frithjof Brand-Jacobsen, *Searching for Peace. The Road to Transcend*, London: Pluto Press, 2002, p. 152.

[3] Olivier Ramsbotham and Hugh Miall, Tom Woodhouse, *Contemporary Conflict Resolution*, Cambridge: Polity Press, 2011, p. 10.

relations.[4] Conflicts are dynamic and can develop rapidly into the next level of hostility, with internal and external factors as decisive turning points in the course of events. Economic crises, weak state institutions, demographic pressures and other social challenges may contribute to growing radicalism followed by the inability of the state authorities to tackle the internal and external security issues effectively. In South Asia, as in any other part of the world, politics and security are driven by economic and social dynamics.[5]

The escalation of the conflict may be presented within the framework of a general theoretical approach, but importantly, it must be highlighted that all conflicts have their own distinguished characteristic features, correlated with local/regional geopolitical, economic, social, ethno-religious or demographic specificity. The latter approach is a major starting point for a case study analysis. The key elements of reconciliation and peace building mark a de-escalation of conflict behaviour and positive changes in attitudes by eliminating the clashing interests which have a benign influence on improving bilateral interactions. The tragic historical events and deeply rooted antagonism have negatively affected the bilateral attitudes on both sides of the border.

Certain factors contributing to conflict transformations and dynamics can be enumerated. The model adopted for the needs of this chapter recognizes nine following stages:

Figure 1. Conflict escalation and de-escalation model

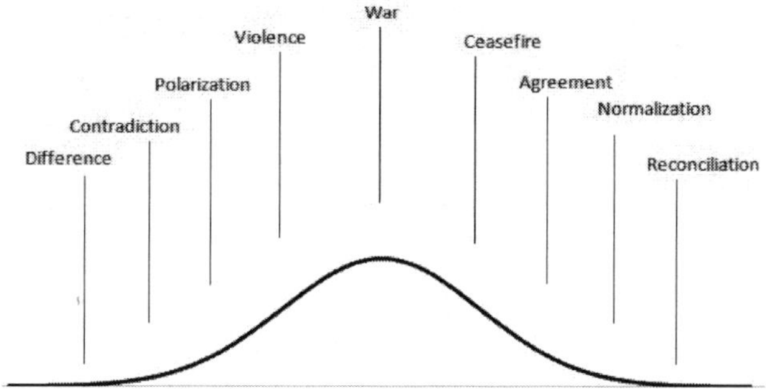

Source: O. Ramsbotham, H. Miall, T. Woodhouse, *Contemporary Conflict Resolution*, Cambridge: Polity Press, 2011, p. 13.

---

[4] William I. Zartman and Guy Olivier Faure, 'The Dynamics of Escalation and Negotiation,' in *Escalation and Negotiation in International Conflicts*, ed. William I. Zartman and Guy Olivier Faure, Cambridge: Cambridge University Press, 2005, p. 4.

[5] S.D. Muni, 'Asia's Rise: the Challenge of Stability,' in *Political and Security Dynamics of South and Southeast Asia, Singapore*, ed. Daljit Singh, Singapore: ISEAS Publishing, 2007, p. 5.

The protracted, historically inherited conflict between India and Pakistan has witnessed all the above-mentioned phases except normalization and reconciliation. Due to the constant escalation and de-escalation phases, the conflict cycle has been embedded in moving back and forth between the following phases: polarization, violence, war (escalation phases), ceasefire and agreement (de-escalation phases). Certain examples of each phase are worth presenting:

i. polarization takes place when antagonistic parties are formed and rivalry becomes manifest; gradually it may (but does not have to) lead to further escalation – for example, the Muslim League and Congress activities in pre-Partition era; military exercises and massive troop mobilizations – for example, 'Operation Brasstacks,' a major military exercise conducted by the Indian Army in 1986–1987;
ii. violence is connected with an outbreak of hostilities, preceded by polarization, not always accompanied by the use of armed forces, for example limited skirmishes along the ceasefire line (Line of Control), a proxy war using non-state actors (such as Lashkar-e-Taiba, lit. 'Army of the Good,' LeT);
iii. war erupts when the armed forces of both countries are engaged on a full scale – e.g. the first (1947–1948) and the second (1965) Kashmir wars or the 1971 war; an extra dimension to the conflict was added in the late 1990s due to the nuclear factor – in 1999 the Kargil War took place against the backdrop of recent nuclear tests;[6]
iv. ceasefire is accompanied by the end of hostilities, withdrawal of forces, discussing the principles of re-established bilateral relations – e.g. the India-Pakistan ceasefire agreement signed on 30 June 1965;
v. agreement – both sides are ready to accept high level talks, sign bilateral accords aiming at strengthening cooperation; they pledge to resolve disputes by peaceful means – e.g. the Indus Water Treaty (1960), Tashkent Declaration (1966: pledged to return to the *status quo ante* and to refrain from the use of force to settle the Kashmir dispute), Simla Agreement (1972: reaffirmed their commitment to settle the Kashmir dispute bilaterally through peaceful means), SAARC summits or Lahore Declaration (1999: pledged to restart consultations on all issues,

[6] Khurshid Mahmud Kasuri, *Neither a Hawk Nor a Dove. An Insider's Account of Pakistan's Foreign Relations Including Details of the Kashmir Framework*, Karachi: Oxford University Press, 2016, p. 427.

including Kashmir and nuclear aspects, implement the Simla agreement, acknowledge the rule of peaceful coexistence).

The conflict dynamics are shaped by a variety of processes which lead to indirect or direct escalation and de-escalation of relations. Escalation is understood as an observable increase in the intensity of conflict and severity of tactics used,[7] whereas de-escalation is the process aimed at diffusing the tensions, sometimes imposed by a powerful external actor.[8] In general, certain elements of the conflict life cycle are characteristic features of most contemporary international hostilities, thus they may be enumerated within the framework of a theoretical analysis of the problem.

TABLE 1
Theoretical approach to conflict dynamics: escalation and de-escalation factors

CONFLICT DYMAMICS →	ESCALATION	DE-ESCALATION
FACTORS ↓		
INDIRECT	The military muscle-flexing: conducting demonstrative military exercises Foreign policy based on jingoism: aggressive nationalism, threats, emphasizing supremacy over the enemy; tit-for-tat war of words between political/military establishments, demonstrative statements Engaging in arms trade and increasing foreign arms supplies Third party interference in the conflict: verbal support for one side of the conflict, promise of military assistance in case of escalation	Stalemate, inability to gain a military advantage by either of the sides, social pressure to de-escalate tensions The emphasis on strengthening economic, cultural cooperation and development of talks within the framework of existing organizations The awareness that potential escalation of the conflict contradicts the aforementioned goal, especially when the conflict involves neighbouring countries

[7] Ami C. Carpenter, *Community Resilience to Sectarian Violence in Baghdad*, New York: Springer, 2014, p. 53

[8] Louis Kriesberg and Bruce W. Dayton, *Constructive Conflicts. From Escalation to Resolution*, Lanham: Rowman & Littlefield, 2012, pp. 177–178.

	The enhanced security forces activities in the disputed areas (involving human rights violations) Training and supporting paramilitary outfits, ideology-oriented aggressive outfits, engaging in proxy activities Expressing the territorial claims on an international level The marginalization, exclusion and violation of the rights of religious and ethnic minorities, growing minority-oriented nationalism The internationalization of the conflict by engaging international forum (UN) State-controlled education system aimed at promoting aggressive nationalism, distortion of history in the textbooks	The internationalization of the conflict, outside pressure on negotiations and possible ways of conflict resolution; accepting mediation (for example by the UN) Diplomatic endeavours: unilateral ceasefire, pledge to engage in composite dialogue
DIRECT	The unilateral or bilateral breaking-off of the negotiations The skirmishes along the border between paramilitary units or regular army The cross-border influx of militants and/or arms, guerrilla campaigns, training militants The terrorist activities on the territories of the enemy state The unilateral and non-negotiable decision/action with direct negative effects for the enemy state Direct military attack with the use of regular armed forces and/or violent non-state actors	Significant reduction in combat capabilities – for example, as a result of long term stalemate, urgent necessity to compromise and start negotiations Personal contribution and engagement of the world leaders in conflict negotiations and resolution Enhancing economic cooperation, introduction of new tools, signing MoU's or bilateral accords Facilitating cross border people-to people contact, academic and cultural cooperation, making borders 'invisible' Signing the agreements which set the objectives and principles of bilateral cooperation

Based on: Agnieszka Kuszewska, 'Dynamika konfliktów międzynarodowych: konflikt w fazie eskalacji,' *Sprawy Międzynarodowe*, no. 4/2009, p. 81.

3. India–Pakistan conflict dynamics: Internal and External Factors

As previously mentioned, there are several factors which influence the dynamics of contemporary security challenges: power politics among the states, domestic instabilities and rising importance of non-state actors. These elements have a far-reaching influence on the India-Pakistan conflict, where internal and external factors, which have an impact on its dynamics, can be enumerated. It is worth emphasizing that there are profound interconnections between phenomena which occur within the states and the geopolitical as well as regional situation. The border between internal and external factors is sometimes fluid because in the contemporary world, the internal situation is strictly interconnected with external factors. Undoubtedly, the Kashmir conflict – the most important bone of contention in bilateral relations – has a strong influence on the internal and foreign policy of India and Pakistan.

The Kashmir issue has always been the crucial point of reference in India's and Pakistan's regional security strategy. The historically-inherited, protracted conflict has had a direct impact on shaping the security situation in South Asia since 1947. Although it entered phases of escalation and de-escalation, neither side has managed to come up with a solution acceptable for India, Pakistan and the Kashmiris. Moreover, it serves as an excuse for those elements of the establishments in both states that are not interested in improving bilateral relations. The tensions sharply escalated after the Indian security forces killed Burhan Wani, a local militant leader popular in Jammu and Kashmir, on 8 July 2016.

The violence which erupted in Indian Jammu and Kashmir following Wani's death, prompted an immediate reaction from the policymakers on both sides of the border. Unsurprisingly, it clearly showed that the positions of India and Pakistan have not changed over the decades. Pakistan remains a firm proponent of holding a plebiscite in Jammu and Kashmir in accordance with the UN resolutions, knowing well that this idea will most probably never materialize. Neither country is in fact willing to comply with the basic obligation of withdrawing their security forces from their respective areas of Kashmir. Nevertheless, for Pakistan, the idea of a referendum and the 'self-determination of suppressed Kashmiris' living on the Indian side serves as a useful tool in its Kashmir strategy. Sartaj Aziz, a Pakistani adviser on foreign affairs, confirmed this stance in the aftermath of Wani's death by saying that the 'verdict on the future of Kashmir' can only be given by the 'people of

Kashmir not by the external affairs minister of India.'[9] He emphasized that the United Nations Security Council had promised the Kashmiris the right to determine their future. In the same month, the Pakistani prime minister Nawaz Sharif addressed a rally in Muzaffarabad (the capital city of 'Azad' Kashmir) and announced that Jammu and Kashmir will soon become part of Pakistan. He added that the freedom movement cannot be stopped and will be successful as he prayed for the people of Kashmir suffering from the brutality of the Indian forces. Earlier that month Pakistan had issued a protest against India in the United Nations accusing New Delhi of a massive violation of human rights in Kashmir. Indian external affairs minister Sushma Swaraj replied immediately accusing Islamabad of supporting terrorist activities in Kashmir and warned that its goal of detaching Kashmir from India 'will not be realized to the end of eternity.' She also added that 'all of Kashmir belongs to India.' The September 2016 Uri attack against Indian forces deployed in Kashmir, further escalated the already increasingly aggressive rhetoric.

The internal factors escalating the conflicts are strictly connected with domestic instabilities and challenges. Pakistan, a state seesawing between military dictatorship and civilian rule, continuously faces the risk of political turmoil. Growing radicalization and the activities of terrorist groups pose a serious threat to the state's stability, with the civilian government unable to effectively manage the situation. The army and Pakistani intelligence agency, the Inter-Services Intelligence (ISI) have gained immeasurable privileges and succeeded in having a decisive impact on Pakistan's foreign strategy.

State-supported Islamic radicalization (e.g. Gen. Zia-ul Haq's regime) and the policy of using violent non-state actors by Pakistani military establishment in proxy wars and the regional strategy towards Afghanistan and in Indian Kashmir has a long history dating back to the partition of the subcontinent. This has led to the armed conflicts between India and Pakistan and shaped the South Asian security environment. In this context two major problems should be highlighted.

Firstly, the activity of various violent non-state actors, such as the Pakistani Taliban – Tehrik-e Taliban Pakistan (TTP) – should be mentioned. This group seeks to expel the Pakistani government and introduce harsh Sharia laws

---

9 All quotations in this paragraph are from: 'Pakistan Gives Shut-up Call to India on Kashmir,' *The Nation*, 25 July 2016 (http://nation.com.pk/national/25-Jul-2016/pakistan-gives-shut-up-call-to-india-on-kashmir, access 05.10.2016) and 'Not Long Till Kashmir Becomes Part of Pakistan: Nawaz,' *The Express Tribune*, 22 July 2016 (http://tribune.com.pk/story/1147098/not-long-till-kashmir-becomes-part-pakistan-pm-nawaz/, access 16.11.2016).

in Pakistan. It has orchestrated terrorist attacks in Pakistan against state institutions and civilians. The Afghani Taliban: Quetta Shura and the Haqqani Network, which found a safe haven in Pakistan and have received strong support from the ISI and the army. The anti-Shia terrorist outfits, such as Lashkar-e Jhangvi (LeT), a predominantly Punjabi group, which primarily attacks the Shia minority in Pakistan, but cooperates with the Taliban and has an alliance with Islamic State (ISIS)[10]. The Kashmiri jihadists are terrorist outfits infiltrating Indian Jammu and Kashmir (especially in the 1990s, when anti-Indian insurgency escalated), carrying out terrorist attacks on Indian territory, for example Jaish-e-Mohammed (JeM) or Lashkar-e-Taiba (LeT, renamed Jamaat-ud-Dawa when the former was banned in Pakistan).

Secondly, growing religious radicalization and nationalism in both India and Pakistan in the context of structural differences between the two states has had an impact on religious minorities, such as open aggression against minorities, marginalization and persecution – for example, the anti-Muslim mob attacks and pogrom in Indian Gujarat in 2002, the forced conversions of the Hindu minority to Islam in Pakistan. It must be emphasized that the system of education is co-responsible for promoting a strong national ideology and creating a sectarian, exclusionary world view: 'On both sides of the border Indian and Pakistani children are being educated in an exclusive, nationalistic and religiously inspired way which automatically puts them in conflict with each other. Their shared past has been distorted beyond recognition in some of the history textbooks. As children and their families generally believe what they are taught at school and what is written in state-sanctioned education materials, one can safely assume that a lot of the lies will be swallowed without question.'[11] This quotation speaks volumes of how the generations of young Indians and Pakistanis are educated in the way that enhances the possibility of opting for violent means of interactions.

External factors in India-Pakistan relations are the result of power politics among the states in the region. The crucial external element which influences the dynamics of the India-Pakistan conflict and shapes the security environment in the region are the China and Afghanistan factors. In this regard, initiatives and strategies related to China-Pakistan joint security/trade

[10] Kunwar Kuldune Shahid, 'An Alliance Between Islamic State and Lashkar-e-Jhangvi in Pakistan Was Inevitable,' *The Diplomat*, 15 November 2016 (http://thediplomat.com/2016/11/an-alliance-between-islamic-state-and-lashkar-e-jhangvi-in-pakistan-was-inevitable/, access 16.11.2016).

[11] Cohen, *Shooting for a Century*, p. 133.

cooperation and the strategy of India and Pakistan towards Afghanistan are particularly important.

China has been a major ally of Pakistan and their 'all-weather friendship' has its India-centric foundations[12] in the Cold War era. This wide-ranging alliance includes arms trade and multi-faceted military and economic cooperation. China's assistance in developing nuclear technology enabled Pakistan to become a nuclear power. Furthermore, China helped Pakistan to modernize its conventional deterrence capabilities against India.[13] The current China-Pakistan Economic Corridor (CPEC), a multi-billion dollar infrastructure investment mega-project, has already been announced as an important game changer for the regional security environment. The CPEC is a part of a major Chinese development initiative, known as 'One Belt, One Road,' aimed at connecting Asia with Europe, the Middle East and Africa. It is strictly connected with China's permanent search for global energy resources and might help solve Pakistan's grave energy crisis. For China, Pakistan is a staunch ally crucial for counterbalancing India's emerging regional military and economic aspirations. It does not, however, impede the growing India-China economic cooperation.

The strategy of India and Pakistan towards Afghanistan has its roots in the Cold War power game when South Asia was an important element of the rivalry between the United States and the Soviet Union, especially since the end of the 1970s, when the war in Afghanistan started. The long-term military and security related cooperation between the United States and Pakistan has strengthened the position of the Pakistani army and ISI in the regional strategy. Military dictators such as General Zia ul-Haq or General Pervez Musharraf turned out to be useful allies in Washington's regional interests, although they took power in undemocratic ways. The 'strategic depth' policy of the Pakistani establishment towards Afghanistan had a decisive impact on its political and military support for the Taliban regime in the 1990s and subsequent assurance of a safe haven for the Afghan Taliban in the post 2001-era. The mujahideen warriors were used to precipitate the insurgency in Indian-administered Kashmir in 1989 and 1990. Seeking a 'strategic depth' in Afghanistan turned out to be counterproductive for Pakistan's *raison d'être*

[12] Andrew Small, *The China-Pakistan Axis. Asia's New Geopolitics*, New York: Oxford University Press, 2015, pp 5–8.

[13] Syed Rifaat Hussain, 'Sino-Pakistan Ties: Trust, Cooperation and Consolidation,' in *The New Great Game. China and South and Central Asia in the Era of Reform*, ed. Thomas Fingar, Stanford: Stanford University Press, 2016, p. 131.

and its internal security; until today the relations between Afghanistan and Pakistan remain strained and apprehensive.

India's economic and structural assistance to Afghanistan as well as the amicable relations between these two states are regarded with tremendous suspicion by Pakistan. Pakistani policy makers accuse India of attempts aimed at diplomatic and economic encirclement, and limiting Pakistan's role in the region. There is no doubt that Afghanistan will remain a theatre of rivalry between New Delhi and Islamabad.

The selected direct and indirect factors regarding the dynamics of the India-Pakistan conflict are presented below in Table 2.

TABLE 2
Practical approach to conflict dynamics: selected escalation and de-escalation factors in India-Pakistan relations

CONFLICT DYMAMICS →	ESCALATION	DE-ESCALATION
FACTORS ↓		
INDIRECT	US-India Nuclear Deal, 2006 Foreign policy based on the jingoistic attitude on the Indian and Pakistani side (escalation in 2016) Engaging in the arms trading and increasing foreign arms supplies (Russia-India, United States-Pakistan, China-Pakistan, etc.) China's ongoing assurances of friendship and support for Pakistan China-Pakistan Economic Corridor (CPEC), which crosses disputed territory in Pakistan-administered Kashmir India-Iran-Afghanistan trade corridor deal, which aims at turning Iranian port of Chabahar into a transit hub bypassing Pakistan, 2016	Stalemate: inability to gain a military advantage by either of the sides The emphasis on the strengthening economic and cultural cooperation, bilateral initiatives The awareness that potential escalation of the conflict contradicts the above-mentioned goal, especially when the conflict involves neighbouring countries Outside pressure on negotiations and possible ways of conflict resolution Internationalization of the conflict: offering mediation (UN Secretary General)

	Massive human rights violations by Indian security forces in Jammu and Kashmir, with escalation in 2010 and 2016 Pakistan's vociferous support for the Kashmiri cause, self-determination, activities of militants in Kashmir Bilateral accusations of human rights abuses (Indian abuses in Jammu and Kashmir, Pakistani in Baluchistan) The expression of the territorial claims and mutual accusations on an international level: Human Rights in Geneva, General Assembly Communal aggression: mob attacks against the Muslim minority in India, the Hindu minority in Pakistan; economic exclusion and persecution of the minority communities in both states State-controlled textbooks, the negative portrayal of religious minorities, focusing on the historical periods which are most glorious for the particular religious group; promoting nationalism and unification within religious identity – Hindus in India, Muslims in Pakistan; adjusting history to friend-foe concept by distorting it (Islamization, Hinduization)	Outlawing terrorist organizations, for example LeT and JeM by Pervez Musharraf in 2002
DIRECT	The unilateral or bilateral breaking-off of the negotiations The wars between India and Pakistan (1947–48, 1965, 1971, 1999) The regular cross-border skirmishes along the Line of Control, exchange of fire with casualties	The auspices and mediation of the World Bank (then the International Bank for Reconstruction and Development) in signing the Indus Waters Treaty, a water-sharing treaty between India and Pakistan, 1960

	The major terrorist attacks in India carried out by Pakistan-based groups: India's Parliament (2001) Mumbai (2008) Indian unilateral decision to withdraw from SAARC summit in Islamabad (November 2016)	The 2003 ceasefire: negotiating confidence building measures, introducing a bus service in Kashmir reuniting families divided by the Line of Control 2004 SAARC summit in Islamabad: pledge by the seven member states to implement a South Asian Free Trade Area between 2008-10 2004 Atal Bihari Vajpayee and Pervez Musharraf joint statement: the two countries will revive a composite dialogue on all contentious issues, including Kashmir, and will work on CBMs The 'cricket diplomacy' as the commendable step towards reconciliation: the high level visits on the occasion of India-Pakistan cricket matches; e.g. Pervez Musharraf in India, 2005 Narendra Modi – Nawaz Sharif unexpected 'family' meeting in 2015

Author's study.

4. Conclusion

In this paper, a theoretical and practical approach to the conflict dynamics analysis has been presented. The uniqueness of India-Pakistan relations and the security environment of South Asia draws the constant attention of political analysts worldwide, especially when the tension between India and Pakistan escalates. It is the only region in the world with a protracted conflict between two nuclear states, negatively affecting the chances for the regional development. Due to the complexity of geopolitical conditions and the quagmire of challenges in India and Pakistan relations, political, economic and social factors have to be taken into consideration while discussing the possible de-escalation initiatives. The research on conflict escalation and de-escalation processes has to be carried out with special reference to these factors and through the prism of strategies based on establishment-enforced bilateral rivalry and mistrust.

The current state of escalated relations leads to the conclusion that there are extremely limited prospects of coming up with acceptable solutions, strengthening interregional economic and security related cooperation or successfully undertaking any new progress-oriented initiatives. In 2016, the chances of re-establishing the peace process and implementing confidence building measures are bleak, in the context of growing jingoism and religion-based nationalism on both sides of the border. This leads to direct open hostility and threatens conflict escalation, where conventional war, despite the nuclear deterrence, might be a scenario we should not unequivocally reject.

The partition of the subcontinent paved the way to territorial disputes and left the legacy of profound hostility between the two states, skillfully ratcheted up by political and military establishments on both sides of the border. Today the situation resembles a Cold War reality: in bilateral relations security concerns play a pivotal role with huge sums spent on defence purposes and a concurrent negligence of developmental initiatives. The Kashmir conflict has remained the primary source of tension and it may be assumed to be the most probable pretext for any future Indo-Pakistani belligerence. Both countries have avoided major wars since the nuclearization of their bilateral relations, but it has not prevented against regular outbreaks of serious crises and, taking into consideration the current situation, further escalation should not be excluded.

The analysis of escalation and de-escalation phases in India and Pakistan rivalry enables an explicit conclusion to be drawn: peace in the subcontinent is highly elusive and will remain so in the foreseeable future. The dynamically evolving direct and indirect internal and external factors should be taken into consideration while discussing the (grim) prospects for normalization and reconciliation between India and Pakistan.

Bibliography

Akbar, Mobash Jawad, *Tinderbox. The Past and Future of Pakistan*, New Delhi: HarperCollins, 2011.

Behera, Ch. Navnita, *Demystifying Kashmir*, Washington: The Brookings Institution Press, 2006.

Carpenter, C. Ami, *Community Resilience to Sectarian Violence in Baghdad*, New York: Springer, 2014.

Cohen, P. Stephen, *Shooting for a Century. Finding Answers to the India-Pakistan Conundrum*, Noida: HarperCollins, 2013.

Fingar, Thomas (ed.), *The New Great Game. China and South and Central Asia in the Era of Reform*, Stanford: University Press, 2016.

Galtung, Johan, Carl G. Jacobsen and Kai Frithjof Brand-Jacobsen, *Searching for Peace. The Road to Transcend*, London: Pluto Press, 2002.

Hussain, Syed Rifaat, 'Sino-Pakistan Ties: Trust, Cooperation and Consolidation,' in *The New Great Game. China and South and Central Asia in the Era of Reform*, ed. Thomas Fingar, Stanford: Stanford University Press, 2016, p. 131.

Kasuri, Khurshid Mahmud, *Neither a Hawk Nor a Dove. An Insider's Account of Pakistan's Foreign Relations Including Details of the Kashmir Framework*, Karachi: Oxford University Press, 2016.

Keay, John, *Midnight's Descendants. A History of South Asia Since Partition*, New York: Basic Books, 2014.

Kriesberg, Louis and Bruce W. Dayton, *Constructive Conflicts. From Escalation to Resolution*, Lanham: Rowman & Littlefield, 2012.

Kunwar Kuldune Shahid, 'An Alliance Between Islamic State and Lashkar-e-Jhangvi in Pakistan Was Inevitable,' *The Diplomat*, 15 November 2016 (http://thediplomat.com/2016/11/an-alliance-between-islamic-state-and-lashkar-e-jhangvi-in-pakistan-was-inevitable/, access 16.11.2016).

Kuszewska, Agnieszka, 'Dynamika konfliktów międzynarodowych: konflikt w fazie eskalacji' (in Polish: 'International Conflict Dynamics: Conflict in the Phase of Escalation'), *Sprawy Międzynarodowe*, no. 4/2009, pp. 80–81.

Muni, S.D., 'Asia's Rise: the Challenge of Stability,' in *Political and Security Dynamics of South and Southeast Asia*, ed. Daljit Singh, Singapore: ISEAS Publishing, 2007, p. 5.

'Not Long Till Kashmir Becomes Part of Pakistan: Nawaz,' *The Express Tribune*, 22 July 2016 (http://tribune.com.pk/story/1147098/not-long-till-kashmir-becomes-part-pakistan-pm-nawaz/, access 16.11.2016).

'Pakistan Gives Shut-up Call to India on Kashmir,' *The Nation*, 25 July 25, 2016 (http://nation.com.pk/national/25-Jul-2016/pakistan-gives-shut-up-call-to-india-on-kashmir, access 05.10.2016).

Ramsbotham, Oliver, Hugh Miall and Tom Woodhouse, *Contemporary Conflict Resolution*, Cambridge: Polity Press, 2011.

Small, Andrew, *The China-Pakistan Axis. Asia's New Geopolitics*, New York: Oxford University Press, 2015.

Zartman, I. William and Guy Olivier Faure, 'The Dynamics of Escalation and Negotiation,' in *Escalation and Negotiation in International Conflicts*, ed. William I. Zartman and Guy Olivier Faure, Cambridge: Cambridge University Press, 2005, p. 4.

Justyna Wiśniewska-Singh

Chair of South Asian Studies, Faculty of Oriental Studies, University of Warsaw

First-Person Narrative in the Early Hindi Novel

The first-person narrative, crucial for autobiographical accounts, was completely absent during the initial period of novel writing in Hindi – i.e. from 1870[1] onwards. However, an unfinished work by Bharatendu Harishchandra (Bhāratendu Hariścandra; 1850–1885[2]) *Ek kahānī kuch āp bītī kuch jag bītī* (*A Story of What Has Happened to Me and Others*) published in 1876[3] will be mentioned here as an exception. Subsequent attempts at mastering this narrative technique took place in 1889, 1893, 1906, 1907, 1909 and 1914.[4] This paper alludes to these works and while analysing one of them – *Mādhavī-Mādhav vā Madan-Mohinī* (*Madhavi and Madhav, Madan and Mohini*) published in 1909 – it seeks to explore, firstly, how

[1] *Devrānī jehānī kī kahānī* (*Tale of the Younger and the Elder Sister-in-Law*) by Gaurīdatt (1836–1905) was published in 1870 and is considered by some scholars as the first novel in Hindi. Gopāl Rāy, *Hindī upanyās kā itihās*, Nayī Dillī–Paṭnā–Ilāhābād: Rājkamal Prakāśan, 2009, pp. 13, 17, 27. Cf. Ronald Stuart McGregor, 'The Rise of Standard Hindi and Early Hindi Prose Fiction,' in *The Novel in India: Its Birth and Development*, ed. Thomas Welbourne Clark, London: George Allen and Unwin, 1970, p. 153. McGregor is one of the scholars claiming that *Parīkṣā guru* (*Experience Is the Only Teacher*) by Śrīnivās Dās (1850–1887) published in 1882 is 'the first work in Hindi which can fairly be described as a novel.'

[2] Vasudha Dalmia, *The Nationalization of Hindu Traditions: Bhāratendu Hariśchandra and Nineteenth-century Banaras*, New Delhi: Oxford University Press, 2005, p. 10.

[3] Rāy, *Hindī upanyās kā itihās*, p. 38. Hemant Śarmā, 'Editor's Introduction' [to *Ek kahānī kuch āp bītī kuch jag bītī*], in *Bhāratendu samagra*, ed. Hemant Śarmā, Vārāṇasī: Pracārak Granthāvalī Pariyojnā, 1989, p. 981. Cf. Dalmia, *The Nationalization of Hindu Traditions*, p. 298. According to Dalmia it appeared in April 1877.

[4] Rāy, *Hindī upanyās kā itihās*, p. 124.

crucial the author's choice of the narrative mode is for the novel itself and, secondly, what the advantages and limitations of this form of narration are. Apart from those, more or less successful, literary experiments during the period of the early endeavours at novel writing, the primacy of third-person narration was unquestioned.

Before discussing novels written in the first-person, it will be useful to scrutinize the features of narration in the majority of works written at the turn of the 19th century. The scope of prose fiction at that time ranged from the genre of didactic novels to romance and detective stories. Both in didactic works and those of popular entertainment, the narrative is marked by the more or less noticeable presence of an omniscient narrator who sees everything that happens and knows the thoughts and feelings of all the characters. In didactic novels, the narrator tends to make observations on contemporary social conditions and to express general views about human life, whereas in romances and detective stories, the narrator's commentary is limited owing to the fact that the description of the sequence of events is in the foreground. Nevertheless, it is also true that there were attempts at writing works of the romance type that touched on social issues. Regardless of the novel's subject matter, the narrator recounts the events in the story, indicates the utterances of particular characters and describes the locations and protagonists. However, there are relatively fewer descriptions than a European reader would expect – for example, one does not have the chance to learn what the main characters look like due to the fact that descriptions in early Hindi novels are sparse and their major function is to highlight the feelings of a protagonist. A good example of this strategy is the passage from *Candrakāntā* (*Chandrakanta*),[5] the first bestseller in Hindi, depicting Prince Veerendra Singh pining for his beloved Princess Chandrakanta. It may be also noted here that the first part of this novel was published in 1888, while all four came out in 1891 separately and in one volume in 1892.[6] The number of editions prove the novel's unprecedented popularity as there

[5] For more on the phenomenon of this extremely popular novel, see: Arthur Dudney, 'Keeping the Magic Alive: How Devakīnandan Khatrī's Chandrakāntā, the First Hindi Best-seller, Navigates Western Modernity and the Fantastical,' 2009 (retrieved on 30.04.2013 from http://www.columbia.edu/itc/mealac/pritchett/00urduhindilinks/txt_dudney_chandrakanta.pdf). Francesca Orsini, *Print and Pleasure: Popular Literature and Entertaining Fictions in Colonial North India*, Ranikhet: Permanent Black, 2009, pp. 198–225. Justyna Wiśniewska, 'Pierwsza popularna powieść w języku hindi,' *Przegląd Orientalistyczny*, no. 1–2, 2009, pp. 63–71.

[6] Rāy, *Hindī upanyās kā itihās*, p. 68 and Orsini, *Print and Pleasure*, p. 201.

were 37 editions until 1961.[7] It is customarily repeated after Ramchandra Shukla (Rāmcandra Śukla), a Hindi literary critic, that *Candrakāntā*'s author, Devakinandan Khatri (Devakīnandan Khatrī; 1861–1913[8]), 'created more readers in the Hindi language than any other writer.'[9] The statement applies both to *Candrakāntā* and to its two sequels in spite of their intricate plot and multitude of characters. Nevertheless, the romantic theme remains in the foreground as the passage highlighting the emotions of Prince Veerendra Singh indicates:

> Where the prince and Tej Singh sit, the river is very wide and on its banks there is a dense forest of *sal* trees in which thousands of peacocks and langurs, with their shrieks and laughter add to the beauty of the forest. Prince Veerendra Singh sits dejected. Suffering the anguish of separation from Chandrakanta, frequent shrieks of the peacocks strike him like arrows, the laughter of monkeys sounds like a thunderbolt and the light evening breeze feels like a hot wind. Sitting quietly, he sighs to himself.[10]

A description in a novel *Adhkhilā phūl* (*Half-Blossomed Flower*) by a renowned poet Ayodhya Singh Upadhyay 'Hariaudh' (Ayodhyāsiṁh Upādhyāy 'Hariaudh'; 1865–1947[11]), discussed later in this paper, performs a similar function. Here the narrator gives an account of a scorching day,

---

[7] McGregor, *Hindi Literature of the Nineteenth and Early Twentieth Centuries*, p. 100. Cf. Meenakshi Mukherjee, *Realism and Reality: The Novel and Society in India*, New Delhi: Oxford University Press, 2005, s. 64. According to Mukherjee during the same period there were 45 editions with an estimated number of 180 000 printed copies.

[8] Madhureś, *Devakīnandan Khatrī*, Dillī: Sāhitya Akādemī, 2002, pp. 11, 13.

[9] *Jitne pāṭhak unhõne utpann kie utne aur kisī granthkār ne nahī̃.* Rāmcandra Śukla, *Hindī sāhitya kā itihās*, p. 476. English translation by Mukherjee, *Realism and Reality*, p. 64.

[10] *Jahā̃ kumār aur Tejsih baiṭhe haĩ nadī bahut cauṛī hai aur us par sākhū kā baṛa bhārī ghanā jaṅgal hai jismẽ hazārõ mor tathā laṅgūr apnī-apnī boliyõ aur kilkāriyõ se jaṅgal kī śobhā baṛhā rahe haĩ. Kũvar Vīrendrasiṁh udās baiṭhe haĩ, Candrakāntā ke virah mẽ morõ kī āvāz tīr-sī lagtī hai, laṅgūrõ kī kilkārī vajra-sī mālūm hotī hai, śām kī dhīmī-dhīmī ṭhaṇḍī havā lū kā kām kartī hai. Ve cupcāp baiṭhe (...) ũcī sā̃s le rahe haĩ.* Devakīnandan Khatrī, *Candrakāntā*, Dillī: Sanmārg Prakāśan, 2000, p. 36. English translations of Chandrakanta are mostly after Manju Gupta but whenever Manju Gupta has strayed from the original, the translation has been modified. Devakīnandan Khatri, *In the Mysterious Ruins: A Novel*, Star Publications: New Delhi, 2004, pp. 45–46 (with changes).

[11] Sisir Kumar Das (ed.), *A History of Indian Literature: 1800–1910 Western Impact: Indian Response*, Delhi: Sahitya Akademi, 2000, p. 322.

which corresponds with the emotions of the heroine Devhuti. While her husband has been missing for three years, another man seeks her favour. Devhuti is about to read a letter from this man. The narrator concludes: 'You people have just seen a summer midday, exactly the same is a state of mind of Devhuti.'[12]

Significantly, such introductory passages at the beginning of a chapter are often set in time and describe either a season or a time of the day. While analysing another novel, McGregor perceives them as a 'point of contact with older literary traditions,' alluding to 'older Hindi poetry, in which the changing seasons form a framework within which the heroine's changing emotions are presented.'[13]

In *Parīkṣā guru*[14] (*Experience Is the Only Teacher*) by Śrīnivās Dās (1850–1887) published in 1882, a description of Western – i.e. not traditionally Indian – clothes and furnishings emphasizes the main character's attitude towards new fashions from the West. Madanmohan, the main protagonist of *Parīkṣā guru,* is depicted as ostentatiously extravagant and fascinated with Western things. Significantly, the very first chapter of the book reveals his interest in buying foreign, often useless articles as he visits an Englishmen's shop and makes a purchase of a purely decorative but very expensive curio made in France. Madanmohan comments on it, saying: 'I buy good things. Once I like something, then I do not care about the price.'[15] In this novel, we also find a long passage naming the items in Madanmohan's collection. They include furniture and decorative items at home and in the summerhouse, a row of fountains, artificial waterfalls and an aquarium in the garden, along with English carriages in his stable.[16] Because of such lengthy passages also including the narrator's comments on social issues and human life in general, 'there is little dialogue until quite late in the book' and the reader

---

12 *Āp logõ ne abhī ek jeṭh kī dopahar dekhī hai – ṭhīk vahī gat Devhūtī ke jī kī hai.* Upādhyāy 'Hariaudh,' *Adhkhilā phūl*, in Ayodhyāsih Upādhyāy 'Hariaudh,' *Racnāvalī*, ed. Śāhī, vol. 6, Nayī Dillī: Vāṇī Prakāśan, 2010, p. 60.

13 McGregor, 'The Rise of Standard Hindi and Early Hindi Prose Fiction,' pp. 154-155.

14 For more on this novel, see: Dalmia, 'A Novel Movement in Hindi: *Parīkshā guru*,' in *Narrative Strategies. Essays on South Asian Literature and Film*, ed. Vasudha Dalmia and Theo Damsteegt, New Delhi: Oxford University Press, 1999, pp. 169–184. Amrik S. Kalsi, '*Parīkṣāguru* (1882): The First Hindi Novel and the Hindu Elite,' *Modern Asian Studies*, vol. 26, no. 4, 1992, pp. 763–790.

15 *Maĩ to acchī cīz kā gāhak hū̃. Cīz pasand āye pīche mujhko qīmat kī kuch parvā nahī̃ rahtī.* Śrīnivās Dās, *Parīkṣā guru*, Ilāhābād: Lokbhāratī, 2002, p. 9.

16 Ibid., p. 23.

is much 'a passive spectator' as McGregor aptly points out.[17] Thus, the narrator's voice remains in the foreground. McGregor acknowledges that as far as *Parīkṣā guru* and most other early Hindi novels are concerned, 'the borrowing from the earlier-founded drama of its convention of representing dialogue' is an interesting aspect in terms of presentation of the narrative.[18]

In the already quoted *Candrakāntā*, a description of Chapala, Princess Chandrakanta's skilful attendant, lacks individual features but refers, at first, to the abilities of *aiyār*s, the clever helpers of the main characters, adding to the catalogue of skills of these stock characters. In the introduction to the novel, its author, Devakinandan Khatri, writes that *aiyār*s could 'change their form, deal in magic potions, sing, play, discharge commissions, bear arms, spy, and had many arts besides.'[19] At the same time, the second part of the same passage describes the heroine in a conventional way:

> Chapala was no ordinary woman. Apart from beauty and grace, she was strong too. Confrontation with a few men or capturing them was no difficult task for her as she was adept in handling arms and armament. Apart from being well-versed in the art of spying, she possessed a number of other qualities. She was a master singer and musician, expert in dancing and fond of making fireworks and what not – there was no craft which Chapala did not know. Her fair complexion, a well-built body, delicate hands and feet – the mere thought of them made one fear that if they were hit with flowers, it would be tantamount to killing her. Whenever she had to venture out, she would on purpose spoil her good looks by painting them up or by disguising her appearance.[20]

---

17 McGregor, 'The Rise of Standard Hindi and Early Hindi Prose Fiction,' p. 155.

18 Ibid.

19 *sūrat badalnā, bahut sī davāõ kā jānnā, gānā-bajānā, dauṛnā, astr calānā, jāsūsõ kā kām denā vaġairah bahut-sī bātẽ jānā karte the*. Khatrī, *Candrakāntā*, Dillī: Sanmārg Prakāśan, 2000, p. 6 ('Bhūmikā'). English translation by McGregor, 'The Rise of Standard Hindi and Early Hindi Prose Fiction,' p. 156.

20 *Capalā koī sadharāṇ aurat na thī. Xūbsūratī aur nazākat ke sivāy usmẽ tāqat bhī thī. Do-cār ādmiyõ se laṛ jānā yā unko giraftār kar lenā uske liye ek adnā kām thā, śastr-vidyā ko pūre taur se jāntī thī. Aiyārī ke fan ke alāvā aur bhī kaī guṇ usmẽ the. Gāne aur bajāne mẽ ustād, nācne mẽ māhir, ātiśbāzī banāne kā baṛā śauq, kahā̃ tak likhẽ – koī fan aisā na thā jisko Capalā na jāntī ho. Raṅg uskā gorā, badan har jagah se suḍaul, nāzuk hāth pā̃v kī taraf xayāl karne se yahī zāhir hotā thā ki ise ek phūl se mārnā xūn karnā hai. Usko jab kahī̃ bāhar jāne kī zarūrat paṛtī thī, to apnī xūbsūratī jānbūjh kar bigāṛ ḍāltī yā bheṣ badal letī thī*. Khatrī, *Candrakāntā*, p. 52. English translation by Manju Gupta. Khatri, *In the Mysterious Ruins*, pp. 68–69 (with changes).

In this and nearly all other works the narrator, far from being objective, comments on and evaluates the actions and motives of the characters:

Now this group of devils left for Vijayagarh. They had every intention of going to Naugarh too. Let's see where they go and what they do.[21]

At the same time, in the majority of books written at the end of the nineteenth and the beginning of the twentieth century the narrator addresses the readers directly to explain some facts, sum up what has happened, recap earlier incidents or introduce new facts or characters like in this excerpt from *Candrakāntā*:

> Till it is identified who the delicate woman, walking in front of other women and keeping a book in her hand, is and where she lives, till then we shall use a name 'Vankanya' (a forest-maiden) when writing about her.[22]

The omniscient narrator acts here like an oral storyteller (*qissāgo*)[23], where the influence of the oral tradition is evident. In most passages, like in the one cited above, he refers to himself using the first-person plural pronoun (ham) while in two novels by Ayodhya Singh Upadhyay 'Hariaudh' with the main narration in the third-person, the first-person singular pronoun (*maĩ*) appears. Interestingly, the earliest works – i.e. *Devrānī jeṭhānī kī kahānī* (*Tale of the Younger and the Elder Sister-in-Law*) by Gauridatt (Gaurīdatt) published in 1870 and *Bhāgyavatī* (*Bhagyavati*) written by Shraddharam Philauri in 1877 (Śraddhārām Phillaurī; 1833–1881[24]) and published in 1887[25] – lack such self-reference from the narrator. However, *Devrānī jeṭhānī kī kahānī* contains a phrase, which performs none of the above-mentioned functions and seems highly conventional instead: 'You should know that

---

21 *Ab yah śaitānõ kā jhuṇḍ Vijayagaṛh kī taraf ravānā huā. In logõ kā irādā Naugaṛh jāne kā bhī thā. Dekhiye, kahā̃ jāte haĩ aur kyā karte haĩ*. Khatrī, *Candrakāntā*, p. 36. English translation by Manju Gupta. Khatri, *In the Mysterious Ruins*, p. 45.

22 *Vah nāzuk aurat jiske hāth mẽ kitāb hai aur jo sab auratõ ke āge-āge ā rahī hai, kaun aur kahā̃ kī rahne vālī hai jab tak yah na mālūm ho jāy tab tak ham usko Vankanyā ke nām se likhẽge*. Khatrī, *Candrakāntā*, p. 136. English translation by Manju Gupta. Khatri, *In the Mysterious Ruins*, p. 171 (with changes).

23 For more on storytelling tradition and popular oral genres, see: Orsini, *Print and Pleasure*, pp. 106-159.

24 Das (ed.), *A History of Indian Literature*, p. 460.

25 Rāy, *Hindī upanyās kā itihās*, p. 28.

one's own life is precious to everyone.'[26] The editor's commentary explains that it is 'a natural style of a storyteller,'[27] thus attributing this sentence, or rather a formula,[28] to the oral tradition. In both these works, the narrator's voice remains fully hidden behind the story.

Nevertheless, in later works we encounter a gradual shift in the position of the narrator in relation to the story. This, in turn, contributed to the further development of the Hindi novel. For example, if we compare two prose works by Ayodhya Singh Upadhyay 'Hariaudh' – *Ṭheṭh hindī kā ṭhāṭ* (*A Tale Devised in Pure Hindi*) published in 1899 and *Adhkhilā phūl* (*Half-Blossomed Flower*) published in 1906 – we notice some differences. While addressing his audience directly, in the first of them the narrator refers to himself, with just a few exceptions, using the first-person plural pronoun (*ham*), whereas in the latter he switches here and there from the first-person plural pronoun (*ham*) to the first-person singular pronoun (*maĩ*). In *Adhkhilā phūl*, the omniscient narrator sporadically introduces new facts from the point of view of the characters, pretending to have assumed their perspective.

> Surely [by now] you understand who this woman and Harmohan are. But for those of you who do not, let me explain: the woman is Parbati, her daughter – Devhuti, her son – Devkishor, and the father of both is Harmohan. People assumed Harmohan was dead, and who am I[29] to have an opinion? There was no sign of him, and I[30] thought what all the others in the village did.[31]

---

[26] *Tum jāno apnī jān sabko pyārī hai.* Gaurīdatt, *Devrānī jeṭhānī kī kahānī. Hindī kā pratham upanyās (varṣ 1870 mẽ prakāśit)*, ed. Puṣpapāl Siṁh, Nayī Dillī: Remādhav Pablikeśans, 2006, p. 50.

[27] *Kissāgoī kī sahaj śailī.* Puṣpapāl Siṁh, *Sandarbh*, in ibid., p. 64.

[28] For more on the concept and function of formula in oral tradition and an example of formulaic analysis of a poem originated in Rajasthan, see: Aleksandra Szyszko, *The Three Jewels of the Desert. The Ḍholā-Mārū Story: A Living Narrative Tradition of Northern India*, Warsaw: Dom Wydawniczy Elipsa, 2012, pp. 87–146.

[29] Lit. 'we.'

[30] Lit. 'we.'

[31] *Yah strī aur Harmohan kaun haĩ? Yah to āp log samajh hī gaye hõge. Par jo na samjhe hõ to, maĩ batlātā hū̃. Strī Pārbatī hai – laṛkī Devhūtī hai – laṛkā Devkiśor hai – aur in donõ kā bāp Harmohan hai. Harmohan ko logõ ne marā samjhā, ham kyā samjhẽ? Jab patā nahī̃ lagā; to ham aur kyā samjhẽge, gā̃v vālõ kā sāth ham bhī dete haĩ.* A. Upādhyāy 'Hariaudh,' *Adhkhilā phūl*, p. 59.

In the first part of the above-mentioned passage the narrator refers to himself by using the first-person singular pronoun (*maĩ*) distinguishing himself from 'the others in the village' and explaining the facts from the point of view of the omniscient narrator. At the same time in the latter part both the pronoun and the narrative perspective change. Although the first-person plural pronoun (*ham*) in Hindi can denote both one and more than one person, its use at the end of the quotation brings the narrator closer to 'the others in the village,' justifying his apparent lack of knowledge concerning what had happened to Harmohan. Moreover, this brings about an element of suspense and induces curiosity in the reader by means of the narrative, whereas in works like *Candrakāntā* such an effect is achieved mainly by introducing unexpected turning points; though Ayodhya Singh Upadhyay 'Hariaudh' also introduced some events by a lucky coincidence.

Comparing two more passages from the beginning and the end of *Adhkhilā phūl*, one notices more instances of the narrative perspective shifting. The first chapter of the novel begins with a description of a hot, humid night and is followed by an account of a small house. Before the narrator goes on to introduce the characters living there, he states: 'I[32] want to go and see what is going on there right now,'[33] attracting the readers' attention and bringing them closer to the conversation, which follows the house's description. Finally, towards the end of the novel, there is even less distance between the narrator and the story being related as he starts witnessing what is happening and uses mostly a first-person narrative. As far as the grammatical form is concerned, both the first-person plural pronoun (*ham*) and the first-person singular pronoun (*maĩ*) appear. The last page of the book opens with the passage:

> After I had read [the writing on] the stone, I felt a great urge to see the temple. I washed my hands and feet, took some flowers, and entered the temple. I cannot explain the state that overtook me when I saw the statue of the Goddess there.[34]

---

32 Lit. 'we.'

33 *ham vahī̃ cal kar dekhnā cāhte haĩ, is ghaṛī vahā̃ kyā hotā hai*. Ibid., p. 31.

34 *Patthar paṛhkar mujhko mandir dekhne kī baṛī cāh huī. Maĩ hāth-pā̃v dhokar aur kuch phūl lekar mandir ke bhītar gayā. Vahā̃ jākar devī kī mūrti dekhne pīche merī jo gat huī, maĩ us ko kisī bhā̃ti nahī̃ batlā saktā*. Ibid., p. 141.

The novel ends with two paragraphs of the narrator's concluding remarks in the third-person. As far as shifting the narrative perspective in *Adhkhilā phūl* is concerned, Ayodhya Singh Upadhyay 'Hariaudh' proved himself to be a skilful prose writer, although the novel is mainly analysed in terms of its experimentation with a language style void of borrowed words.

The earliest prose text of the incipient stage of novel writing in Hindi exclusively in the first-person narrative is an unfinished work by Bharatendu Harishchandra. Merely two pages long, *Ek kahānī kuch āp bītī kuch jag bītī* is told from the perspective of a first-person narrator. It appeared in 1876 in a literary magazine *Kavivacansudhā* edited by the writer. The narrator, a young and well-born but inexperienced boy surrounded by apparent well-wishers and agents of all kinds, begins his story by addressing the readers:

> Who I am and in what clan I was born, you will only find out afterwards. What interest could you people have, it could be the lament of any one at all, you just want to read on, you are only concerned with amusing yourselves. For the time being I will only disclose that the tithi[35] I was born on is considered auspicious both by the Jains and the Vaidiks. On a day in samvat[36] 1930, when I was twenty-three years old, I was sitting at the window, it was spring and a cool breeze was blowing.[37]

In the very first sentence, the narrator uses the first-person plural pronoun (*ham*), which, as has already been mentioned, can refer in Hindi both to many persons and to one person, then he switches to the first-person singular pronoun (*maĩ*). Such an inconsistency, not uncommon for the Hindi language,

[35] *Tithi* – a lunar day or a 30th part of the whole lunation, its average duration is slightly less than 24 hours. Monier Monier-Williams, *A Sanskrit-English Dictionary Etymologically and Philologically Arranged with Special Reference to Cognate Indo-European Languages*, Delhi: Motilal Banarsidass, 1999, p. 446; *Brill's Encyclopedia of Hinduism*, vol. 2, Leiden–Boston: Brill, 2010, p. 293.

[36] *Samvat* – a year, esp. of the Vikram era (beginning in 58 B.C.). Monier-Williams, *A Sanskrit-English Dictionary*, p. 1114.

[37] *Ham kaun haĩ aur kis kul mẽ utpann haĩ āp log pīche jānẽge. Āp logõ ko kyā, kisī kā ronā ho paṛhe calie, jī bahlāne se kām hai. Abhī maĩ itnā hī kahtā hū̃ ki merā janm jis tithi ko huā vah jain aur vaidik donõ mẽ baṛā pavitr din hai. Sam. 1930 mẽ maĩ jab teīs baras kā thā, ek din khiṛkī par baiṭhā thā, basant ṛtu, havā ṭhaṇḍī caltī thī?* Hariścandra, *Ek kahānī kuch āp bītī kuch jag bītī*, in *Bhāratendu granthāvalī* (tīsrā khaṇḍ), ed. Vrajaratnadās, Kāśī: Nāgarīpracāriī Sabhā, 1953, p. 813. English translation by Dalmia, *The Nationalization of Hindu Traditions*, p. 298.

also occurs in other works of this period – for example, in the novels by Ayodhya Singh Upadhyay 'Hariaudh.' The narrator of *Ek kahānī kuch āp bītī kuch jag bītī* conveys a realistic but highly personal account, using shorter sentences that are informative as well as longer, descriptive ones.[38] Gopal Ray (Gopāl Rāy) considers this fragment to be a novel (*upanyās*) revealing Bharatendu's talent as a writer of fiction, and claims that the experiences of the protagonist described in it are based on episodes from the author's life, as Bharatendu was himself a young and wealthy man surrounded by hangers-on.[39] Some scholars, like Hemant Sharma, perceive *Ek kahānī kuch āp bītī kuch jag bītī* as Bharatendu's autobiography (*ātmacaritr*).[40] This may be also owing to the fact that the date of birth of the protagonist probably coincides with the date of birth of Bharatendu – i.e. in 1873 – since the character was twenty-three years old in samvat 1930. Moreover, the term *āp bītī*, literally 'what has befallen oneself, the story of one's own experiences,'[41] denotes autobiography both in Hindi and Urdu.[42] Vasudha Dalmia in her analysis of *Ek kahānī kuch āp bītī kuch jag bītī* perceives the work as a 'novel venture' and writes that because of the first-person narration employed here and the space and the time being specified, it 'has a frankly autobiographical character' and 'is not conceived of as a work of fiction.'[43] In the opening passage, immediately following the words quoted above, the narrator 'is obviously concerned with sharing an intimately experienced perception with the reader,' as Vasudha Dalmia aptly describes it:

> The evening in full blossom, the sky with the moon on one side and the sun on the other, both red, a strange mood had been created, on the street vendors of kaserū roots, sugar-cane and flowers called out. I was also shot through with the longings of youth, indifferent to the ups and downs of the times, immersed in the intoxication of

---

38 Dalmia, The Nationalization of Hindu Traditions, p. 299.

39 Rāy, *Hindī upanyās kā itihās*, pp. 38–39.

40 Śarmā, 'Editor's Introduction' [to *Ek kahānī kuch āp bītī kuch jag bītī*], p. 981.

41 Ronald Stuart McGregor, *The Oxford Hindi-English Dictionary*, New Delhi: Oxford University Press, 2003, p. 87.

42 Metcalf analyses the Urdu autobiography of Muhammad Zakariyya entitled simply *Āp bītī*. Barbara D. Metcalf, 'The Past in the Present: Instruction, Pleasure, and Blessing in Maulana Muhammad Zakariyya's Aap Biitii,' in *Telling Lives in India: Biography, Autobiography, and Life History*, ed. David Arnold and Stuart Blackburn, Bloomington: Indiana University Press, 2004, pp. 116–143.

43 Dalmia, *The Nationalization of Hindu Traditions*, p. 298.

> my connoisseurship, surrounded by all the parasitic sycophants of the world, listening to my own praises, though even at this tender age I could well recognize love.[44]

Apart from Bharatendu Harishchandra's attempt at what could have possibly been, whether fictional or not, the first life-history in modern standard Hindi, the primacy of the third-person narration in the early endeavours at novel writing was unquestioned. Gopal Ray in his history of the Hindi novel mentions that during the period of 1891–1917 the first-person narrative mode was employed in five novels, including three by Kishorilal Goswami[45] (Kiśorīlāl Gosvāmī; 1865–1932[46]), *Mādhavī-Mādhav vā Madan-Mohinī* (*Madhavi and Madhav, Madan and Mohini*), analysed later in the paper, being one of them. The other two writers of the time who composed their works using the first-person narrative were Bhuvaneśvar Miśra and Chandraśekhar Pathak (Candraśekhar Pāṭhak).[47] According to Gopal Ray, Devakinandan Khatri also experimented with this narrative mode in *Bhutnath* (*Bhūtnāth*)[48], a sequel to *Candrakāntā*, in an effort to present a biography of the eponymous character as his own account. The early experiments at 'the autobiographical technique,' as the scholar refers to it, were however not fully successful, because writers were prone to forget about the limitations of the use of the first-person narration. For example, at some point of narration they would begin to present facts not corresponding with the knowledge of the narrator and thus typical for a viewpoint of an omniscient storyteller. Nevertheless, according to Gopal Ray, this narrative technique is creative and useful since it enables a writer to make his story credible.[49] The editors of the volume *Telling Lives in India* also pay attention to the advantages

---

[44] *Sā̃jh phūlī huī, ākāś mẽ ek or candramā dūsrī or sūrya par donõ lāl lāl, ajab samā bā̃dhā huā, kaserū, gaṇḍerī aur phūl becnevāle saṛak par pukār rahe the. Maĩ bhī javānī kī umaṅgõ mẽ cūr, zamāne ke ū̃c nīc se bexabar, apnī rasikāī ke naśe mẽ mast, duniyā ke muftxore sifārśiyõ se ghirā huā apnī tārīf sun rahā thā, par is choṭī āvasthā mẽ bhī prem ko bhalī bhā̃ti pahcāntā thā.* Hariścandra, *Ek kahānī kuch āp bītī kuch jag bītī*, p. 813. English translation by Dalmia, *The Nationalization of Hindu Traditions*, pp. 298–299.

[45] Rāy, *Hindī upanyās kā itihās*, pp. 89, 106, 109,124.

[46] McGregor, 'The Rise of Standard Hindi and Early Hindi Prose Fiction,' p. 162.

[47] Rāy, *Hindī upanyās kā itihās*, p. 124.

[48] Ibid., pp. 69, 77, 124. In fact Devakinandan Khatri wrote and published only part of this novel before his death, then it was completed by his son Durgaprasad Khatri (Durgāprasād Khatrī).

[49] Ibid., p. 124.

provided by the first-person narrative mode. As David Arnold and Stuart Blackburn point out,

> Life stories, far from being mere fabrications, are seen to be imbued with an extra dose of 'truth.' Narratives, in this view, are not just entertaining fictions but meaningful explorations of life which reveal emotional and social realities that otherwise elude identification and explanation.[50]

The novel *Mādhavī-Mādhav vā Madan-Mohinīu* can be reasonably referred to as a combination of topics typical of the prose fiction of the time – i.e. ranging from didactic novels, romances and detective stories. There is a subplot of a kidnapped and then luckily found boy, a happy ending as the novel finishes with the marriages of both eponymous couples, being an illustration of love-cum-arranged marriage, but at the same time it is a didactic work set out to expose wrong social practices and promote proper ones. McGregor rightly writes that Goswami was 'prone to try to combine with his melodramatic subject matter a social commentary of didactic type.'[51] Although he also argues that the 'readers were little interested'[52] in such social commentaries, the novel *Mādhavī-Mādhav vā Madan-Mohinī*, not mentioned by him, makes for interesting reading and, artistically speaking, is fairly successful. However, in the context of this paper the most important fact is that this novel differs from the majority of the works of the same period as far as its narrative is concerned. It is a fictional life history told by the main character and narrator in the first-person singular. In the opening chapter entitled *Introduction of myself* (*Merā paricay*), a young Brahman, Madhavprasad Sharma, presents himself:

> My name is Madhavprasad Sharma. The residence of my father and his forefathers was in the city of Agra situated on the bank of the River Yamuna but I don't live in Agra now. My mother died when I was small. That is why I wasn't able to learn what mother's love is. My father would work as an accountant for a merchant of Lucknow. When on holiday once in a few months, he would come

50 Arnold and Blackburn, 'Introduction. Life Histories in India,' in *Telling Lives in India*, ed. Arnold and Blackburn, p. 4.

51 McGregor, *Hindi Literature of the Nineteenth and Early Twentieth Centuries*, p. 101.

52 Ibid.

> home and stay a week. When my mother died, I spent some time at my maternal uncle's house. Then my father took me along to Lucknow. There I was admitted to an English school and started learning in the first class. That time I was not older than sixteen.[53]

The same chapter informs the reader that the main protagonist was not able to continue his education in college because it was too expensive and he started working as a school teacher but after his father's death he decided to leave the city and reached Delhi. At the train station he meets a rich merchant, Ramprasad, who gives him shelter in his house.

The novel alludes to several social problems but as soon as the main character reaches Ramprasad's house in the second chapter, the narration reveals that adolescent widows, facing no restrictions at all, pose a threat not only to the protagonist himself but also to the society. Madhavprasad encounters in Ramprasad's house two young widows and is astonished by the fact that they do not look and behave like widows. Moreover, the younger widow, named Sarasvati, tries to seduce Madhavprasad, to his great distress. The protagonist explains his feelings in the following way:

> I have already introduced [you], to some extent, to her flirtatious nature. Alas! This wretch (…) was indeed a beauty (…) but she embodied to the maximum all that is inappropriate for a young widow! I shivered on seeing her appearance, behaviour, attitude, flirtatious glances and coquetry (…).[54]

---

[53] *Merā nām hai, Mādhavprasād Śarmā. Yamunā ke kināre basī huī Āgrā nagarī mẽ mere pitā-pitāmah-ādi pūrvpuruṣõ kā nivās thā, kintu ab maĩ Āgrā mẽ nahī̃ rahtā. Bahut thoṛī umr mẽ merī mātā kā svargvās huā thā; islie mātā kā sneh kaisa hota hai, yah maĩ na jān sakā. Mere pitā Lakhnaū ke yahā̃ munīmī karte the. Chuṭṭī milne par ve tīsre-chauthe mahīne ghar āte the aur das-pā̃c din rah jāte the. Mātā ke pralokvās hone par kuch dinõ tak maĩ apne māmā ke yahā̃ rahā, iske bād pitā mujhe apne sāth Lakhnaū le gae. Vahā̃ par maĩ ek ā̃grezī skūl mẽ bhartī huā aur enṭrens klās mẽ paṛhne lagā. Us samay merī umr solah varṣ se adhik na thī.* Kiśorīlāl Gosvāmī, *Mādhavī-Mādhav vā Madan-Mohinī*, Dillī: Anubhav Pablikeśan, 2010, p. 1.

[54] *Maĩ pahle hī iske cañcal svabhāv kā kuch paricay de āyā hū̃. Hāy, yah nigoṛī (...) sundarī thī (...) par vidhvā yuvatiyõ ke lie jo ḍhaṅg anucit hai, ve hī is kambaxt mẽ kūṭ-kūṭ kar bhare the! Maĩ uske raṅg, ḍhaṅg, hāv, bhāv kaṭākṣ aur cañcaltā ko dekhkar ekdam se kā̃p uṭha (...).* Gosvāmī, *Mādhavī-Mādhav vā Madan-Mohinī*, pp. 23-24. For the analysis of social issues in this novel, see: Justyna Wiśniewska-Singh, 'Marriage in Early Twentieth Century Northern India: Hindi Literature vis-à-vis Social Transformations,' *Asian Journal of Women's Studies*, vol. 22, no. 1, 2016, pp. 35–47.

Madhavprasad, a newcomer in the household of Ramprasad, discovers that the other widow is in a relationship with someone. The affair comes to light only after she becomes pregnant. Madhavprasad helps the family and covers up all the traces of the performed abortion. I would argue that it is not a matter of coincidence but a conscious choice of the writer that Madhavprasad enters the household of another community, as Ramprasad, a wealthy merchant from Delhi, is from a completely different caste and environment. The narrator indicates that restrictions concerning widows in Ramprasad's house were ignored to a large extent as both young widows were not treated differently than the rest of the family and were even allowed to adorn themselves.[55] Therefore, as the main protagonist perceives it, it was due to the lack of restrictions that one of the widows was able to have an affair and the other tried to seduce him. Here we arrive at the main concern of *Mādhav-Mādhavī vā Madan-Mohinī* – i.e. the notion of a widow's remarriage. The novel illustrates an extremely conservative attitude to this practice. Moreover, Madhavprasad perceives the widowhood of Sarasvati from a traditional point of view, explaining it as a result of her deeds in an earlier birth. Thus, he advises her to observe the rules required of widows and devote herself to God as there is no possibility of improving her plight in the present life. He does not admit that another solution is possible since he is strongly against a widow's remarriage, which leads him to call it 'the disease of adultery.'[56] It is worth noticing that it is the first-person narrator and the protagonist at the same time who expresses such an opinion and not a third-person narrator who is outside the story, as was usual in earlier works. The passage depicts Madhavprasad warning Sarasvati against improper behaviour.

> Listen, Sarasvati! Take my words as the truth that in this life you will acquire nothing but the feeling of burning pain and no happiness of true love whatsoever. Therefore recover at this very moment and following restrictions imposed on a widow, purify your soul. If you act accordingly, you will surely be a happy woman in the next life.[57]

---

55 Gosvāmī, *Mādhavī-Mādhav vā Madan-Mohinī*, p. 11.

56 Ibid., p. 25.

57 *Suno Sarasvatī! Tum merī bāt sac jāno ki is janm mẽ sivā jalne ke aur tumhẽ sacce prem kā sukh kadāpi nahī̃ prāpt hogā, islie tum ab bhī samhal jāo aur vaidhavyavrat kā pālan karke apnī ātmā ko pavitr karo, yadi aisa tum karogī to avaśya hī par janm mẽ tum sukhinī hogī*. Ibid., pp. 63–64.

While analysing the novel *Mādhav-Mādhavī vā Madan-Mohinī* it should be mentioned that in the introductory remarks the author offers a comment, stating that this work describes true social events though the names of places and characters have been changed.[58] Moreover, the narrator of the novel acknowledges what he himself has written is his biography (*jīvan carit*, *jīvan vr̥tānt*).[59] He states this fact almost at the end of the novel, explaining that this is the way to overcome the trauma of the past events and to do penance for his sins because he cannot afford to have an expensive *puja*[60] performed. Madhavprasad appears here as a reliable narrator, especially since he has access to the entire house of his host and to the women's part of the house as well. Moreover, Madhavprasad's account is very convincing. All in all, why not believe a decent Brahman, particularly, as readers know from the very first sentence of the book, since he belongs to the Brahman community and exemplary conduct is expected of him?

Although there are certain advantages of the use of the life-historical narrative, we can not say whether Kishorilal Gosvami was himself aware of them. Quoting the words of Stuart Blackburn as an example, one of the assumptions, underlying recent research on life histories, makes readers believe 'that autobiographies speak directly to us and that biographies are based on "true-life" experience; for this reason, it is thought that these life-historical forms (…) are somehow imbued with the veracity of the spoken word.'[61] This very idea should be understood as the greatest advantage of a life-historical narrative. As far as its limitations are concerned, the difficulty is that due to the limited viewpoint of a narrator some facts remain beyond his knowledge. I would argue that the use of life-historical account and the first-person narration in *Mādhav-Mādhavī vā Madan-Mohinī* is a conscious narrative strategy employed here by the writer – Kishorilal Gosvami. It should also be mentioned that the author was himself a Brahman; this is possibly why he set the story – i.e. the subplot connected with widows – within the merchant (*vaiśya*) community of Delhi, attributing the corrupt practices, depicted in the novel, to others. There could have been even more reasons

58 Gosvāmī, 'Viśeṣ vaktavya,' in *Mādhavī-Mādhav vā Madan-Mohinī*, p. v.

59 Gosvāmī, *Mādhavī-Mādhav vā Madan-Mohinī*, pp. 208, 252.

60 Puja – (*pūjā*) denotes worship activities 'directed generally toward a divinity or a group of divinities.' *Brill's Encyclopedia of Hinduism*, vol. 2, p. 380.

61 Stuart Blackburn, 'Life Histories as Narrative Strategy. Prophecy, Song, and Truth-Telling in Tamil Tales and Legends,' in *Telling Lives in India*, ed. Arnold and Blackburn, p. 203.

behind the author's choice, especially when we remember that Ramchandra Shukla accused Kishorilal Gosvami of depicting immoral practices in his novels.[62] Interestingly, the editor of the latest edition of *Mādhav-Mādhavī vā Madan-Mohinī*, quotes Shukla's opinion on the first page of the introduction to the novel.[63] Thus, using Madhavprasad's life-history as a central plot and claiming to describe true social events, Kishorilal Gosvami distracts the readers' attention from himself.

Summing up, we can say that while tracing and analysing the earliest examples of the use of the first-person narrative in Hindi prose fiction and comparing them with the features of the third-person narrative used in the majority of works written at the end of the nineteenth and the beginning of the twentieth century, the literary experiment with the narrative technique initiated by Bharatendu Harishchandra seems to take on a new dimension. Significant both historically and artistically, it opened the spectrum of possibilities wide for writers in Hindi, and in other Indian languages too, who experimented with a new literary form. Apart from the already mentioned advantage of a life-historical text – i.e. the idea of its veracity – this form provides further possibilities. Firstly, as Stuart Blackburn puts it, 'life history is a readily understood template suitable for storytelling'[64] and, in fact, all the works mentioned in this paper refer to their characters' lives, although novels written in the first-person present life-histories from within the story, giving prominence to the point of view of the narrator. Secondly, its other salient feature is the notion that 'the life of an individual is a vehicle for revealing wrongdoing and naming the guilty.'[65] This, in turn, is exactly what the story of *Mādhav-Mādhavī vā Madan-Mohinī* incorporates. Moreover, the above discussed few instances of works in the first-person narrative written in Hindi during the period under discussion contributed to the development of Hindi novel, one of the most important literary genres of the modern era. To specify to what extent, remains, however, the subject for further research on this topic.

---

62 Śukla, *Hindī sāhitya kā itihās*, p. 477.

63 Madhureś, *Bhūmikā*, in Gosvāmī, *Mādhavī-Mādhav vā Madan-Mohinī*, p. vii.

64 Blackburn, 'Life Histories as Narrative Strategy,' p. 204.

65 Ibid., p. 205.

BIBLIOGRAPHY

Arnold, David and Stuart Blackburn, 'Introduction. Life Histories in India,' in *Telling Lives in India: Biography, Autobiography, and Life History*, ed. David Arnold and Stuart Blackburn, Bloomington: Indiana University Press, 2004, pp. 1–28.

Arnold, David and Stuart Blackburn (eds), *Telling Lives in India: Biography, Autobiography, and Life History*, Bloomington: Indiana University Press, 2004.

Blackburn, Stuart, 'Life Histories as Narrative Strategy. Prophecy, Song, and Truth-Telling in Tamil Tales and Legends,' in *Telling Lives in India: Biography, Autobiography, and Life History*, ed. David Arnold and Stuart Blackburn, Bloomington: Indiana University Press, 2004, pp. 203–226.

Brill's Encyclopedia of Hinduism, ed. Knut A. Jacobsen, associate ed. Helene Basu, Angelika Malinar, Vasudha Narayan, vol. 2, Leiden–Boston: Brill, 2010.

Das, Sisir Kumar (ed.), *A History of Indian Literature: 1800–1910 Western Impact: Indian Response*, Delhi: Sahitya Akademi, 2000.

Dās, Śrīnivās, *Parīkṣa guru* (*Experience Is the Only Teacher*), Ilāhābād: Lokbhāratī, 2002 (1st published 1882).

Dalmia, Vasudha, *The Nationalization of Hindu Traditions: Bhāratendu Hariśchandra and Nineteenth-century Banaras*, New Delhi: Oxford University Press, 2005.

Dalmia, Vasudha, 'A Novel Movement in Hindi: *Parīkshā guru*,' in *Narrative Strategies. Essays on South Asian Literature and Film*, ed. Vasudha Dalmia and Theo Damsteegt, Oxford University Press, New Delhi 1999, pp. 169–184.

Dudney, Arthur, 'Keeping the Magic Alive. How Devakīnandan Khatrī's *Chandrakāntā*, the First Hindi Best-seller, Navigates Western Modernity and the Fantastical,' 2009, (retrieved on 30.04.2013 from http://www.columbia.edu/itc/mealac/pritchett/00urduhindilinks/txt_dudney_chandrakanta.pdf).

Gaurīdatt, *Devrānī jeṭhānī kī kahānī. Hindī kā pratham upanyās (varṣ 1870 mẽ prakāśit) (Tale of the Younger and the Elder Sister-in-law)*, ed. Puṣpapāl Siṁh, Nayī Dillī: Remādhav Pablikeśans, 2006 (1st published 1870).

Gosvāmī, Kiśorīlāl, *Mādhavī-Mādhav vā Madan-Mohinī* (*Madhavi and Madhav, Madan and Mohini*), ed. Madhureś, Dillī: Anubhav Pablikeśan, 2010 (1st published 1909).

Gosvāmī, Kiśorīlāl, 'Viśeṣ vaktavya,' in *Mādhavī-Mādhav vā Madan-Mohinī*, ed. Madhureś, Dillī: Anubhav Pablikeśan, 2010, p. v.

Hariścandra, 'Bhāratendu,' *Ek kahānī kuch āp bītī kuch jag bītī*, in *Bhāratendu granthāvalī* (tīsrā khaṇḍ) [Collected Works by Bharatendu (Third Volume)], ed. Vrajaratnadās, Kāśī: Nāgarīpracāriṇī Sabhā, 1953, pp. 813–815.

Kalsi Amrik S., '*Parīkṣāguru* (1882): The First Hindi Novel and the Hindu Elite,' *Modern Asian Studies*, vol. 26, no. 4, 1992, pp. 763–790.

Khatrī, Devakīnandan, *Candrakāntā*, Dillī: Sanmārg Prakāśan, 2000 (1st published 1892).

Rāy, Gopāl, *Hindī upanyās kā itihās* (*History of Hindi Novel*), Nayī Dillī–Paṭnā–Ilāhābād: Rājkamal Prakāśan, 2009.

Madhureś, *Devakīnandan Khatrī*, Dillī: Sāhitya Akādemī, 2002.

McGregor, Ronald Stuart, *Hindi Literature of the Nineteenth and Early Twentieth Centuries*, Wiesbaden: Otto Harrassowitz, 1974.

McGregor, Ronald Stuart, 'The Rise of Standard Hindi and Early Hindi Prose Fiction,' in *The Novel in India: Its Birth and Development*, ed. Thomas Welbourne Clark, London: George Allen and Unwin, 1970.
McGregor, Ronald Stuart, *The Oxford Hindi-English Dictionary*, New Delhi: Oxford University Press, 2003.
Metcalf, Barbara D., 'The Past in the Present: Instruction, Pleasure, and Blessing in Maulana Muhammad Zakariyya's Aap Biitii,' in *Telling Lives in India: Biography, Autobiography, and Life History*, ed. David Arnold and Stuart Blackburn, Bloomington: Indiana University Press, 2004, pp. 116–143.
Monier-Williams, Monier, *A Sanskrit-English Dictionary Etymologically and Philologically Arranged with Special Reference to Cognate Indo-European Languages*, Delhi: Motilal Banarsidass, 1999.
Mukherjee Meenakshi, *Realism and Reality: The Novel and Society in India*, New Delhi: Oxford University Press, 2005.
Orsini, Francesca, *Print and Pleasure: Popular Literature and Entertaining Fictions in Colonial North India*, Ranikhet: Permanent Black, 2009.
Siṁh, Puṣpapāl, *Sandarbh*, in *Gaurīdatt, Devrānī jeṭhānī kī kahānī. Hindī kā pratham upanyās (varṣ 1870 mẽ prakāśit)*, Puṣpapāl Siṁh (ed.), Remādhav Pablikeśans, Nayī Dillī 2006, pp. 59–66.
Śarmā, Hemant, 'Editor's Introduction [to *Ek kahānī kuch āp bītī kuch jag bītī*],' in *Bhāratendu samagra* (*Collected Works by Bharatendu*), ed. Hemant Śarmā, Vārāṇasī: Pracārak Granthāvalī Pariyojnā, 1989, p. 981.
Śukla Rāmcandra, *Hindī sāhitya kā itihās*, Kāśī: Nāgarīpracāriṇī Sabhā, 1961 (1st published 1929).
Szyszko (Turek), Aleksandra, *The Three Jewels of the Desert. The Ḍholā-Mārū Story: A Living Narrative Tradition of Northern India*, Warsaw: Dom Wydawniczy Elipsa, 2012.
Upādhyāy 'Hariaudh,' Ayodhyāsiṁh, *Adhkhilā phūl*, in *Racnāvalī*, vol. 6, ed. Sadānand Śāhī, Nayī Dillī: Vāṇī Prakāśan, 2010.
Wiśniewska, Justyna, 'Pierwsza popularna powieść w języku hindi' ('First Popular Novel in Hindi Language'), *Przegląd Orientalistyczny*, vol. 1–2, 2009, pp. 63–71 [in Polish].
Wiśniewska-Singh, Justyna, 'Marriage in Early Twentieth Century Northern India: Hindi Literature vis-à-vis Social Transformations,' *Asian Journal of Women's Studies*, vol. 22, no. 1, 2016, pp. 35–47.

Maria Skakuj-Puri

Independent scholar

Writing the Self: Literary Strategies in Dalip Kaur Tiwana's Autobiographical Writings

It is reported that at a 'meet-your-writer' program at Punjab University in April 1989, Dalip Kaur Tiwana[1] mesmerized the audience with her academic brilliance and then revealed why she wrote. This is what she said: 'Some write to find a meaning of their existence, others to forget it. I write to understand man's journey from the past to the present – *kitthõ ture sī te kitthe ā gaye*.'[2] In this paper, I would like to draw on this statement and show not only how it sums up Dalip Kaur Tiwana's personal view of history, with its ebbs and flows, all merely a background for human life-stories, whether fictional or not, but also informs her purely literary strategies. However, before continuing, let me briefly introduce her to those that might not be familiar with her person or her writing.

Born in 1935 in Rabbon village of eastern Punjab, to the family of well-to-do landowners, Dalip Kaur Tiwana grew up between the ancestral village and the city of Patiala, where she did her schooling and where she went to college. She obtained – the first woman to do so – a first class MA degree in Punjabi literature, and then, again as the first woman in the

1 Throughout the paper I use the English version of Dalip Kaur Tiwana's and other writers' names.

2 Lit.: 'Where did he come from and where is he now.' Quotation after: Nirmal Sandhu, 'National Honor for Punjabi Language,' *The Tribune*, 26.1.2002. In Punjabi transcription, I follow Anna Sieklucka as given in her *Język pendżabski*, Warszawa: Dialog, 1998. I would also like to thank Dr Jakub Wilanowski-Hilchen for going through Punjabi transcriptions.

region, a PhD in the same subject from Punjab University, Chandigarh. In 1963, she joined Punjabi University, Patiala, as a lecturer, and stayed on to become a professor, then Head of the Department of Punjabi, and finally Dean of the Faculty of Languages, before retiring from active teaching. Today she is considered to be one of the most influential Punjabi writers, with more than 30 novels, 14 collections of short stories, a long, stand-alone poem[3] published as a separate entity, a couple of books of literary criticism and innumerable scholarly articles to her credit, not to mention her autobiographical writings.

Tiwana began writing while still in college, starting with short stories for a student magazine. However, her true debut came with *Agnī prīkhyā* (*An Ordeal by Fire*), a novel published in 1969. It was followed a year later by *Eho hamārā jīvaṇā* (*This Is Our Life*), published later in English as *And Such is Her Fate*[4] and even serialized for the TV, for which she received the 1971 Sahitya Akademi Award. By 1995, when she turned sixty, she had already published 19 more novels. Then came the shock of her brother's suicide, in 1994, that rendered her mute, and her next work of fiction, actually a set of 6 novellas, under the umbrella title *Kathā kaho Urvaśī* (*Tell the Tale, Urvashi*[5]) came 5 years later, in 1999.

Tiwana's autobiography, *Nãge pairõ dā safar* (*A Journey on Bare Feet*) – which is the focus of this paper – was published in 1981,[6] with 12 earlier novels paving its way. It opens with a dedication (for some reason omitted from the English translation) that says: 'Long before being recorded in the annals of history, history gets written down on the bodies of people. This autobiography (*sva-jīvanī*) is dedicated to those who have endured having history written on their bodies.'[7] Between the title, *A Journey on Bare Feet*,

[3] *Vid in vid āūṭ* (*Within Without*, 1975), though a long poem, is usually listed as a novel and Dalip Kaur Tiwana herself calls it a novel in her literary autobiography: *Pūchte ho to suno*, New Delhi: Navyug Publishers, 2001 (1st published in 1995), p. 114. There is an unpublished Polish translation of this work done by Artur Karp and available on academia.edu.

[4] English translation by Jai Ratan, Punjabi University, Patiala, 1980.

[5] English translation (tr. Bhupinder Singh, Orient BlackSwan, New Delhi) appeared only in 2016.

[6] I give 1981 after 'Autobiography (Punjabi)' in *Encyclopedia of Indian Literature*, vol. 1, pp. 284–285, chief editor: Amresh Datta, Sahitya Akademi, New Delhi 1987 (1997, 2003); other sources sometimes give also different dates: 1979, 1980 and 1981.

[7] *Itihās itihās de saphiā ute likh jāṇ tõ bahut cir pahilā̃ kujh lokā̃ de pīdhiā̃ upar likhiā jā̃dā hɛ. Iha sva-jīvanī samarpit hɛ unnā̃ lokā nū̃ jihaṛe itihās nū̃ āpne pīdhiā upar likhiā jāṇā jarde ne.* Dalip Kaur Tiwana, *Nãge pairõ dā safar*, Chandigarh: Lokgeet Prakashan,

and the dedication – with its evocation of suffering and forbearance – the framework for reading the life-history of its protagonist is firmly set.

A close reading of the first chapter shows clearly how Tiwana casts her autobiography into the world. Its seemingly simple sentences made up of commonplace words and its recourse to repetition bear testimony to Tiwana's masterful use of language and perfectly foreground author's special interests (for example, her attitude to patriarchy or her advocacy for self-dependence of women), thus setting up her agenda for the whole book, probably her complete oeuvre. The proposed analysis of Tiwana's autobiography as well as brief insights into her other texts offered during the course of this paper are greatly influenced by Veena Das and her close reading of women's testimonies, in order to mine them for things said and unsaid, as demonstrated in her essay 'The Act of Witnessing: Violence, Poisonous Knowledge and Subjectivity.'[8]

Let us begin the exercise by quoting *in extenso* from the opening passage of Tiwana's autobiography in Jai Ratan's slightly modified English translation,[9] and then follow it with a brief textual examination:

> When I pause to look back into my past, my first memory is of a rich house in which a meek-looking woman lived. I called her mother (*mā̃*). She was also my father's mother (*Te oh bāpū jī dī vī mā̃ sī.*)[10]
> It never ceases to amaze me how a poor and humble woman like her came to live in a rich house. It may be because she was not my *bābā jī*'s first wife. Or, maybe his family was so well-off that it was no longer of consequence whether he married into a rich family or not (….).[11]

2001 (1st published in 1981), p. 5. Cf. Shauna Singh Baldwin, *What the Body Remembers*, New York: N.A. Talese, 1999.

[8] Veena Das, 'The Act of Witnessing: Violence, Poisonous Knowledge and Subjectivity,' in *Violence and Subjectivity*, eds. Veena Das, Arthur Kleinman, Mamphela Ramphels and Pamela Reynolds, Berkeley–Los Angeles–London: University of California Press, 2000, pp. 205–225.

[9] I quote mostly after Jai Ratan but whenever I feel he strays from the original, I modify the translation slightly. I also dispense here with quoting whole relevant passages in Punjabi.

[10] Imbedded Punjabi quotations come from the relevant passages of the Punjabi original of the autobiography, here: Tiwana, *Nā̃ge pairõ dā safar*, p. 7.

[11] Tiwana, *A Journey on Bare Feet*, p. 1

The opening lines, in fact just three and a half sentences in Punjabi, infuse the text with a tone of wistfulness, while resolutely drawing the reader right into the middle of a story peopled by a plethora of characters: the mysterious and yet unidentified first person narrator, the meek-looking (or else: poor and humble – *garīb/a/nī*) woman – whom the narrator calls mother (*mā̃*); the narrator's *bāpū jī*, to whom again the meek-looking woman is – inexplicably – mother as well; and the fourth – undoubtedly the most important person – *bābā jī* – the meek woman's husband and the master of the rich household, who we are told could choose to marry a second time and, moreover, anywhere he wanted. In no time the robust Punjabi narrative presents us with a net of criss-crossing relationships, pointing to a large and entangled familial setting.

In the subsequent paragraphs the narrator keeps the focus on the meek-looking woman who is undoubtedly the most important person in the narrator's life. The narrative continues:

> In this large village house which had seven rooms on an upper storey and coloured glass panels and chandeliers, where they weighed gold in ordinary scales, this woman didn't even have the money to buy a box of matches. For days together she used to be in a quandary, not being able to summon the courage to ask for the money. She would carefully nurse an ember of fire in cow-dung cake to light the fire for the next meal.[12]

However, this tale of austerity does not seem to preclude a sense of prideful belonging and in the very next paragraph we hear the meek woman recalling joyfully: 'At the wedding of your elder aunt...' (*Jadõ terī vaḍḍī būā jī dā viāh sī...*)[13] and so on, adding one more piece to the family puzzle – the narrator has a *būā*, a paternal aunt, her relationship to the meek woman yet unknown. A few lines further on, it appears that the meek woman has a younger daughter (*choṭī dhī*) – hence probably an older one too – and a son (*mũḍā*), who:

> would get angry at her for going about the house in bare feet. (...) Too timid to stand up to her son and daughters she would hold my finger, tiny girl that I was (....) 'Don't they realize that if I wear

[12] Ibid., pp. 1–2.

[13] Tiwana, *Nãge pairõ dā safar*, p. 7.

> shoes in the house they will wear out at the heels?' she would ask. 'It makes no sense to me.'[14]

So by the time we turn to the second page of the book, we already know that the title of the autobiography is a debt owed to this frugal, rich-poor, barefooted, nameless village woman, and that the narrator is actually a 'tiny girl' (*nikkī jihī kuṛī*). This intelligence is immediately followed by another disclosure, where the meek-looking woman's identity *vis-à-vis* the narrator is at last revealed – she is the narrator's grandmother (*dādī mā̃*). This is how it comes about:

> 'You are my younger sister,' my *bapuji* would often joke with me. When I was very small my grandmother (*dādī mā̃*) breast-fed me. (...) I was too young to know why my grandmother had nursed me[15] in place of my mother (*bībī*).[16]

Though the meek-looking woman is the little narrator's paternal grandmother, the narrator addresses her lovingly as 'mother' (*mā̃*) – imitating others – most probably her own father and the servants, and foregrounding their closeness; the appellation *dādī mā̃* is reserved only for the authorial digressions. Side by side, almost as if by accident, we get a quick peek into the workings of a rural, well-to-do, patriarchal family, where the granddaughter of the house, tiny as she is, seems to have more confidence than the perennial daughters-in-law – her grandmother (*mā̃*, *dādī mā̃*) and her own mother (called here *bībī*) – who is still absent from the narrative. Instead, there follow further attestations to the close bond between the granddaughter and the grandmother, with the 'tiny girl' acting as a faithful confidant and an intermediary to the powers-to-be. Let us consider this telling exchange:

---

14 Tiwana, *A Journey on Bare Feet*, p. 2.

15 In her very terse and cryptic manner, Tiwana imparts here some powerful information steeped in strong criticism of the patriarchy: the first born is a girl, the wife has thus not yet done her duty to the family – to enable her to be available to her husband at any time without having to be bothered with a crying and hungry infant girl, her mother-in-law takes care of the baby and the wife takes care of getting pregnant as soon as she can – hopefully with a boy this time.

16 Tiwana, *A Journey on Bare Feet*, p. 2.

> One day when she[17] told me: 'Ask your grandfather to take me for a dip in the holy Ganga before I die,' I retorted: 'Why don't you ask him yourself?'
> Eventually, she picked up the courage to broach the subject. 'Gulab Kaur's father,' she said, 'your granddaughter says we should go and take a dip in the holy river.'
> Grandfather who was putting on a vest suddenly turned to look at her. Grandmother wilted under his gaze.
> 'No, no, I leave it to you,' she stammered.[18]

The patriarchal setting with the looming figure of an all-powerful though benevolent grandfather, a devoted and loving grandmother, the good-for-nothing father (as it turns out, he is a hopeless alcoholic without any sense of duty, hell-bent on squandering ancestral wealth on drinking), and the rest of the family provide a safe, familiar space to the *nikkī jihī* – girl Deep – our future writer. Her mother, whom we only meet in the next chapter, is mentioned almost as an afterthought, when the elder *būā jī* and her husband, the *phupphaṛ*, come to the village to take Deep with them to Patiala as they have no children of their own. Obviously she is not consulted and has no say in the matter of her own child, then some four years old.[19] This is how Tiwana brings her into the story:

> A dark and youthful attractive woman, who used to go about the house, unobtrusively attending to her chores, and of whom I had never taken much notice, emerged from among the other women and led me to the back room. 'So you're going?' she asked me. She hugged me, stroked my head, my face, my arms and kissed me on my cheeks. Then she suddenly burst into tears.
> 'Don't forget me,' she said, 'keep sending me news of yourself. How will I live without you? Tell your grandfather that you don't want to go.' She was my mother (*bībī*).[20]

I have deliberately quoted at length from the opening parts of the autobiography to convey the sense how the writing style and the construction

[17] The original Punjabi has bare 'she' here, while the Jai Ratan translation substitutes it for 'my grandmother' giving the game of naming/non-naming away.

[18] Tiwana, *A Journey on Bare Feet*, p. 2.

[19] Ibid., p. 8.

[20] Ibid., pp. 6–7.

of the text take recourse to a novelistic, one is almost tempted to say, fictional build-up. The start, as we have seen, is made by casting memory as far back as it would go, in becoming once again the 'tiny girl' of the past who can then set down in simple, slightly disjoined, childlike sentences what her child's eyes see, allowing the narrator to roll out the story following a sequence of importance attuned to a child's vantage point. There is little doubt that to tell the story of her life, from the earliest memories going back to her little four-year-old self (which, by quick reckoning, gives us the year 1939) until the moment of divorce, which takes place in 1967–1968 as the author tells us herself in the closing paragraphs of the book, Tiwana chooses to write novelistically. In this way, though the rough material is all there in the form of her life, the author is free to build up her persona according to the rules of fiction – anyway she wants – moving slowly, though almost exclusively in chronological order, tracing her growing up year by year and calibrating her verbal delivery accordingly.

There is a careful economy of language, which brings to mind Krishna Sobti with her measured choice of words and deliberate attention to unfolding the story so as to sustain the reader's interest in what comes next. Almost holding our breath, we read of Deep's life in her *phupphaṛ*'s, or 'father's sister's husband's' household in Patiala, with her *vaḍḍī būā*, or 'father's sister,' and her co-wife, the first wife of her husband. Soon Deep is calling her Aunt *bejī* (another name for 'mother'), or rather *choṭī bejī* ('younger mother'), and her husband's elder wife, with the joint family logic – *vaḍḍī bejī* – 'older or senior mother.' Meanwhile, her own mother in the village delivers a third daughter and once again has to face the humiliation of not having produced a son and heir, with both her husband and his family beginning to look for an opening to contract another marriage thus causing her mother even more grief. These developments seal Deep's fate and she is virtually adopted by her *phupphaṛ*. At twelve,[21] as is the custom, she is married off, as it transpires, into a household where both father and son prove to be drunkards – but luckily, thanks to her age, she does not have to stay there yet, and can return home and go back to school. Revolted by drinking, which destroyed her father and which frightened her during her short visit to the in-laws at the time of marriage, she stubbornly hopes for a life free of all the obnoxious predicaments hinted at in the opening chapter – the common

[21] Incidentally, this is 1947, the year of independence and partition – which, however, find no mention in the story focused on the personal.

lot of women in her still feudal society. So she takes fate in her own hands, persists with her studies and secures a job as a college lecturer. In the end, we find her assuming responsibility for the whole family – her widowed aunts in Patiala, her own mother, now widowed too, her younger sisters and her long awaited little brother, born after five girls. Steadily ignored by her in-laws, who for years have no need of her, she refuses to go to her husband's house and ultimately agrees to a divorce. With this incident the book draws to an end but not before the author confesses: 'This happened in 1967–68, the year in which my first novel *Agnī prīkhyā* appeared.'[22]

The very name of this first novel is very telling: *An Ordeal by Fire*, referring here to Sita's tribulations. Linking her own life-story to that of Sita to provide herself a frame for closure and speaking of her heroine but also of herself, Tiwana concludes her autobiography thus:

> In this novel,[23] I took a close look at the process of becoming/creation (*sirje jāṇ de karam*) and of annihilation (*fanāh hoṇ de karam*). One who recreates oneself from the debris of life does not only drift away from people but also moves beyond one's own self. That is why the heroine (*nāyikā*) of this novel asks, 'Who am I? And who are these people?' This question posed by a thinking man assumes cosmic overtones when he asks himself, who is he? In fact, I should have started my autobiography on this note. It is for the first time that I feel that I am 'I'.[24]

Although now would seem like the right moment to end, I would like, however, to be permitted to add a couple of words more before signing off.

Apparently, urged on by her readers, in 1995, Tiwana followed *Nãge pairõ dā safar* of 1981 (*A Journey on Bare Feet*) with another autobiographical piece of writing *Pūchte ho to suno* (*Since You Have Asked, Listen*). This was furnished with a very specific subtitle – *Sāhitak svā-jīvanī* (*A Literary Autobiography*).[25] Cast in a different mould than the novel-like *Nãge pairõ dā safar*, this book too begins with an emotional recalling of author's young

---

22 Tiwana, *A Journey on Bare Feet*, p. 164.

23 It is not really clear whether 'novel' here refers to her novel *Agnī prīkhyā* or to *Nãge pairõ dā safar*, or both.

24 Tiwana, *A Journey on Bare Feet*, p. 165.

25 With time literary autobiography became quite a rage in Punjabi letters with many writers penning them. Punjabi University Press, Patiala, has actually a series that publishes such autobiographies – all with similar covers and all titled *sva-jīvanī*.

self, specifically the incident of her being taken away from her biological mother (we are given here an additional poignant fact: at that time she was barely learning to walk[26]), and strongly worded criticism of her father, his drinking and his lack of responsibility. It then retells the story of her college education but enriched by details of literary readings (the first book mentioned by name is *Āg kā daryā* (*River of Fire*, 1959) by Qurratulain Hyder which made a great impression on her[27]). From there, Tiwana meanders on to her own writing, her academic career and Punjabi literary scene. The narrative framework is once again well though out and this time constructed in the manner of an oral telling or a recital, thus more episodic, with chapters and paragraphs often starting with formulaic expressions: *kahīde ne, ākhde ne* ('they say'), *mɛ̃ ākhiā hɛ ki* ('I say'), *mɛ̃ ākhiā hɛ nā* ('as I say'), *ek varī* ('once), or even *tusī̃ puchde ho* ('since you ask').

Of special interest here are Tiwana's reminiscences of Amrita Pritam (1919–2005) and Ajeet Cour (1934), two other well-known Punjabi women writers with autobiographies to their name. Amrita Pritam's autobiography, *Rasīdī ṭikaṭ* (*Revenue Stamp*), came out in 1976, some 5 years before Tiāwana's, while Ajeet Cour's *Khānābadoś* (*A Nomad*, published in English as *Pebbles in a Tin Drum*), appeared in 1983,[28] some three years after Tiwana's own autobiographical novel. Tiwana is of course familiar with both. Acknowledging Amirta Pritam's contribution in the field of literature, she writes: 'It is not possible to speak of Punjabi literature without talking of her (Amrita Pritam).'[29] But as to Amrita Pritam's impact on her own writing, she makes it clear: 'I am not influenced by her style because her style is so personal that if someone else were to use it, it would look merely a poor imitation (*nakal*).'[30] Of Ajeet Cour, she says: 'Whenever I read her stories, I feel that nobody can match her way with words (*ãdāz e biān*) in Punjabi.'[31] And confesses she cried while reading her autobiography.[32]

26 *Ākhde ne riṛan tõ aje masā̃ khaṛan hī laggī sī jadõ vaḍḍī būā ne ā vāsatā pāiā ki ieh beṭī mɛ̃nū de dio...* Tiwana, *Pūchte ho to suno*, p. 7.

27 Ibid., p. 11. *Āg kā daryā* was first published in Urdu in 1959, from Lahore.

28 *Khānābadoś* received Sahitya Akademi Award in 1985.

29 Tiwana, *Pūchte ho to suno*, p. 64.

30 *Mɛ̃ us dī bolī tõ vī prabhāvit nahī̃ kiõ ki usdī bolī edhī nijī hɛ ki koī dūsrā je usnū̃ vartegā tā̃ uh usdī nakal lagegī.* Ibid., p. 64.

31 *Mɛ̃ āp jaõ usdīā̃ kahāṇīā̃ paṛhīā̃ lagiā ajihā ãdāz e biān pãjābī vic hor kise kol nahī̃.* Ibid., p. 66.

32 *Par jadõ 'khānābadoś' vic mɛ̃ 'van zīro van' āg bujāū̃ laeī fon nābar paṛiā tā̃ bahut roeī.* Ibid., p. 66. 'One Zero One' is the first chapter of this book.

However, Tiwana's literary works, including her novel-like autobiography, are a class apart.

Boldly premised on a desire to serve merely as a link in a larger metanarrative charged with recording the journey called life, of *kitthõ ture sī te kitthe ā gaye*, Tiwana's self-set task for each of her stories, including her autobiographical novel, is to bear witness to women's lives. So, this brings us to our last question: 'how does she do it?' At first she turns the question into a joke, saying: 'with pen and paper' – 'I take some paper and a pen and sit down to write a novel or a story, what else.'[33] But then grows serious, and explains how an idea – a 'seed' (*bīj*) – takes root in her mind and grows into a story. To illustrate this process, she recounts how once her mother casually mentioned a girl they both knew, one Virpal, saying: 'Her husband is dead but Virpal refuses to take off her nose-pin. (...) "It is he who died. I am not dead."'[34] And that was that. Then a couple of months later, Tiwana met Virpal by chance on a bus. It was October, the *shradh*s were on and they were going to Pehowa.[35] On seeing her, Virpal broke down. Overtime, all these little details germinated into a story *Tīllī dā niśān*[36] (*Mark of the Nose-Ring*) with Virpal metamorphosed into Kiranjeet.[37] And once again a gesture of a woman who would not know how to go about verbalizing

---

33 *Kāgaz lɛ ke te pɛn lɛke likhaṇ bɛṭh jā̃dhī hā̃ te nāval kahānī likh lɛ̃ndī hā̃, hor kī.* Ibid., p. 43.

34 *Ādmī mar giā par Vīrpāl ne nak 'cõ tīllī nahī̃ lāhī. (...) 'Oh mar giā. Mɛ̃ te nahī̃ marī!.'* Ibid., p. 43.

35 Pehowa/Pahewa is a pilgrimage site near Kurukshetra in Haryana, where during a specific period falling in September-October people go to pay *shradh* (*sarādh*), or ritual homage, to their ancestors. The details of this journey, which the author undertakes with her mother for the sake of the soul of her father, and where, on the bus, they meet Virpal, are given by Tiwana in *Pūchte ho to suno*, p. 43 (*sarādhā̃ de din āe. Mɛ̃ te bejī pahoe gae*) and then incorporated almost verbatim in: Dalip Kaur Tiwana, *Tīllī dā niśān*, Arsi Publishers, Delhi, 2000, p. 43 (*Āssū dā mahīnā ā giā. Sarādh caṛ pae. Ihnā̃ dinā̃,vic lok āpṇe moiā̃ mukiā̃ dī gatī karvāṇ pahoe jā̃de han.*) and Tiwana, *Mark of the Nose-Ring*, in *Twilight. Mark of the Nose-Ring. (Two novellas by Dalip Kaur Tiwana)*, tr. Jai Ratan and Narinderjeet Kaur, National Book Trust, New Delhi, 2009, p. 111 (*In October the shradhs were on when people went to Pahewa to pay ritual homage to their ancestors*). I thought it is significant that a woman, who refused to take off a nose-ring as a mark of respect for her dead husband, still does make the traditional pilgrimage for the sake of his soul. Similarly, Tiwana, very critical of her father and his drunken and irresponsible ways, does the same for him.

36 Punjabi original was published in 1970; English translation as *Mark of the Nose-Ring* by Jai Ratan, in *Twilight. Mark of the Nose-Ring. Twilight* has been done by Narinderjeet Kaur.

37 *Pūchte ho to suno*, pp. 43–44.

her feelings beyond an emotionally charged outburst (*Oh mar giā. Mɛ̃ te nahī̃ marī!*) was turned by Tiwana into a literary masterpiece – a powerful narrative made up of almost bare but very evocative description of events and scraps of conversation, devoid as usual of overt authorial comments.

Apparently Tiwana's all narratives, including her autobiography, are worked out in such a way – starting from women-centred, real life situations, they are ultimately transformed into sophisticated literary artefacts. Had *Nãge pairõ dā safar* not been subtitled autobiography and had the names of the protagonists not been preserved, only those in the know would have read it as anything other than a novel written in the first person, for as one can see, its author equipped it with all the makings of that fictional genre.

BIBLIOGRAPHY

Cour, Ajeet, *Khānābadoś*, New Delhi: Navyug Publishers, 1982.
Cour, Ajeet, *Pebbles in a Tin Drum*, tr. Masooma Ali, New Delhi: HarperCollins Publishers India, 1998.
Das, Veena, 'The Act of Witnessing: Violence, Poisonous Knowledge and Subjectivity,' in *Violence and Subjectivity*, eds. Veena Das, Arthur Kleinman, Mamphela Ramphels, Pamela Reynolds, Berkeley–Los Angeles–London: University of California Press, 2000, pp. 205–225.
Encyclopedia of Indian Literature, chief ed. Amaresh Datta, vol. 1, New Delhi: Sahitya Akademi, 1987.
Hyder, Qurratulain, *Āg kā daryā: nāvil*, Delhi: Urdu Kitab ghar, 1984 (1st published 1959).
Pritam, Amrita, *Rasīdī ṭikaṭ*, New Delhi: Nagmani Prakashan, 1976.
Pritam, Amrita, *The Revenue Stamp*, tr. Krishna Gorowara, New Delhi: Vikas Publishing House Ltd., 2016 (1st published in 1994).
Sandhu, Nirmal, 'National Honor for Punjabi Language', *The Tribune*, 26.1.2002.
Sieklucka, Anna, *Język pendżabski*, Warszawa: Wydawnictwo Akademickie DIALOG, 1998.
Singh, Shauna Baldwin, *What the Body Remembers*, New York: N.A. Talese, 1999.
Tiwana, Dalip Kaur, *Agnī prīkhyā*, Chandigarh: Lokgeet Prakahshan, 2001 (1st published in 1967).
Tiwana, Dalip Kaur, *And Such is Her Fate*, tr. Jai Ratan, New Delhi: Diksha Books, 1990.
Tiwana, Dalip Kaur, *Eho hamārā jivṇā*, Chandigarh: Lokgeet Prakashan, 2001 (1st published in 1968).
Tiwana, Dalip Kaur, *Kathā kaho Urvaśī*, Chandigarh: Lokgeet Prakashan, 2001 (1st published in 1999).
Tiwana, Dalip Kaur, *Mark of the Nose-Ring, in Twilight. Mark of the Nose-Ring (Two novellas by Dalip Kaur Tiwana)*, tr. Jai Ratan and Narinderjeet Kaur, National Book Trust, New Delhi, 2009.

Tiwana, Dalip Kaur, *Nãge pairõ dā safar*, Chandigarh: Lokgeet Prakashan, 2001 (1st published in 1981).
Tiwana, Dalip Kaur, *Pūchte ho to suno*, Chandigarh: Lokgeet Prakashan, 2001 (1st published in 1995).
Tiwana, Dalip Kaur, *Tell the Tale Urvashi*, tr. Bhupinder Singh, New Delhi: Orient BlackSwan, 2016.
Tiwana, Dalip Kaur, *Tīllī dā niśān*, Delhi: Arsi Publishers, 2000 (1st published in 1970).
Tiwana, Dalip Kaur, *Vid in vid āūṭ* (*Within Without*), Chandigarh: Lokgeet Prakashan, 1975.

Monika Browarczyk

Department of South Asian Studies, Adam Mickiewicz University, Poznań

Sobti Meets Haśmat. *Ham Haśmat* by Krishna Sobti as an Experiment with Life Writing Form

Krishna Sobti needs no introduction: she is one of the most widely acclaimed Hindi writers, often addressed as the grand dame or the doyenne of Hindi literature. Numerous translations of her works into English as well as other Indian languages have secured her recognition outside the Hindi lore. Nevertheless, for those unfamiliar with her biography, here are a few facts. She was born in 1925 in Gujarat (Western Punjab, now in Pakistan), studied at the Fatehchand College in Lahore and after the Partition worked for two years as a governess with a Rajput royal family in Mount Abu; she then found employment in the Delhi Administration as an editor in the Adult Literacy Department and in 1980 she resigned from her job to dedicate herself exclusively to writing. Fiercely protective of her creative independence, Sobti, nonetheless, often takes a pro-active stance in the pan-Indian public sphere, sharing her opinions on matters of social, political and religious conflicts.[1]

[1] Cf. for instance: 'two more writers – Hindi author Krishna Sobti and Malayalam novelist Sarah Joseph – returned their Sahitya Akademi awards (...). Sobti also returned the Akademi's fellowship, the highest honour of the premier institution. The writers cited the recent Dadri lynching and the killing of Kannada author and Sahitya Akademi Award winner M. M. Kalburgi as the reasons for their decision. Referring to the Dadri incident and the subsequent statements by BJP ministers, Sobti told *The Sunday Express* that the country cannot afford another "Dadri and Babri;"' Ashutosh Bharadwaj, http://indianexpress.com/article/india/india-news-india/two-more-writers-return-sahitya-akademi-awards-another-

Sobti repeats again and again that she could have never imagined herself doing anything other than writing.[2] Her debut short story *Lāmā* was published in 1944 in a literary magazine *Vicār*, and since then she has never stopped writing. She has published numerous short stories, essays and novels,[3] for as she explains: 'Writing for me is the main activity of my life, not an alternative.'[4]

Sobti continuously experiments with language registers, style and form. The critics have acclaimed Sobti's distinctive manner of writing – altered punctuation, use of neologisms or words, phrases and syntax constructions drawn from Hindi dialects as well as Punjabi or Urdu – all masterly woven into a unique and distinguishable idiom, different for each of her works. Portraits of strong women protagonists are also seen as trademarks of her writing. Sheila Sandhu – a Punjabi from Lahore, and Sobti's long time publisher (for many years she was the managing director of Rajkamal Prakashan, a Delhi-based Hindi publishing house), and one of her close friends – wittily characterized Sobti's creative individuality thus: '[she] writes in Hindi with the sensibility of Urdu and the impertinence that comes from being a Punjabi.'[5]

Sandhu is one of the many persons portrayed in the first of the three volumes of Sobti's reminiscences *Ham Haśmat* (*Me, Haśmat*), originally

---

resigns; access 11.10.2015. In 2010, distancing herself from the establishment, Sobti declined the Padma Bhushan, or the highest award of the government of India.

2 'I never considered the prospect of not writing. You see I have no other skills.' Tarun Bhattacharya and Jayeeta Sharma, 'Interview with Krishna Sobti,' in *The Wordsmiths*, ed. Meenakshi Sharma, New Delhi: Katha Rupa and Co, 1996, p. 108.

3 A list of her novels in chronological order (along with my literal translations of their titles or their published English translations where available) is as follows: *Ḍār se bichuṛī*, 1958 (*Memory's Daughter*, tr. Smita Bharti, Meenakshi Bharadwaj, 2007); *Mitro Marjānī*, 1966 (*To Hell with You Mitro*, tr. Gita Rajan, Raji Narasimhan, 2007); *Yārõ ke yār* (*Everybody's Buddy*), 1968; *Tin pahāṛ* (*Three Mountains*), 1968; *Sūrajmukhī andhere ke*, 1972 (*Sunflowers of the Dark*, tr. Pamela Manasi, 2008); *Zindagīnāmā*, 1980 (*Zindaginama*, tr. Neer Kanwal Mani, 2016); *Ai laṛkī*, 1991 (*Listen Girl!*, tr. Shivanath, 2002); *Dilodāniś*, 1993 (*The Heart Has Its Reasons*, tr. by Reema Anand and Meenakshi Swami 2010), and *Samay sargam*, 2000 (*The Music of Solitude*, tr. Vasudha Dalmia, 2013). *Sikkā badal gaya* (*A Coin Got Changed*), *Nafīsā* and *Badalõ ke ghere* (*The Encircling Clouds*, tr. Jai Ratan, 2003) are a few of Sobti's acclaimed short stories. Sobti was also involved – as a consultant – in a production of Durdarshan serial on Partition, *Buniyād* (*Foundation*, directed by Ramesh Sippy, written by Manohar Shyam Joshi, first aired in 1986.

4 Bhattacharya and Sharma, 'Interview with Krishna Sobti,' p. 111.

5 Sheila Sandhu, 'Crossroads after Crossroads,' in *Women Who Dared*, ed. Ritu Menon, New Delhi: National Book Trust, no date, p. 19.

published in 1977,[6] the book which is the focus of this paper. In these pen-portraits (*rekhācitr*) – though Sobti herself disapproves of the label given by the editors, and this will be discussed later – she depicts some of the figures of the Hindi literary scene and some other acquaintances. The collection includes among others satirical descriptions of parties, of a village council, and an utopian dream of Delhi Transport Authority's improved services. Sobti willingly bestows the authorship of these three volumes on her literary male *alter ego*, or Haśmat, a first-eye-witness to the encounters and events described in these sketches.

It is the role allotted to Haśmat that makes *Ham Haśmat* an intriguing case study for the concept of 'the self in performance' in life writings, with the self constantly narrating itself through an invented persona.[7] I would like to take a closer look at this narrative construction of *Ham Haśmat* and address multiple readings of 'the self in performance' present in it. Assuming the figure of Haśmat and sketching literary portraits of others, Sobti adapts two parallel strategies for inferring her self-narrative. *Prima facie*, it is a construct of her male alter ego, or Haśmat, as the active participant in the described events, who thus assumes the 'eye-witness' authority to pen the sketches. However, when we examine the text closely, the connection between Sobti and Haśmat woven within the narrative discloses a multi-layered positioning of the author-cum-protagonist-cum-narrator-cum-alter ego. More interestingly, in the very last essay in the collection – i.e. in *Sobti Meets Haśmat* (*Mulāqāt Haśmat se Sobtī kī*)[8] – Sobti openly discusses her own self and her creative works, disarming the strategy of employing the persona of Haśmat, and taking over his voice while telling her own story.

Before we proceed further with the analysis of *Ham Haśmat*, let us take a look, for the sake of argument, at two other women writers who did not write autobiographies *per se*, but who also, like Sobti, penned reminisces

[6] The fourth edition – supplemented with three later essays on Nagarjun, Govind Mishra and Manohar Shyam Joshi – was published in 1999. The latter two volumes of *Ham Haśmat* were published in 1999, and 2012 respectively: *Ham Haśmat*, vol. 1, Naī Dillī: Rājkamal Prakāśan, 1999 (1st published 1977); *Ham Haśmat*, vol. 2, Naī Dillī: Rājkamal Prakāśan, 1999, and *Ham Haśmat*, vol. 3, Naī Dillī: Rājkamal Prakāśan, 2012.

[7] Theoretical reflections on autobiography genre have been recently driven by concepts of performativity, cf. Monika Browarczyk, 'From the Other One to the Only One. Prabha Khaitan and Her Autobiography,' *Cracow Indological Studies*, vol. 17, 2015, pp. 207–208.

[8] Sobti, 'Mulākāt Haśmat se Sobtī kī,' in *Ham Haśmat*, vol. 1, pp. 252–271.

of other people's lives, namely Shivrani Devi Premchand, the author of *Premcand: ghar mẽ* (*Premchand at Home*, 1956)[9] and Mahadevi Varma, the author of *Atīt ke calcitra* (*Moving Images of the Past*, 1941) and *Smṛti kī rekhāẽ* (*Contours of Memory*, 1943).[10]

Alaka Chudal argued that for Shivrani Devi Premchand sharing her memories of Premchand at home was, in fact, a pretext for telling her own story and that she purposefully employed the narrative strategy of seducing readers interested basically in Premchand to tell them about her own life.[11] The collections of Mahadevi Varma, i.e. portraits of street vendors, beggars and servants, provoked a debate between Francesca Orsini and Rupert Snell. For Orsini, Mahadevi Varma was basically a shy, 'reticent autobiographer,' while Snell strongly disagrees with this view. According to him Varma, in fact, constantly revealed her self, in a most consummate and sophisticated manner – i.e. through her unmistakably distinguishable style of a cultured and learned intellectual.[12]

Alaka Chudal's argument in defence of autobiographical expression in Shivrani Devi's text and the discussion between Orsini and Snell on Varma's works reflect a wider debate on the plausible reluctance of women – Indian women in general, and Hindi women writers in particular – to produce outright autobiographies, that is to say narrations with explicit focus on the self and unequivocally communicated by the self. However, the works of Shivrani Devi, Mahadevi Varma and Krishna Sobti can be also taken as an example and a proof of the existence in the Hindi oeuvre of a variety of modes of narrating the self, attesting therein to the indubitable presence of life writing forms authored by women.

In a long interview published in 1996, when asked about Haśmat, Sobti explained that he was her 'spiritual double' and described her first encounter with Haśmat as follows:

---

[9] Shivrani Devi Premchand, *Premcand: ghar mẽ*, Dillī: Ātmārām eṇḍ sans, 2012 (1st published 1956).

[10] Mahadevi Varma, *Atīt ke calcitra*, Ilāhābād: Lokbhāratī 2008 (1st published 1941); *Smṛti kī rekhāẽ*, Ilāhābād: Lokbhāratī, 2008 (1st published 1943).

[11] In her paper presented at the EASAS workshop 'Opening Up Intimate Spaces; Women's Writing and Autobiography in India,' held in Poznań, Poland in 2016.

[12] Francesca Orsini, 'The Reticent Autobiographer: Mahadevi Varma's Writings,' in David Arnold and Stuart Blackburn (eds.), *Telling Lives in India. Biography, Autobiography and History*, Delhi: Permanent Black, 2004, pp. 54–82; Rupert Snell, unpublished material.

> 'Ek Daavat me Shirkat,' the first piece by Hashmat, was written after a party. There were quite a few people there – many of them writers. I felt I was different from them. Most of them seemed to be asking the same old questions in the same tired idiom. By the time I got home something had been transformed within me. That night there was a new presence at my table and I found myself writing with a sort of masculine hand. I felt threatened – What was I doing? Was I crossing over for good to something new and different? Later I realised Hashmat was there to stay. Fortunately Hashmat and Sobti decided to respect each other, to coexist peacefully.[13]

Sobti has proclaimed many a time that she does not perceive herself as a woman writer. This is one of the reasons for her troubled relations with some Indian feminists, who want to frame her as a flagship of women's literature in Hindi. Creative writing, according to Sobti, is an exercise reaching beyond the dichotomy of genders; literature can either be praiseworthy or bad, and therefore being authored by a man or a woman is an issue of no consequence for her. According to Sobti, the figure of Ardhanarishvar (Skt. Ardhanārīśvara) – a half-woman and a half-man that symbolizes the perfect unity of both genders or perhaps the completeness of a human being – is the most appropriate metaphor for a writer:

> My intellectual and creative responses have been deeply rooted to an eclectic and integrated human experience. I have always been conscious of two distinct elements merging in me. I believe in the concept of Ardhanarishvar – both male and female elements are combined creatively in content, language, style, and imagination.[14]

Interestingly, these reflections of Sobti on the epicene quality of a writer resonate with the thoughts of Virginia Woolf expressed in her essay *A Room of One's Own*, a text of immense significance to the feminist discourse on

[13] Bhattacharya and Sharma, 'Interview with Krishna Sobti,' p. 116. 'Dāvat mẽ śirkat,' in *Ham Haśmat*, vol. 1, pp. 100-116. This sketch presents a satirical description of a party where 'famous, more famous and less famous writers' of Delhi meet, and their wives show off their stylish cloths and expensive jewellery; it is also the first occasion for Haśmat to meet Sobti.

[14] Ibid., s. 111. Sobti seems to refrain here from religious connotations of the term. Ardhanārīśvara is one of the epithets of Śiva, who in this form reveals another dimension of divinity, that beyond dichotomous distinctions of human categories and thus beyond human understanding.

women's writings.[15] Woolf pondering over the words of the English Romantic poet Samuel Taylor Coleridge on the androgynous nature of great minds, seems to arrive at the supportive conclusion of it.[16] It is not possible, however, to decisively resolve whether Sobti's views were informed by Woolf's text or not, and so far I have not come across any references to it in Sobti's writings. It is quite plausible that to express her unique take on the role of gender in creative writing, Sobti generally drew intuitively on the Indian concept of Ardhanarishvar.

In this discussion on the androgynous quality of a writer's personality, a different opinion was put forward. It suggested that the very process of writing was an act of a highly gendered nature, which – for a woman writer – necessitated the shedding of one's femininity, so as to make space for the male within. Amrita Pritam (1919–2005) – a well-known Punjabi poet and writer and Sobti's erstwhile close-friend[17] – writes in her autobiography (originally published in Punjabi in 1976, later translated into Hindi and English):

> In the totality of myself as a writer, the woman in me has had only the secondary role to play. So often have I nudged myself into an

[15] I owe an acknowledgement to Dr. Tara Puri, who referred me to this essay. Virginia Woolf, *A Room of One's Own*, https://ebooks.adelaide.edu.au/w/woolf/virginia/w91r/chapter6.html (access 15.10.2016).

[16] 'Coleridge perhaps meant this when he said that a great mind is androgynous. It is when this fusion takes place that the mind is fully fertilized and uses all its faculties. Perhaps a mind that is purely masculine cannot create, any more than a mind that is purely feminine, I thought. But it would be well to test what one meant by man-womanly, and conversely by woman-manly, by pausing and looking at a book or two. Coleridge certainly did not mean, when he said that a great mind is androgynous, that it is a mind that has any special sympathy with women; a mind that takes up their cause or devotes itself to their interpretation. Perhaps the androgynous mind is less apt to make these distinctions than the single-sexed mind. He meant, perhaps, that the androgynous mind is resonant and porous; that it transmits emotion without impediment; that it is naturally creative, incandescent and undivided. In fact one goes back to Shakespeare's mind as the type of the androgynous, of the man-womanly mind, though it would be impossible to say what Shakespeare thought of women. And if it be true that it is one of the tokens of the fully developed mind that it does not think specially or separately of sex, how much harder it is to attain that condition now than ever before.' Ibid.

[17] Their ways parted over a court battle for copyrights. In 1984, Sobti filed a court case for the copyright to the title of her novel *Zindagīnāmā* (lit. 'a book of life') Pritam used the same word in the title of her own work. The case was finally decided in favour of Pritam in 2011, after her death and more than two decades of judiciary battle.

> awareness of the woman in me. The writer's role is obvious. But the existence of that other being I have increasingly discovered through my creative works. (...) This secondary role as a woman, however, rakes up no quarrels with my main being as a writer. Rather, the woman in me has in a disciplined manner learned to accept that secondary role.[18]

The reflections of Woolf, Sobti and Pritam present their individual understanding of the convoluted connections between cultural constructs of genders and the process of creative writing, and do not exhaust multiple and diverse approaches of others, both male and female, writers, academics and readers to the issue of creative writing and its ability to touch the universal human experience without or within the binary distinctions of genders.

However, returning to *Ham Haśmat*, it seems that the male persona of Haśmat is one of Sobti's many attempts to attain in her self-narrative – in yet another manner and with a twist – the wholeness of human experience. At the same time, this does not in any way imply that Sobti is unaware of the tensions that women have to face in Indian society:

> Our Hindi [literature] world has a peculiar relationship with its women. They want to feel free with you... make you wait on them. This used to irritate me a great deal. Now I know that they cant just treat you as an equal – either they are patronising or they put you on a pedestal. Though I must confess they did not treat me quite like that. Probably, because I was too much of an individual. I didn't have the inhibitions that most women feel in a predominantly male set up. (...) Men do not allow women to share the world they inhabit, and the region outside the house becomes almost exclusively male. Which is why I have chosen to live alone and inhabit both worlds – the one within the walls of my house and the other one beyond it.[19]

Reading *Ham Haśmat*, we are introduced to Haśmat on many different levels of the text. Bits of his made-up biography sink in as we continue reading the essays; that is how we learn that Haśmat is married, does odd-jobs and is constantly worried about his finances, has one decent set of

---

[18] Amrita Pritam, *The Revenue Stamp. An Autobiography*, tr. Krishna Gorowara, New Delhi: Vikas, 2015, pp. 32-33.

[19] Bhattacharya and Sharma, 'Interview with Krishna Sobti,' p. 118.

clothes, enjoys a drink or two and an occasional puff on a cigarette, writes but has never published anything. Haśmat's style is at times flowery and polite, at times witty and ironical, and at yet other times straightforward. He willingly expresses opinions – either in his conversations, or in narration of events, else in commentaries. In due time all these build up the shape of a trickster-like persona: lively, inquisitive, sarcastic, funny and critical, with deep potential for introspective and self-reflective thinking. Haśmat seems to be an amusing companion, and for Sobti it must have been a diverting and refreshing exercise – as she describes it – to write 'with new presence at the table,' with Haśmat's 'sort of masculine hand.'[20]

From the information scattered throughout the text, Haśmat comes across as a self-proclaimed literati of the Hindi bohemian circles of the 1960s and 1970s. He relishes endless group debates, one-to-one conversations, visits to friend's houses, lounging at coffee-houses, eating at restaurants, hanging out at parties, and attending some official gatherings of artists and intellectuals. It is while frequenting these venues and conversing with people that Haśmat offers his audience a 'peep' – or *tāk-jhā̃k*, after all it is one of his favourite activities, usually done *baṛī tamīz se* or 'in a very polite manner'[21] – into the world of Hindi literature populated by writers, artists, critics, publishers, academics (and one academic-cum-translator – a Russian, Barannikov, met at the party at the Sahnis). Conceivably Haśmat inhabits a parallel, virtual world, as he shares some of Sobti's favourite past-times, elements of her life style, friends and acquaintances, but the ultimate common ground is their dedication to literature, serious and deep involvement with all the components of the process of creative writing.

Haśmat describes his encounters not only with Hindi writers (e.g. Nirmal Varma, Bhisham Sahni, Krishna Baldev Vaid, Govind Mishra, Manohar Shyam Joshi and Nagarjun) with an artist – Ramesh Pateriya, an editor of Punjabi literary magazine from Pakistan, Amzad Bhatti, and a publisher (Sheila Sandhu) but also with those on the margins of artistic circles, people whose life paths criss-cross Haśmat's: a Punjabi taxi driver in Delhi, a Kashmiri porter in Shimla, a *nān* baker from Old Delhi, a Brahmin in search of job in New Delhi, and a waiter from a Delhi restaurant. Haśmat also frequents other, somewhat unexpected, places, like a kitty party of women from high-society in Delhi, and a village council meeting.

20 Ibid.

21 Sobti, *Ham Haśmat*, vol. 1, p. 82

Haśmat is passionate about life and literature, and in spite of some financial struggles that he hints at, enjoys his wanderings and exploits of the world, shares a dislike of literary critics, academics and publishers with other writers, enjoys endless debates with his intellectual friends, admires them and argues with them. While narrating his encounters and explorations, Haśmat sets the tone for the discourse as that of critical admiration for writers and the diversity of their writings, disdain for the glittering world of opportunists and an understanding for those less privileged socially.

Haśmat is very much aware of the audience he performs for, whom he keeps addressing directly throughout the text, often in asides peppered with polite *Lakhnavī tahzīb*-like[22] expressions, which give a touch of stylish etiquette to his manner of speech (interchangeably interspersed with colloquial phrases, and this fusion of different speech registers at times creates a comic effect). The narrative is repeatedly interjected with *sahabo* or 'gentelmen,' and phrases like *āpkī duā se*, or 'through your grace.' Haśmat presumes that his audience takes a deep interest in literature and those who create it, as he discusses not only the works, style, composition and vocabulary of particular writers, but also their appearance, clothes, smiles, laughter, rooms, bookshelves, wives – i.e. their way of living, their manner of writing and their interactions. In this way, the imaginatively sketched pen-portraits expand the literary frames set by the genre.

A patchwork of Haśmat's sketches, every one of them composed in a different stylistic mode, yet connected through the persona of Haśmat, is sown together into a canvass that purposefully reveals the constant human and creative interactions within the community of writers, artists and intellectuals, heralding the mechanisms of intertextuality at work.

It seems that Haśmat strongly believes in *birādrī*, or the fraternity of writers, repeatedly mentioned in the narrative, a community of wordsmiths who share common interests and argue over contradictory views, form attachments and react to undercurrent tensions; their thoughts on different creative approaches and intellectual reflections are interflowing freely between them.

Haśmat, thus, echoes Sobti's belief in an all-encompassing involvement with literature, which has to be lived every day, day in and day out, and

[22] The expression *lakhnavī tahzīb*, or 'refined culture of Lakhnau,' reflects a widespread belief that court culture of Lakhnau princely state was an epitome of sophisticated etiquette, good manners and elaborate poetic style.

not merely indulged during the process of writing, and this is perhaps why Sobti does not approve of the label 'pen-portraits' given by the publishers to the *Ham Haśmat* sketches, somewhat denigrating their literary gravitas:

> But they are much more than the portraits of the people I know and they are not fiction either. See, a writer lives a literature apart from the one she creates – a large area where we writers interact with other writers, read each other's works. Hashmat was an attempt to find meaning in this area. I did take a few liberties with my contemporaries – as Hashmat I almost felt I was an author! What I wanted to do was to preserve that sense of all of us being a community of writers.[23]

The audience invoked throughout the text seems to be easy to define: its members are plausible admirers of literature, and perhaps of writers too; however, it is not that clear how to identify or label the one communicating with the audience. *Ham*, which appears in the title *Ham Haśmat* and then throughout the text, is nominally a pronoun of the first person plural; however, it can regularly be used in certain registers of both Hindi and Urdu for the first person singular. In several parts of *Ham Haśmat* and in the very last essay of the series, *ham* appears to indicate Sobti (or the author credited on the book cover), whereas in others it points readers to Haśmat, the alter-ego or even to its plural meaning, hinting at the combined voice of both Sobti and Haśmat – i.e. a complex, heterogeneous, multilayered persona of the self. *Ham* in some passages can also be read as inclusive and include us – i.e. the readers of the narrative.

The image of Haśmat and the image of the self in the narrative are blurred. The borders between them, if any, are not clear-cut, which is one of the intriguing features of this experiment with the life writing form that Sobti undertook. We readers do not know who the persona of Haśmat is; in some essays it seems to be a figment of Sobti's imagination, just another protagonist brought to life by her narrative.[24] Sometimes Haśmat appears

[23] Bhattacharya and Sharma, 'Interview with Krishna Sobti,' p. 116.

[24] The first essay that was written focusing on Haśmat's persona, i.e. *Dāvat mẽ śirkat*, is partly narrated in the third person singular or plural, which might prove that originally Haśmat was designed as a protagonist. However, there are some passages in the text, where Haśmat employs this form of address, i.e. third person singular, when talking to or about himself.

as if co-existing with Sobti and occasionally as if merging with her. Sobti, in this manner, creates a unique narrative of the self that is in the constant process of performance. Haśmat, the persona that narrates lived experiences and witnessed events, functions as a multilayered avatar of the self. It might be the self that is heterogeneous; or possibly the self that does not want to be completely revealed to the others. This self-narrative, overall, invites multiple interpretations.

Haśmat appears to be a particular example of a gendered self, a persona that allows Sobti to escape the dichotomous divisions she is being framed into by the society at large, and it is not without meaning that Haśmat hints at a Muslim cultural background.[25] It seems to be yet another hint at an idea deeply ingrained in Sobti's writings – i.e. the idea of the cultural richness of Punjab, and India in general, informed by different religious traditions of Hinduism, Islam and Sikhism, which are indispensable elements of the Punjabi Indian identity, in spite of the historical trauma of the Partition.[26]

Haśmat as 'the other' of Sobti, her 'double,' offers her the freedom of constructing a particular autobiographical narrative. On the one hand, the persona may reflect her qualities, as well as elements of her life style that she wishes to unveil in front of the readers, and on the other, it may be endowed by the author with any coveted ability and enjoy the eccentricities of a bohemian life without the author being judged for her choices. Therefore, Sobti describes Haśmat as follows: 'We both have different identities, I protect

[25] Cf.: 'It first came to me as a sound. In Urdu it [Haśmat] refers to a person who is his/her own boss. Interestingly the same name can be used for both 'servant' and 'master.' You know the first piece really shocked me – Hashmat's language was nothing like mine. I guess I had absorbed it somewhere.' Bhattacharya and Sharma, 'Interview with Krishna Sobti,' pp. 116–117.

[26] Cf.: 'A creative writer has to transform experience into something that is history from below. When politics, religion and humanism are transmitted in literature human faith is transformed. (...) I do feel in my inner recesses a certain richness that is a part of our common heritage. Nanak, Baba Farid, Amir Khusro, Jayasi, Bulle Shah, Waris Shah, Shah Latif – can we divide this whole lots of poets between yours and ours? No doubt we divided the territory – but tradition, music, art, and literature are not like geographical areas: they continue to remain undivided, indivisible. A novelist makes use of his or her experiences many years after the event. (...) it was necessary to look beyond immediate horror – that it was necessary to salvage something that remained untouched by violence.' Alok Bhalla, 'Memory and History. Krishna Sobti in Conversation with Alok Bhalla, in *Crossing Boundaries. Memory and History on the Partition*, ed. Geeti Sen, New Delhi: Orient Longman, 1997, p. 56.

and he reveals; I am ancient, he is new and fresh; we operate from opposite directions.'[27]

Ham Haśmat mentions two encounters of Sobti and Haśmat. In the first sketch that Sobti associates with Haśmat's writing – i.e. *Dāvat mẽ śirkat* (*Attending a Party*) – Sobti plays with the concept of her alter ego and narrates a brief meeting of Haśmat with a stranger, whose vanity strikes him. Haśmat notices 'a fine lady all elegantly dressed in a black gown, who was ordering a coke'[28]; on inquiring Haśmat learns it is Madam Sobti:

> Seeing her for the first time in such a gathering Haśmat, to judge her better, stepped back. Let us find who really is this one, hiding behind all that façade of energy. A stiff body and a polite way of talking. Haśmat at once realized that there must be a dangerous kind of vanity hidden behind this personality. This kind of look in her eyes that everyone is her subject. He almost felt compelled to approach her and whisper in her ear: 'My lady, the time of kingdoms is over. Please, do change your temper and attitude!'[29]

However, the second encounter recorded in the collection is very different from the earlier brief meeting with a stranger at a party, satirically narrated above. *Haśmat Meets Sobti*, the essay closing the collection, is very different from the other sketches. Here Sobti takes over the reins of the narration and but for the title (is meeting here equal to the merging of Sobti's and Haśmat's voices?) and probably for the closing words *xudā hāfiz* ('May God protect you!,' or a traditional parting phrase, expressing good wishes towards the readers), Haśmat virtually disappears from the text.

Haśmat Meets Sobti, both a self-confession and a writer's testimony, reveals certain interesting details of the creative process of writing. The narrative seems to be divided into two streams that interflow and merge in the closing sections: an opening, introspective soliloquy directed at the

---

27 Bhattacharya and Sharma, 'Interview with Krishna Sobti,' p. 102.

28 *kāle libās mẽ sājī-ḍhākī ek xātūn kok kī farmāiś kar rahī thī*. Sobti, *Ham Haśmat*, vol. 1, p. 105:

29 *Aise mazme mẽ inhẽ kyõki pahlī bār dekhā thā, islie jā̃c parṭāl ke lie haśmat pīche ho lie. jis asliyat par dhamkamvālā yah khol hai, patā to lage āxir cīz hai kis pāye kī. kāṭhi kaṛiyal aur guftagū śāistā haśmat jaldī hī samajh gaye ki is vyaktitv ke nīce ḍhakā gumān baṛā xatarnak ķism kā honā cāhie. Nigāh kuch aisī ki sabhī unkī riyāyā haĩ. Beixtiyār tabīyat huī ki unke kān mẽ jākar kahẽ: 'Riyasatẽ to khatm ho gayī̃ huzūr! Thoṛa mizāj aur andāz badlie.'* Sobti, *Ham Haśmat*, vol. 1, p. 105:

self, which the self does also articulate, and a subsequent section – i.e. a monologue addressed to the audience that focuses on revealing certain aspects of creative practices.

To demonstrate how the narrative develops, I will briefly examine the opening passages. The monologue opens with some verses and develops into a brief reflection on the hardship of life experiences caused by the influence of Saturn, or Śānī, the planet that in India is believed to bring ill-luck, and have an adverse influence on the author's life. Then the narrative explains the difference between self-judgment and the opinions of others:

> When I look at myself with the eyes of others, I see an arrogant and vain woman, dressed in a shining gown, with an air of being different from others.
> When I scrutinize myself, I see a simple, self-contained person, on whom neither god, nor time has shown much mercy, and in spite of that – drawing strength from her own self – still vivacious.[30]

In the first part of the sketch, reflections on the past and the present intermingle with fragments of recollected memories, bitter judgments of the bygone, ambiguous indications of painful experiences or unfulfilled dreams and some glimpses of earlier happy moments. The narration flows, bringing up vague scenes from the past, which transform into polyvalent metaphors and evoke oblique images. At times both types of scenes, those induced from the past and the purely imaginary, become so intertwined that it becomes difficult to distinguish between them. Puzzling questions about past developments – and what sense, if any, they had – keep surfacing haphazardly.

Metaphors and images appearing here are often connected with depictions of flowing (water), waves, estuary, streams, water[31] – associations not unusual for someone coming from the land of five rivers – bring an array of reflections on the passing of time, death and memories of the past. The imagery is also synesthetic, combining the impression of one sense with others – so

---

30 *Dusrõ kī nazar se apne ko dekhtī hũ to ek magrūr ghamaṇḍī aurat, camak-damakvālā libās aur apne ko dūsrõ se alag samajhnevālā andāz. / Apnī nazar se apne ko jā̃ctī hũ to ek sīdhī-sādī xuddār śaxsiyat. Vaqt aur xudā donõ hī jis par zyādā meherbān nahī̃ – phir bhī apne jigre ke zor se zindādil.* Sobti, *Ham Haśmat*, vol. 1, p. 253:

31 Respectively: Sobti, *Ham Haśmat*, vol. 1, pp. 253, 261, 254, 255.

we have, for example, visual images tinted with aural sensations and so on. This kind of imagery gives polyvalent meanings to interpretations of the past, as haunting memories of the lost homeland and horrors of the Partition are buried somewhere deep within the texture of this self-narrative.

At some point in the account of the past, the reminiscences are overtaken by reflections on literature. Description of the writing process reveals some details of the writer's technique and the particulars of work on specific novels.[32] There is also a telling passage on society's biased judgment of a single woman living an independent life. Glimpses of some journeys follow and those focus on pleasant as well as disturbing moments.

The sketch ends with an image of a chest – Punjabi brides leaving their ancestral homes are described in earlier passages, so it is probable that a chest, or *sandūq*, here hints at a dowry chest. This opens a very polyvalent metaphorical image that summons back the water and air of the lost homeland in Punjab, all of it safely locked away:

> A fragrant smell of this land is locked in this chest. A novel.
> I do not dare to open this novel written long time back. Thousand times, I threatened myself into it, I bullied myself, I coaxed myself, but it did not work.
> I am helpless in front of myself.
> And still I am waiting for that moment, when I will be able to open it with my live hands.
> Friends, if it ever opens, then we shall meet again.
> Khuda hafiz! [May God protect you!][33]

(Maybe that moment did happen, the chest did open, when Sobti published *Zindagīnāmā* in 1980, an epic story of pre-independence Punjab, the work that earned her the Sahitya Akademi award).

Ham Haśmat is a unique creative experiment with a life writing form. Sobti seems to perform the self in this narrative through a construct of a heterogeneous, multilayered persona, but appears to drop that guard in

---

[32] Sobti, *Ham Haśmat*: *Ḍār se bichuṛī*, p. 258; *Yārõ ke yār*, pp. 259 and 263; *Mitro Marjānī*, p. 259; *Sūrajmukhī andhere ke*, pp. 260–262.

[33] *Is sandūq mẽ us dhartī kī xuśbū band hai. ek upanyās./ Us purāne likhe upanyās ko kholne kī himmat nahī̃ hotī. apne ko lākh ḍarāyā hai, dhamkāyā hai, phuslāyā hai, par kuch bhī kārgar nahī̃ hotā./ apne āge hī bebas hū̃./ phir bhī intazār hai us ghaḍī kī – jab zindā hāthõ se use khol sakū̃./ dosto, zindagī mẽ vah kabhī khul gayā to phir mulāqāt hogī. / xudā hāfiz!* Sobti, *Ham Haśmat*, vol. 1, p. 271.

the last, partly self-confessional sketch. The narrative taken as a whole interrogates multilayered construction of the self and interconnections of this construct with various patterns provided by society, culture, and gender, amongst others.

BIBLIOGRAPHY

Bhalla, Alok, 'Memory and History. Krishna Sobti in Conversation with Alok Bhalla,' in, *Crossing Boundaries. Memory and History on the Partition*, ed. Geeti Sen, New Delhi: Orient Longman, 1997, pp. 55–78.

Bhattacharya, Tarun and Jayeeta Sharma, 'Interview with Krishna Sobti,' in *The Wordsmiths*, ed. Meenakshi Sharma, New Delhi: Katha Rupa and Co, 1996, pp. 99–158.

Bharadwaj, Ashutosh, 'Two More Writers Return Sahitya Akademi Awards,' in *The Indian Express*, http://indianexpress.com/article/india/india-news-india/two-more-writers-return-sahitya-akademi-awards-another-resigns/ (access 11.10.2015).

Browarczyk, Monika, 'From the Other One to the Only One. Prabha Khaitan and Her Autobiography,' *Cracow Indological Studies*, vol. 17, 2015, pp. 203–229.

Francesca Orsini, 'The Reticent Autobiographer: Mahadevi Varma's Writings,' in David Arnold, Stuart Blackburn (eds.), *Telling Lives in India. Biography, Autobiography and History*, Delhi: Permanent Black, 2004, pp. 54–82.

Pritam, Amrita, *The Revenue Stamp. An Autobiography*, tr. Krishna Gorowara, New Delhi: Vikas, 2015.

Sandhu, Sheila, 'Crossroads after Crossroads,' in *Women Who Dared*, ed. Ritu Menon, New Delhi: National Book Trust, no date, pp. 8–25: p. 19.

Shivrani Devi Premchand, *Premcand: ghar mẽ*, Dillī: Ātmārām eṇḍ sans, 2012 (1st published 1956).

Sobti, Krishna, 'Dāvat mẽ śirkat,' in *Ham Haśmat*, vol. 1, Naī Dillī: Rājkamal Prakāśan, 1999, pp. 100–116.

Sobti, Krishna, *Ham Haśmat*, vol. 1, Naī Dillī: Rājkamal Prakāśan, 1999 (1st published 1977).

Sobti, Krishna, *Ham Haśmat*, vol. 2, Naī Dillī: Rājkamal Prakāśan, 1999.

Sobti, Krishna, *Ham Haśmat*, vol. 3, Naī Dillī: Rājkamal Prakāśan, 2012.

Sobti, Krishna, 'Mulāqāt Haśmat se Sobtī kī,' in *Ham Haśmat*, Vol. 1, Naī Dillī: Rājkamal Prakāśan, 1999, pp. 252–271.

Varma, Mahadevi, *Atīt ke calcitra*, Ilāhābād: Lokbhāratī, 2008 (1st published 1941).

Varma, Mahadevi, *Smṛti kī rekhāẽ*, Ilāhābād: Lokbhāratī, 2008 (1st published 1943).

Woolf, Virginia, 'A Room of One's Own,' https://ebooks.adelaide.edu.au/w/woolf/virginia/w91r/chapter6.html (access 15.10.2016).

Notes on Contributors

Monika Browarczyk, PhD, is Assistant Professor at the Unit of South Asian Studies of Adam Mickiewicz University in Poznań. From 2005 to 2008 she taught Polish at Delhi University under the auspices of the Indo-Polish cultural exchange program. At present she conducts research on Hindi life writings by women and has several publications on this subject to her credit. Her publications include translations from Hindi into Polish: she edited and co-translated a volume of selected poems by Harivansh Rai Bacchan (2013), and of Polish literature into Hindi (with Maria Skakuj-Puri) such as poems of Adam Zagajewski (2011) and Andrzej Stasiuk's *Galitsyā kī kathāẽ* (2014). Contact: monikabr@amu.edu.pl.

Piotr Borek teaches Hindi language and literature at the Department of Languages and Cultures of India and South Asia, Institute of Oriental Studies, Jagiellonian University in Kraków. He has published several articles within the scope of Hindi literary studies. He is currently completing his PhD research on the historical-political discourse in Bhūṣaṇ's poetry.
Contact: piotr.borek@me.com.

Agnieszka Kuszewska is Associate Professor of political science at the University of Social Sciences and Humanities in Warsaw. Her research and teaching focus on the issues of security in South Asia, the political challenges of contemporary India and Pakistan, international conflicts and human rights (Kashmir). She is the author of three books (in Polish: *Understanding Pakistan. Radicalization, Terrorism and Other Challenges*, 2015; *India and Pakistan in International Relations. Conflicts, Strategies*

and Security, 2013, and *India-Pakistan Conflict over Kashmir*, 2010) along with over forty articles and research papers in her field of research.
Contact: akuszewska@swps.edu.pl.

Olga Nowicka is a PhD candidate at the Department of Languages and Cultures of India and South Asia, Institute of Oriental Studies, Jagiellonian University in Kraków, working on her doctoral thesis concerning regional hagiology and the Advaita Vedānta monastic tradition in Kerala. She is the author of several articles on Indian culture.
Contact: olga.nowicka00@gmail.com.

Maria Skakuj-Puri is an independent scholar and translator with degrees in Indology from the University of Warsaw and Islamic Studies from Jamia Millia Islamia in New Delhi. Her publications include a book on Delhi, *Everyday Life in Delhi* (in Polish, 2011), and translations from Polish into Hindi, such as a selection of Adam Zagajewski's poems (*Parāyī sundartā mẽ*, 2011, with Monika Browarczyk), stories by Olga Tokarczuk (*Kamre aur anya kahaniyā̃*, 2014) and a novel by Andrzej Stasiuk (*Galitsyā kī kathāẽ*, 2014, with Monika Browarczyk). At present she is finalizing a translation, from Hindi to English, of Kunwar Narain's long poem *Ātmajayī* and working on the Hindi translation of Olga Tokarczuk's novel *Drive Your Plough Over the Bones of the Dead.*
Contact: mariaskakujpuri@gmail.com.

Katarzyna Skiba is a PhD candidate at the Institute of Sociology, Jagiellonian University in Kraków and a former research fellow of the École française d'Extrême-Orient in Pondicherry. She is the author of several articles on the social history of Kathak dance. She has also researched and published on contemporary South Asian dance in Great Britain.
Contact: katarzyna.skiba@yahoo.com.

Danuta Stasik is Professor of Hindi language and literature at the Faculty of Oriental Studies at the University of Warsaw. Her main research interests are the history of Hindi literature and literary criticism, the Rāmāyaṇa tradition, Rāmbhakti in North India and the Indian diaspora in the West, particularly as represented in Hindi writing. She is the author of over 70 research papers and articles in different books and journals in English, Polish and Hindi. Her books include *The Infinite Story. The Past and Present of the Rāmāyaṇa*

Tradition in Hindi Literature (2009), *Out of India. Image of the West in Hindi Literature* (1994), a grammar of the Hindi language in Polish (1st published in 1998), a textbook of Hindi in Polish in two parts (1st published in 1994 and 1997) and a bilingual collection – Polish translations with Hindi originals – of Kunwar Narain's poems (2013).
Contact: d.stasik@uw.edu.pl.

Bożena Śliwczyńska is Associate Professor at the Faculty of Oriental Studies, University of Warsaw. She specializes in Classical (Sanskrit) and Modern (Bengali and Malayalam) South Asian Studies. Her research concentrates on Indian drama and theatre with special reference to the Kūṭiyāṭṭam temple theatre. Within the scope of her scholarly interest lies the concept of ritual-in-change as well as Bhakti devotional practice (Gauḍīya Vaiṣṇavism). She is the author of two monographs: *The Gītagovinda of Jayadeva and the Kṛṣṇa-yātrā. An Interaction between Folk and Classical Culture in Bengal* (1994) and *Tradition of Temple Theatre Kūṭiyāṭṭam* (in Polish, 2009) and of a number of articles.
Contact: b.sliwczynska@uw.edu.pl.

Aleksandra Turek, PhD, is Assistant Professor at the Chair of South Asian Studies, Faculty of Oriental Studies, University of Warsaw. Her research interests include the Hindi language and literature, particularly its early modern forms, with a special emphasis on the language, literature and culture of Rajasthan. She is the author of *The Three Jewels of the Desert. The Ḍholā-Mārū Story: A Living Narrative Tradition of Northern India* (2012) and a number of articles on Rajasthan.
Contact: a.turek@uw.edu.pl.

Justyna Wiśniewska-Singh, PhD, teaches Hindi language at the Chair of South Asian Studies, Faculty of Oriental Studies, University of Warsaw. She has published several articles on the beginnings of the novel genre in Hindi and is currently working on a book on this subject.
Contact: j.wisniewska@uw.edu.pl.